FOUR-DIMENSIONALISM

Four-Dimensionalism

An Ontology of Persistence and Time

THEODORE SIDER

CLARENDON PRESS · OXFORD

OXFORD
UNIVERSITY PRESS

Great Clarendon Street, Oxford OX2 6DP

Oxford University Press is a department of the University of Oxford.
It furthers the University's objective of excellence in research, scholarship,
and education by publishing worldwide in

Oxford New York

Athens Auckland Bangkok Bogotá Buenos Aires Cape Town
Chennai Dar es Salaam Delhi Florence Hong Kong Istanbul Karachi
Kolkata Kuala Lumpur Madrid Melbourne Mexico City Mumbai Nairobi
Paris São Paulo Shanghai Singapore Taipei Tokyo Toronto Warsaw

with associated companies in Berlin Ibadan

Oxford is a registered trade mark of Oxford University Press
in the UK and in certain other countries

Published in the United States
by Oxford University Press Inc., New York

British Library Cataloguing in Publication Data

Data available

Library of Congress Cataloging in Publication Data

Sider, Theodore.
Four-dimensionalism: an ontology of persistence and time/Theodore Sider.
p. cm.
Includes bibliographical references and index.
1. Space and time. 2. Time. 3. Fourth dimension. I. Title.
BD632.S522001   115—dc21   2001036027
ISBN 0-19-924443-X

10 9 8 7 6 5 4 3 2 1

Typeset by Hope Services (Abingdon) Ltd.
Printed and Bound in Great Britain by
T. J. International Ltd
Padstow, Cornwall

To my parents,
Arbutus and Ronald

Acknowledgments

I would like to thank the following people for helpful comments: Mark Aronszajn, John G. Bennett, David Braun, Phillip Bricker, Michael Burke, Carol Cleland, Earl Conee, David Cowles, Fergus Duniho, Tim Elder, Fred Feldman, Rich Feldman, Kit Fine, Tove Finnestad, Tamar Szabó Gendler, Ed Gettier, Katherine Hawley, John Hawthorne, Mark Heller, Dave Horacek, Martin Jones, Bonnie Kent, Charles Klein, Kathrin Koslicki, Brian Leftow, David Lewis, Europa Malynicz, Ned Markosian, Neil McKinnon, Trenton Merricks, Mark Moyer, Graham Oddie, Josh Parsons, Cranston Paull, Mike Rea, John Robertson, Adam Sennet, Sydney Shoemaker, Roy Sorensen, Rafael Sorkin, Gabriel Uzquiano, Brian Weatherson, Dean Zimmerman, participants in seminars by Kathrin Koslicki and Yuri Balashov, participants in my seminars at the University of Rochester and Syracuse University, and anonymous referees.

I am especially grateful to Mark Heller, Ned Markosian, Trenton Merricks, Mike Rea, Brian Weatherson, and Dean Zimmerman for extensive comments on the manuscript.

I am grateful for the permission to reproduce certain previously published material. Chapters 3 and 4 contain material originally published in the *Philosophical Review*, 106 (1997), © 1997 Cornell University. Reprinted by permission of the publisher. Some sections of Chapter 5 are taken from an essay that appeared in the *Australasian Journal of Philosophy*, 74: 433–53. In Chapter 5 an extract is taken from my review of André Gallois's book *Occasions of Identity* (Oxford: Clarendon Press, 1998), first published in the *British Journal for the Philosophy of Science* (52 (2001): 401–5).

TS

Contents

List of Figures

Introduction

This book articulates and defends four-dimensionalism: an ontology of the material world according to which objects have temporal as well as spatial parts.

Many others have defended four-dimensionalism. This book contributes new developments of the four-dimensional ontology, new arguments in favor of that ontology, and new lines of defense against objections.

The book is also distinguished by its attention to issues in the philosophy of time and their bearing on the question of temporal parts. The philosophy of time defended is the B-theory, the so-called 'tenseless theory of time'. Rival 'tensed' theories of time, in particular presentism, are rejected. These issues are introduced in Chapter 2, and surface sporadically throughout the rest of the book. In addition to illuminating the debate over four-dimensionalism, Chapter 2 can stand alone as a contribution to the philosophy of time.

The other chapters can also, for the most part, be read on their own. Chapter 1 is an informal introduction to the four-dimensional picture of reality. Chapter 3 explores the debate over temporal parts more deeply and formally, and connects the debate to issues in the philosophy of time. Chapter 4 begins the task of defending four-dimensionalism by setting out all but one of the arguments for temporal parts to be considered. Chapter 5 takes up the final argument for temporal parts: that they are required to solve familiar puzzles involving coinciding objects. This includes, in part, a critical survey of rival accounts of the puzzle cases, including Wiggins-style constitution analyses, mereological essentialism, mereological nihilism, and others. That chapter also defends the identification of everyday objects with instantaneous stages rather than with spacetime worms. Finally, Chapter 6 defends four-dimensionalism from objections.

I feel a bit apologetic for retaining the term 'four-dimensionalism' as a name for the thesis that things have temporal parts. This is one standard usage of the term, but the term is also sometimes used (particularly in Australia) for the B-theory of time, or for the conjunction of the B-theory and the doctrine of temporal parts. The term also has the disadvantage of not wearing its meaning on its sleeve. For example, what I call four-dimensionalism implies the existence of instantaneous objects: temporal slices of spacetime worms. Since temporal slices have non-zero extension in only the three spatial dimensions, someone not familiar with the debate might expect me to be a *three*-dimensionalist. Despite these shortcomings, my terminology is familiar and entrenched enough to be useful, if used with care.

This is a work in speculative ontology. As such, some remarks about methodology are in order. As I said, my goal is to provide an ontology of the material world. I want to describe what kinds of things the material world contains and how they are related, and this at a very high level of abstraction, focusing on issues of parthood, time, and persistence.

Anyone working on topics like mine, using the methods I use, is often asked a question something like this: 'Are you doing *descriptive* or *prescriptive* metaphysics? It can't be the former, because four-dimensionalism is obviously an incorrect description of our ordinary conceptual scheme. So you must be doing *prescriptive* metaphysics. But in that case, what is there for a philosopher to do from the armchair? Leave prescriptions of what conceptual scheme we *should* have to the scientists!'[1]

What I am doing does not fit neatly into either category. I am after the truth about what there is, what the world is really like. So I do not want merely to describe anyone's conceptual scheme, not even if that scheme was thrust upon us by evolution. Nor am I trying to read off an ontology from the pages of the latest physics journals. Even the quickest scan through this book will make it clear that the reasons I provide for my conclusions are largely a priori. Science is certainly relevant to metaphysics since inconsistency with a firmly established scientific theory is as good a reason against a theory as one could ask for. But science invariably leaves many questions open. One of these, I think, is whether things have temporal parts.

I follow the descriptive metaphysician in taking ordinary belief about metaphysical matters seriously, but follow the prescriptive metaphysician in aspiring to more than autobiography. This conception of the

---

[1] The distinction between prescriptive and descriptive metaphysics is from Strawson (1959).

nature of metaphysics is, I suspect, common to many of the practitioners of contemporary analytic metaphysics. Unfortunately, I also share
with my fellow practitioners the lack of a good answer to a very hard
follow-up question: why think that a priori reasoning about synthetic
matters of fact is justified?

I have no good epistemology of metaphysics to offer. It should not be
thought, though, that this uncertainty makes metaphysics a worthless
enterprise. It would be foolish to require generally that epistemological
foundations be established before substantive inquiry can begin.
Mathematics did not proceed foundations-first. Nor did physics. Nor
has ethics, traditionally. It may well be that the epistemological foundations of speculative metaphysics are particularly difficult to secure. But
I have my doubts about epistemologists who say metaphysics is impossible. There is, after all, the bleak history of empiricist theories that
attempt to sharply demarcate the epistemologies of metaphysics and
science. It is notoriously difficult to find a non-arbitrary epistemological
line to draw. Moreover, any theory that rules out the possibility of high-
level philosophical knowledge of the world is just another theory. It may
well be more reasonable to reject such a theory than to give up on metaphysics.

Skeptics often ask too much of metaphysical arguments. A priori
metaphysical arguments should not be faulted for not being decisive.
For suppose the evidential support conferred by such arguments is fairly
weak, though non-zero. Then the support for a typical metaphysical
theory, T, will be weak. But the only support for T's rivals will also be
from a priori metaphysical arguments. Thus T may well be better supported—albeit weakly—than its rivals. One would then be reasonable
in giving more credence to T than to its rivals. Metaphysical inquiry can
survive if we are willing to live with highly tentative conclusions. Let's
not kid ourselves: metaphysics *is* highly speculative! It does not follow
that it is entirely without rational grounds.

I will proceed assuming that reasonable belief in metaphysics is
indeed possible, and that something like the following methodology is
legitimate. One approaches metaphysical inquiry with a number of
beliefs. Many of these will not trace back to empirical beliefs, at least not
in any direct way. These beliefs may be particular, as for example the
belief that I was once a young boy, or they may be more general and theoretical, for example the belief that identity is transitive. One then

develops a theory preserving as many of these ordinary beliefs as possible, while remaining consistent with science. There is a familiar give and take: one must be prepared to sacrifice some beliefs one initially held in order to develop a satisfying theoretical account. But a theoretical account should take ordinary belief as a whole seriously, for only ordinary beliefs tie down the inquiry.

For the remainder of this introduction I will lay out some presuppositions of a more metaphysical nature that will guide the argument of the book. I will argue for these presuppositions whenever I can. Where I cannot, I simply flag them as my own prejudices.

My inquiry will be guided by logical conservatism: for the most part I will not give serious consideration to views that challenge standard logic. (For example, I do not discuss Geach's (1980) view that identity is sortal-relative. I do, however, discuss the view that identity is a temporary relation; see Chapter 5, Section 5.)

A related but more contentious assumption is that modern logic's quantificational apparatus mirrors the structure of reality: I assume an ontology of *things*. Moreover, I assume that there is a single, objective, correct account of what things there are.

This view of quantification is absolutely central to this book. Without it, many of the questions about to be asked would look like pseudo-questions. This may be illustrated by a dispute that intersects the question of temporal parts at several points: the dispute over the conditions under which objects compose some further object.[2] One view—the one I favor—says that any objects whatsoever, no matter how scattered, compose a further object: the mereological sum, or fusion, of those objects. This is the viewpoint of classical mereology. Another view, *nihilism*, says that objects *never* compose a larger object. Reality consists exclusively of mereological simples—things with no proper parts. I say that there is such a thing as the computer keyboard on which I am typing, whereas the nihilist denies this. The nihilist of course admits that there are simples arranged 'keyboard-wise', on which other simples arranged 'Ted-wise' 'type'. But neither the first simples nor the second simples compose any macroscopic object.

We have already met the epistemological skeptic about ontology, who doubts the possibility of reasonable belief about which of these

---

[2] See Peter van Inwagen's *Material Beings* (1990a).

theories is correct. Another skeptic doubts there is any fact of the matter whether either is correct. Or at least, this skeptic doubts that my view and that of the nihilist differ *metaphysically*. Perhaps one of us provides a better description of the meaning of ordinary thing-talk, but our views do not correspond to metaphysically different alternatives. The skeptic might even hold that there are no meaningful metaphysical disagreements at all. If this sort of skepticism is right then most of this book is at best idle, and at worst nonsense. The book attempts to support one theory about what things are in the world against rival theories, whereas this skeptic regards these theories as not genuinely competing.

This vague skeleton of a 'no-conflict' view could be developed in various ways. One version would claim that the world is fundamentally a world of *stuff*, not things. This is not to say that thing-talk is illegitimate, for one is perfectly free to talk about the world of stuff using a thing-language. But there is no one right thing-language, since there is no one right way to divide the world of stuff into things. Speakers of different thing-languages would abide by different rules for using thing-talk, and would make what appear to be conflicting statements about what things exist, but they would not genuinely disagree, for they would be using thing-words differently. One way to talk about stuff would be to use the nihilist's language, and refuse to speak of things with proper parts, but an equally legitimate way would be to speak of stuff using the language of composite things.

It is important to be clear on how radical this view must be, if it is to be a genuine alternative to a thing-ontology. Some philosophers talk as if they defend a stuff-ontology, when really they believe in things in stuff's clothing: 'The world consists of quantities of stuff; we can decide to interpret thing-quantifiers as ranging over any of the quantities of stuff we choose. One could use the thing-quantifiers to range only over small bits of stuff, in which case the nihilist is right. Or one could use the thing-quantifiers to range over *all* the quantities of stuff, in which case there exist scattered objects.' In fact, this view assumes that the world is a world of things: *quantities* of stuff. The alleged different meanings for the quantifiers are simply different *restrictions* on the familiar quantifiers of the thing-theorist. The defender of this view thus takes sides on the question of composition: she agrees with the proponent of unrestricted mereological composition, for she agrees that there are such things as arbitrarily scattered quantities of stuff.

A genuine no-conflict stuff ontology must claim that a truly fundamental description of the world must completely eschew a thing-language. This requires completely eschewing the usual quantifiers and variables—the backbone of contemporary logic. For the fundamental description of the world is not supposed to rule in favor of either side of the dispute over composition. If one cannot say that there exist quantities of stuff, what *can* one say? A whole new language must be developed.[3] Somehow, 'quantifiers' over stuff must be introduced without slipping into talk of things; somehow language must be invented to express all the facts about the world we take there to be, while not slipping into thing-language in disguise.

Suppose—what is not obvious!—that a suitable stuff-ontology could be constructed. Why should we accept it? One reason for moving to a stuff-ontology is inherently unstable. This reason begins with the epistemological skepticism about metaphysics considered earlier— questions about composition are unanswerable. It then adds some sort of prohibition against questions that are, in principle, unanswerable. The no-conflict view then becomes attractive, for it makes these unanswerable questions go away. But upholding stuff-ontology just substitutes one unanswerable question for another: is a stuff- or thing-ontology correct? This question seems no more answerable than questions that face the thing-theorist.

If one gives up this reason to embrace a stuff-ontology, a thing-ontology begins to look more attractive because of the power of the modern logic that presupposes it. Quantificational logic since Frege has proved to be a powerful tool inside and outside of philosophy. Think of contemporary semantic research in linguistics, philosophical logic, or even mathematics. For that matter, think of the conceptual scheme of ordinary thought, which appears to model the world as a world of things. If humans have been so successful with thing-thinking, it takes a strong reason to make us give it up. This is the way epistemic justification works generally. We are entitled to continue believing in the ontology of a successful theory until that theory breaks down and someone shows us a better theory. Someone someday may produce a stuff-theory that looks like a better overall bet, but until then it seems reasonable to continue 'normal science' and think in terms of things.

---

[3] Cortens and O'Leary-Hawthorne (1995) make a start.

A more extreme version of the no-conflict thesis, which purports to dissolve even the stuff versus things dispute, is found in a tradition stemming from Rudolf Carnap's paper 'Empiricism, Semantics and Ontology' (1950).[4] On this view, the stuff-ontologist as well as many different thing-ontologists have different 'frameworks', which employ different meaning-rules governing language use. Within any of these frameworks there are answers to questions about what there is, but any question about which framework is *the* right framework is 'metaphysical' in the pejorative sense of being a pseudo-question. The nihilist and I *think* we disagree. I affirm while the nihilist denies the sentence 'keyboards exist'. But our claims are not contradictory, for we mean different things by this sentence. The meaning of such a sentence is only determined relative to a linguistic framework, that is, a set of linguistic rules; and the nihilist and I employ different linguistic rules.

Of course, not just any set of rules counts as an acceptable framework for describing the world; an astrological framework is clearly inadequate. Carnap's own view would be that a framework is adequate provided it is *empirically* adequate, but less positivistic developments of Carnap's views are possible. Let us think of the view as being developed in some non-positivistic way (though it is not at all obvious just how this will go.)

So '$\exists x\, x$ is a keyboard' is supposed to be true in my framework but not in the nihilist's framework. What sort of shift in meaning could produce this shift in truth value?

Not a shift in meaning of the predicate 'keyboard'. For one thing, no stipulation I could make about the meaning of 'keyboard' would guarantee that the sentence is true in my language. I am free to stipulate any necessary and sufficient conditions for falling under the extension of 'keyboard' that I like, but no such stipulation will guarantee that there is anything satisfying these conditions.[5] This is one moral of the ontological argument for God's existence: stipulating that 'God' is to be synonymous with 'the being than which none greater can be conceived' guarantees that *if* 'God' refers to something then that something is a being than which none greater can be conceived, but no such stipulation can guarantee that there is anything to which 'God' refers. For another,

---

[4] Hilary Putnam (1987*a*, 1987*b*) is a contemporary defender. For a non-verificationist defense of 'no-conflict' theses about other metaphysical disputes, see Peacocke (1988).

[5] Compare van Inwagen (1990*a*: 6–12).

the nihilist and I differ over the truth values of sentences that do not contain any predicates. For example, the nihilist claims that if there were just two simples in the world, the sentence '$\exists x \, \exists y \, [x \neq y \, \& \, \forall z(z = x \vee z = y)]$', which says that there are exactly two things in the world, would be true. I say it would be false; there would exist a third thing, the sum of the two simples.

My framework must differ from the nihilist's by assigning different meanings to the quantifiers themselves. Moreover, it cannot be simply that the nihilist's quantifiers are more restricted than mine. This would not support the no-conflict thesis. Our debate concerns whether, with quantifiers wide open, there are any keyboards. I am happy to agree that someone could choose to restrict her quantifiers to exclude the keyboards; and the nihilist thinks that there are no keyboards, no matter how unrestricted one's quantifiers are. So if '$\exists x \, x$ is a keyboard' is true when the quantifier is suitably unrestricted, the debate between me and the nihilist has been settled, in my favor.

But it is hard to see what other shifts in quantifier meaning there could be, other than shifts in restrictions.[6] This is not an argument, but it is compelling.

Carnap might protest that the different frameworks employ different semantic rules for the quantifiers. Perhaps my framework, but not the nihilist's, contains the rule that if there are some simples arranged keyboard-wise then '$\exists x \, x$ is a keyboard' is to count as true. Surely I will not deny a language community its right to use words any way it chooses!

Certainly, a language community could give the string of symbols '$\exists x \, x$ is a keyboard' a meaning under which it would be true any time there are some simples arranged keyboard-wise. The symbols could be used to mean that there are some simples arranged keyboard-wise, for example. For that matter, a community could use '$\exists x \, x$ is a keyboard' to mean that Quine says there exists a keyboard. But in neither case would '$\exists$' be a (singular) quantifier. I do not deny language users the ability to use words any way they like; what I deny is that there are multiple meanings for '$\exists$', all of which are, in some sense, *kinds of unrestricted quantification*. I simply do not see what these kinds of quantification could be. At the very least, Carnap owes us an explanation of why and in what sense we should consider alternate frameworks as employing kinds of quantification.

---

[6] Compare van Inwagen (forthcoming).

Carnap might concede that any person, x, speaking the language of one of the frameworks would regard speakers of the other frameworks as not meaning quantification by '$\exists$', simply because 'quantification' in x's mouth means quantification in x's framework. But, according to Carnap, no one of the frameworks has a 'privileged position'; none gives a 'better' meaning to quantificational expressions than do the others. This is where, I believe, the debate with Carnap reduces to stalemate. I claim there is only one notion of quantification; Carnap disagrees.

Carnap might try to break the stalemate by questioning the sense of my assertion that there is a single sort of quantification. What could it mean to say that there is a single correct meaning for '$\exists$' (beyond the triviality that just one meaning is *mine*)? This is a serious question for anyone who takes ontology seriously. I will answer by sketching a picture according to which there is a single privileged meaning for (unrestricted) quantificational expressions. The picture will appeal to far more metaphysics than Carnap would allow. I do not pretend to refute Carnap, only to show that the opposing view, that meaningful ontological disagreement is possible, is coherent. The picture requires expounding the last of my presuppositions I want to highlight: David Lewis's (1983c, 1984) 'best-candidate' theory of content.

On this view, meaning is determined by two sources. Nearly everyone agrees that *we* play a role. Perhaps this role is played by convention: a complex pattern of behavior and dispositions of the speaker and her language community. Or perhaps a more individualistic account focused solely on the speaker is correct. The second source is the controversial one: of the many candidate meanings (whatever their ontological status), not all are created equal. Some are intrinsically more eligible to be meant than others. This eligibility is starkly metaphysical in nature: some candidate meanings 'carve nature at the joints' more than others, and it is part of the nature of reference and meaning that candidates that carve nature at its joints are more eligible to be meant. The meaning of a word, then, is the best candidate, where strength of candidacy is based on (1) fit with meaning-determining facts about the speaker or her linguistic community, and (2) intrinsic eligibility on the part of the candidate. For short, meaning supervenes on *use* plus *eligibility*.

There is, of course, room for disagreement about the relative importance of these factors in determining meaning. And perhaps there are other factors beyond use and eligibility. One could claim that causal relations also play a content-fixing role, for instance. All that is important here is that eligibility plays a significant role in securing content.

The best-candidate theory of meaning is plausible for various reasons. One is that, as Lewis argues, it forms the basis of the best reply to a powerful form of meaning skepticism, that of Hilary Putnam's (1981, 1980, 1978, part IV) model-theoretic argument against realism and Saul Kripke's (1982) version of Wittgenstein's private language argument. It is hard to see how we could ever manage to refer to anything at all unless something other than use plays a role in fixing content. Intrinsic eligibility seems a good hypothesis as to the nature of this additional reference-fixer. Another reason to believe the best-candidate theory is that it accounts for successful reference in cases where our definitional beliefs are seriously mistaken (see the discussion of 'contact' on p. 184). At any rate, I presuppose in this book that something like the best-candidate theory is correct.

Carnap's challenge to ontology is that there are many possible linguistic frameworks containing different rules of use for the symbol '∃'. These frameworks agree on a core inferential role of '∃' that is appropriate to existential quantification but differ in other respects, for example over whether '$\exists x\ x$ is a keyboard' follows from 'there are some things arranged keyboard-wise'. If '∃' has different but equally legitimate meanings in all the frameworks, meanings that count as 'kinds of unrestricted quantification', then the ontological enterprise is trivialized for no one framework is correct to the exclusion of the others.

Given the best-candidate theory we can avoid trivialization. The inferential role played by the symbol '∃' in our use of that symbol is only part of what secures its meaning. Another part is the intrinsic eligibility of candidate meanings. Suppose the world comes equipped with 'logical joints' as well as extra-logical ones. In particular, in addition to there being distinguished classes of objects that count as genuinely similar, the world comes 'ready-made' with a single domain **D** of objects: the class of all the objects there are. This class is the most eligible meaning possible for any symbol playing the inferential role of the unrestricted existential quantifier.

(Assuming the existence of the entire set-theoretic hierarchy, **D** cannot be a set since it contains absolutely everything. It must then either be a proper class or not an entity at all. In the latter case, talk of **D**, and talk of **D**'s being the meaning of '∃', must be taken with a grain of salt; what is intended is that the semantic function of '∃' is to range over those things that are 'members' of D. This all could be reworded using plural quantifiers and predicates as follows. There are some things, the Ds, that enjoy the ontological distinction of being all and only the things that exist. The Ds are the most eligible things to be, jointly, the semantic values of '∃'.)

Suppose that D is, in fact, closed under mereological fusions—whenever D contains some things, it also contains a mereological sum of those things. In my framework—that of the mereologist—the symbol '∃', when used with the right intentions to remove restrictions, presumably then expresses unrestricted quantification ranging over the entirety of D. For there is a highly eligible candidate meaning—D—for my symbol '∃' that exactly matches the usage of '∃' in my framework. '∃' also presumably expresses a quantifier over D in the nihilist's framework as well. Although this candidate meaning does not perfectly match the nihilist's usage of '∃', it matches it fairly well. It will, for example, vindicate many patterns of inference that the nihilist deems valid for '∃'. And it makes up for its deficiency in match with usage by being extremely eligible. Thus, we can give sense to the idea that the nihilist could be wrong about what exists. (We could tell a similar story about how *I* could be wrong if D were not closed under fusions.) We can also give sense to the claim made above that '∃' does not mean 'genuine quantification' in a framework that *stipulates* that '∃x x is a keyboard' means that there are simples arranged keyboard-wise. Assuming the stipulation is regarded as a non-negotiable constraint on the meanings of the terms involved, '∃' cannot be interpreted in this framework as meaning the most eligible candidate—a quantifier ranging over D. My claim that '∃' does not express genuine existential quantification is just the claim that '∃' in that community would not be a quantifier ranging over D.

Anyone who is willing to adopt as much metaphysics as has been built into the best-candidate picture can, therefore, make sense of ontological disagreement. Disagreeing parties mean the same thing by their quantifiers—quantification over D—despite disagreeing over what there is. Carnap would not be impressed. He would regard all this talk about joints in reality and D as just the kind of metaphysical nonsense he opposes. But my purpose has not been to convince Carnap, only to provide a model of how genuine ontological disagreement is possible. Note also that this model provides no algorithm for telling when a given ontological disagreement is genuine, or for telling whether a given meta-physical question has a determinate answer. It only provides a way for articulating the claim that questions in fundamental ontology do indeed have answers.

Ironically, the same view that allows for ontology is what makes its epistemology so difficult. If the meaning of the existential quantifier were completely determined by meaning rules, we could reasonably expect to discover general truths about existence by conceptual analysis. But then, the inquiry would seem far less significant. Who would prefer exploring our perhaps parochial conceptual scheme to exploring the fundamental features of reality?

This dilemma for ontology does not apply to every metaphysical inquiry. Arguably, many metaphysical questions are questions of conceptual analysis, for example questions about the nature of free will, causation, and personal identity. The fact that fundamental ontology cannot be viewed in this way is what makes it so interesting.[7]

---

[7] See Sider (2001) for more discussion of this issue.

CHAPTER I

The Four-Dimensional Picture

Think of your life as a long story. Let the story be a rather narcissistic one: cut out all details about everything else except you. So the story begins with an infant (or perhaps a fetus). It describes the infant developing into a child and then an adolescent. The adolescent passes into young adulthood, then adulthood, middle age, and finally old age and death. Like all stories, this story has parts. We can distinguish the part of the story concerning childhood from the part concerning adulthood. Given enough details, there will be parts concerning individual days, minutes, or even instants.

According to the 'four-dimensional' conception of persons (and all other objects that persist over time), persons are a lot like their stories. Just as my story has a part for my childhood, so *I* have a part consisting just of my childhood. Just as my story has a part describing just this instant, so I have a part that is me-at-this-very-instant.[1]

Nearly everyone believes that I have parts. In addition to hands, feet, a head, and other extremities, I have smaller parts as well: cells, molecules, atoms, and subatomic particles. And there are still more: my upper half, for example. There is all of me save my left foot. I also believe in aggregates of things I believe in, and so accept such objects as the sum of my hands and feet, the sum of my brain and my liver, and so on. This view will be defended in due course, but I mention all these parts only to set them aside. These are *spatial* parts, whereas the objects corresponding to parts of my story are my *temporal parts*. And the list of my parts goes on, for in addition to my spatial and temporal parts, I also contain

---

[1] I have in mind in this chapter orthodox four-dimensionalism—that is, the worm theory. My preferred four-dimensionalism is slightly different; see Ch. 5, Sect. 8.

my temporal parts' parts as parts. And (what comes to the same thing) I contain my parts' temporal parts (from the times when they are part of me) as parts. My head's current temporal part—that is, my current temporal part's 'head'—is part of me. And then there are sums of all these objects, for example the sum of my temporal part from my first ten years and the current temporal part of my nose.

My spatial parts extend through time like I do. We call them spatial parts because they are smaller than I, spatially speaking; they are 'cut out of' me along a spatial dimension. Reverse time and space in this description and we obtain a description of my temporal parts, which extend through space like I do but are smaller than I, temporally speaking; they are what you get by slicing me along a temporal dimension. (Talk of cutting and slicing must be taken with a grain of salt: the parts are there whether or not they are physically separated from the whole.) Like me, my current temporal part is 5 feet 9 inches tall, seated in a typing position, and has a full stomach. But it is temporally smaller than I; whereas I extend back in time a number of years, it exists only for an instant. That is, my current *instantaneous* temporal part exists only for an instant. My today-part exists for a day, and my this-year temporal part lasts a year. In each case the temporal part is shorter-lived than I, with one exception: it is common to count me as a temporal part—an 'improper' temporal part—of myself.

A person's journey through time is like a road's journey through space. The dimension along which a road travels is like time; a perpendicular axis across the road is like space. Parts cut the long way—lanes—are like spatial parts, whereas parts cut crosswise are like temporal parts. US Route 1 extends from Maine to Florida by having subsections in the various regions along its path. The bit located in Philadelphia is a mere part of the road, just as it is only a mere part of me that is contained in 1998.

A road changes from one place to another by having dissimilar subsections. Route 1 changes from bumpy to smooth by having distinct bumpy and smooth subsections. On the four-dimensional picture, change over time is analogous: I change from sitting to standing by having a temporal part that sits and a later temporal part that stands.

When you touch a person, you only directly touch a part of that person—the hand, say. According to the four-dimensionalist, there is another sense in which you only directly touch a part of the person. Even if you could somehow touch all of a person's spatial parts at once, you would still fail to touch all the person, for not all the person is *then* to be touched. To touch all of a person you must hold him in an interpenetrating total embrace from his birth until his death; only thus would you have access to all his past and future temporal parts.

This picture of persistence over time I have called four-dimensionalism is also known as the doctrine of temporal parts and the thesis that objects 'perdure'. It has been in the philosophical consciousness for most of this century,[2] and in the minds of non-philosophers as well (e.g. in the opening chapter of H. G. Wells, *The Time Machine*). While it has many adherents it is by no means universally accepted (not even in Australia). Many, in fact, consider it to be wildly counterintuitive. These philosophers prefer instead to regard objects as 'three-dimensional', as 'enduring', as being 'wholly present' at all times at which they exist.[3] Consider the regions of space I occupy throughout my life. According to three-dimensionalists, these regions are not occupied by distinct instantaneous objects, but are rather occupied successively by the *entire* persisting object. More pictures: a perduring object is 'spread out' over a region of spacetime, whereas an enduring object 'sweeps through' a region of spacetime, the whole of the object occupying the region's subregions at different times.

---

[2] The advent of Minkowski spacetime seems to have inspired much interest in the picture on the part of philosophers, although some versions of the doctrine predate Minkowski spacetime. The following philosophers can, with varying degrees of accuracy, be thought of as four-dimensionalists: Armstrong (1980); Balashov (1999, 2000); Broad (1923: 54–5, 63, 1933: 141–66, esp. 166)); Carnap (1967, sects. 128, 159); Cartwright (1975); Goodman (1951, ch. IV, sect. 1); Hawley (1999); Heller (1993, 1992, 1990, 1984); Hudson (1999); Jubien (1993); Le Poidevin (1991); Lewis (1988*a*, 1986*a*: 202–4, 1983*a* (plus postscript B)); Lotze (1887, chs. 1–4); McTaggart (1921: 176–7); Quine (1960, sect. 36, 1963, 1976*b*, 1981: 10–13); Russell (1914: 112 ff., 1927: 243 ff., 284–9); Sider (1997, 1996*a*); Smart (1972, 1963, ch. VII); Whitehead (1920); Williams (1951).

Something like the doctrine can also be found in Jonathan Edwards (1758, part 4, ch. 2); Hume's *Treatise* (1978, book 1, part 4, sects. 2, 6); in Buddhist thought (see Stcherbatsky 1970, ch. XI, 1992, part II, ch. I); and perhaps in Heraclitus, though this is a matter of controversy (see Kirk 1960: 333–9, Guthrie 1962: 449–54).

[3] Three-dimensionalists include: Baker (2000, 1997); Burke (1994*a*, 1994*b*, 1992); Chisholm (1976); Doepke (1982); Gallois (1998); Geach (1972*a*); Haslanger (1994, 1989*a*, 1989*b*, 1985); Hinchliff (1996); Johnston (1987, 1992); Lombard (1994); Lowe (1989, 1988*a*, 1988*b*, 1987, 1983*a*, 1983*b*); Mellor (1998, 1981); Merricks (1999, 1994*a*, 1994*b*); Oderberg (1996, 1993); Rea (2000, 1998, 1995); Simons (1987); Thomson (1998, 1983); van Cleve (1986); van Inwagen (1990*a*, 1990*b*, 1981); Wiggins (1980, 1968); Zimmerman (1999, 1998*a*, 1998*b*, 1997, 1995).

How might the four-dimensional conception be supported? One way is by appeal to its utility in defusing certain classic puzzle cases about identity over time. Three such cases are the puzzle of change, the puzzle of coinciding material objects, and the case of The Ship of Theseus. For the remainder of this chapter I present these cases and show how the puzzles can be resolved by a four-dimensionalist. The discussion will be informal and non-rigorous since the purpose is only to give the flavor of the four-dimensional view. Detailed presentation and (sometimes critical!) evaluation of these and other arguments for four-dimensionalism must wait until Chapters 4 and 5.

Thinking about identity over time begins with the mundane observation that objects regularly persist through change. I will continue to exist tomorrow despite countless changes. I will have ingested and excreted, I will (usually) be wearing different clothes, I may have gotten a haircut. The idea that the *same person* will persist through these changes is intimately tied up with many other parts of our deeply rooted conceptualization of ourselves:

> I can be punished for my past crimes, but no one can be justly punished for anyone *else's* crimes.
>
> I have a certain sort of fear or dread of my future pain, but no one can fear—in the appropriate way—the future pains of others.
>
> While others can wish that I had not done certain things in the past, only I can *regret* my past actions.

The list could be extended; the moral is that the concept of one and the same person persisting over time is intimately connected with many other important notions (such as regret, self-interested concern, and punishment). We cannot lightly give up the idea that persons persist over time. If we did, we would either have to stop extending punishment, fear, regret, and other such concepts, over time, or radically revise our conceptual scheme.

We must, therefore, take challenges to the possibility of persistence over time seriously. One such challenge is that persistence through change is inconsistent with Leibniz's Law. Leibniz's Law states that $x = y$ only if x and y have all the same properties. This law is clearly correct: if we know that the murderer is left-handed and that the butler is right-handed, we are entitled to conclude that the butler is not the murderer.

But now consider any ordinary case of change. Suppose I get a haircut. It would seem that the person before the haircut, call him Longhair, has different properties from the person, Shorthair, after the haircut; one has long hair while the other has short hair. Leibniz's Law then seems to imply that Longhair and Shorthair are distinct, and thus that I do not survive the haircut, since the person after the haircut is not the same person as the person before the haircut.

The puzzle is that Leibniz's Law seems to prohibit anything's surviving any change. Other solutions to this puzzle will be considered in Chapter 4, Section 6; for now I wish only to note that the four-dimensionalist has a nice solution. Leibniz's Law does indeed imply that there are two distinct objects with different properties involved: a temporal part, which we may call 'Longhair', and a distinct temporal part, 'Shorthair'. Longhair is my temporal part before the haircut, and does not survive the haircut; Shorthair is my temporal part after the haircut, and did not exist before the haircut. But it does not follow that *I* do not survive the haircut, for I am not identical to Longhair, nor am I identical to Shorthair. I am a sum of temporal parts that includes both Longhair and Shorthair, and survive the haircut in virtue of including each as parts. Change over time for the four-dimensionalist is thus a matter of dissimilarity between successive temporal parts. As noted above, a changing person can be likened to a changing road with dissimilar subsections.

A second challenge is also based on the rigid demands of Leibniz's Law. Suppose that on Monday an artist obtains a lump of clay, and on Tuesday forms a statue using that clay. It is natural to say that the artist has *created* something, a clay statue, and also natural to say that the creation of the statue does not destroy the lump of clay. After the act of creation, let us name the lump of clay (which is now in statue form) Lump; and let us name the statue Statue. Lump and Statue *seem* to be one and the same object. But if they are to be identical, Leibniz's Law requires them to share all of their properties. Lump and Statue *do* share many properties: they have the same mass, the same shape, the same location, and are made up of the same subatomic particles. But if we turn our attention to *historical* properties, we find differences. Since the statue was created on Tuesday, it did not exist on Monday, but the lump did exist on Monday. Therefore, Statue ≠ Lump, since only Lump has the property *existing on Monday*. But how can this be? How can there exist two things as exactly alike as Lump and Statue? The portion of space in which each is located does not contain room for two such objects.

The problem of how two distinct things could coincide spatially is difficult to solve if one does not accept temporal parts. But given temporal parts, the problem dissipates. At any given time it is only a temporal part of a spacetime worm that is wholly present. Thus it is only temporal parts of Statue and Lump that are wholly present at the time of coincidence. How can these temporal parts both fit into a single region of space? Because 'they' are *identical*. Statue and Lump are of course not identical, for Lump has temporal parts on Monday that are not shared by Statue. It is only their temporal parts on Tuesday (and subsequent days) that are identical. That is, Statue and Lump share a single temporal part on Tuesday. They are like a road and a substretch of that road, as in Figure 1.1. There is no mystery how these roads could be present in the same point in space; they do not crowd each other out because it is only a common segment of the roads that is wholly located in the region in question.

A final case is the classic puzzle of The Ship of Theseus. Consider The Ship of Theseus, made of planks. Surely a ship can survive a single plank's replacement. But imagine replacing The Ship of Theseus's planks one by one until all the original planks are gone, and christen the final ship 'Replacement'. Since replacement of a single plank does not destroy a ship, we obtain a series of true identity statements:

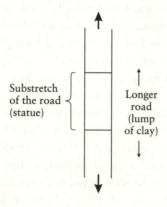

FIG. 1.1. Overlapping roads

The Ship of Theseus = Ship 1
Ship 1 = Ship 2
Ship 2 = Ship 3
.
.
.
Ship $n-1$ = Ship n
Ship n = Replacement

By the principle of the transitivity of identity (if $x = y$ and $y = z$ then $x = z$), The Ship of Theseus = Replacement. This might seem surprising, since these ships share no planks in common, but it does not seem in any way paradoxical. But now imagine that each plank removed during this process was saved in a warehouse. After enough planks accumulated, we began assembling them into a new ship. The plank removed from Ship n was the final plank added to this new ship, which we christened 'Planks'. We now face a difficult question: which ship is the same ship as the original Ship of Theseus? We argued via the transitivity of identity that Replacement is The Ship of Theseus; but Planks also has a powerful claim since it contains all the original planks. Surely a ship could be transported over land by disassembly and subsequent reassembly; the case of The Ship of Theseus and Planks seems parallel. Planks and Replacement cannot *both* be identical to the original ship, for by the transitivity and symmetry of identity (if $x = y$, then $y = x$) it would follow that Planks and Replacement are one and the same ship, when of course they are not.

It would be misleading to say that all of the difficulties surrounding The Ship of Theseus evaporate once we adopt the four-dimensional conception of persistence over time. But the problem becomes tractable.

A four-dimensionalist regards the world as a world of stages. Acceptance of four-dimensionalism is plausibly accompanied by acceptance of another metaphysical principle, the principle of unrestricted mereological composition according to which, for any objects, there exists such a thing as the mereological sum, or fusion of those objects—a larger object that contains those objects as parts. According to this principle, *any* group of objects has a sum, even a group of objects that is very scattered. There exists, for example, a thing that is made up of the coins in my pocket, the Eiffel Tower, and all the polar bears in the world. One could believe four-dimensionalism without accepting unrestricted composition (and vice versa) but most four-dimensionalists accept unrestricted composition;

moreover, I will argue in Chapter 4, Section 9 that the best argument in favor of unrestricted composition can be modified to provide a powerful argument for four-dimensionalism.

Given the principle of unrestricted composition, the four-dimensional world of stages also contains a mereological sum for each collection of stages. We have already met some of these sums: the space-time worms with which the four-dimensionalist identifies everyday objects. But once unrestricted composition is accepted, *any* set of stages has a sum, even sets of stages that are not unified in any particularly interesting way. The world is therefore populated by a host of continuing spacetime worms, of which we name, think of, and quantify over a small minority. The predicate 'person' applies, perhaps, to worms that are psychologically united in a certain way (or perhaps the unity principle is physical; it doesn't matter here). Worms formed from person stages that are not psychologically united, for example the worm that consists of my stages until age 3 and Bill Clinton's stages thereafter, do not fall under the predicate 'person', nor any other everyday predicate, and so are usually ignored.

Let us return to the question of whether The Ship of Theseus is identical to Replacement or Planks. The first thing to note is that there exist spacetime worms corresponding to *each* answer. Consider, for example, the spacetime worm made up of the following stages:

the original Ship of Theseus's stages before replacement occurs
Ship 1's stage after one plank has been replaced
Ship 2's stage after the second plank has been replaced
.

.

Ship *n*'s stage after *n* planks have been replaced
Replacement's stages after the final plank has been put into place.

Call this 'the replacement worm'. And call 'the original planks worm' the worm that consists, at any moment, of the stages of all and only the *original* planks of The Ship of Theseus. This worm is co-located with The Ship of Theseus at the beginning of the process, and is co-located with Planks at the end of the process; it might be thought of as the 'quantity of planks' of which the original Ship of Theseus and Planks are made.

Which is The Ship of Theseus, Replacement or Planks? The answer depends on our concept of a ship.

Perhaps our concept of a ship does not emphasize sameness of planks, and applies to spacetime worms that continue in ship form even if they exchange planks. The replacement worm rather than the original planks worm would then count as a ship, and the correct answer to the question would be Replacement. For when we introduced the term 'The Ship of Theseus', perhaps by saying 'let this ship be named "The Ship of Theseus"', we were actually pointing at many spacetime worms, alike in containing the ostended temporal part, but differing in past and future temporal parts. We selected the replacement worm out of the lot by stipulating that our term was to apply to a *ship*.

On the other hand, perhaps it is a feature of our concept of a ship that ships must retain the same planks. The original planks worm, rather than the replacement worm, might then count as a ship. It would have been the worm christened as 'The Ship of Theseus', and the correct answer to the question would be Planks.

There are many other spacetime worms that begin coinciding with our Ship of Theseus and trace out different paths through spacetime to either Planks or Replacement, for example a worm like the original planks worm but missing the stages when the planks are not all assembled in ship form. This worm goes out of existence after the removal of some of the planks and resumes existence when the discarded planks are assembled to make Planks. Perhaps our concept of a ship applies to one of these other worms. Whether the Ship of Theseus is identical to Replacement or Planks would depend on which of these worms counts as a ship and is thus designated by 'The Ship of Theseus'.

Another interesting possibility is that there may be no determinate answer to the question of which spacetime worms count as ships. Indeterminacy in our concept of a ship would result in a kind of indeterminacy or ambiguity in the expression 'The Ship of Theseus' over several candidate spacetime worms. There might then be no answer to our question of whether The Ship of Theseus is identical to Replacement or Planks, if some of the candidate spacetime worms over which 'The Ship of Theseus' is indeterminate include Replacement's stage after the process of replacement and others include Planks's stage then.

Four-dimensionalism does not, on its own, answer our question, but the *metaphysical* puzzle has been dissolved. We have a perfectly clear metaphysical picture of what happens: the world contains spacetime worms corresponding to both answers to our question. The only remaining question is the merely *conceptual* one of which of these spacetime worms counts as a ship.

From these and other traditional puzzles about identity over time, a powerful case emerges for postulating a four-dimensional world of temporal stages. If we believe in four-dimensionalism, we can dissolve these and other puzzle cases; if we do not, we are left mired in contradiction and paradox. But much remains to be done. The four-dimensional picture of the world must be refined. The four-dimensionalist resolution of the puzzles must be analyzed more carefully. Rival accounts of these and other puzzles must be investigated and criticized, for the case for four-dimensionalism rests on the claim that *only* the four-dimensionalist can give a satisfactory account of the puzzles (or, more cautiously, that the four-dimensionalist gives the *best* account of the puzzles.) Other arguments for four-dimensionalism must be considered. Arguments that have been raised against four-dimensionalism must be answered. These are the tasks of the upcoming chapters.

CHAPTER 2

Against Presentism

Though the central topic in this book is the metaphysics of persistence, I first want to discuss some related issues in the philosophy of time that bear on the question of temporal parts. The goal is to explain and defend a 'B-theory' of time, which I then presuppose for the remainder of the book.

1. TWO ISSUES IN THE PHILOSOPHY OF TIME: ONTOLOGY AND TENSE

There is first the ontological status of the past and future. According to *eternalism*, past and future objects and times are just as real as currently existing ones. Just as distant places are no less real for being spatially distant, distant times are no less real for being temporally distant; the ontological significance of distance is thus a respect in which time is spacelike. Reality consists of a four-dimensional spatiotemporal manifold of events and objects—the so-called 'block universe'. In the block universe, dinosaurs, computers, and future human outposts on Mars are all equally real.[1]

According to *presentism*, on the other hand, only currently existing objects are real. Computers, but not dinosaurs or Mars outposts, exist. Though I think presentism ultimately must be rejected, its guiding intuition is compelling: the past is no more, while the future is yet to be. Presentism is analogous to modal actualism, according to which reality

---

[1] Defenders of eternalism include Goodman (1951, ch. XI); Mellor (1981); Quine (1960, sect. 36); Russell (1915); Smart (1962); Williams (1951).

consists only of actuals. The opposing position in the philosophy of modality, possibilism, according to which reality also contains merely possible things, is analogous to eternalism.[2]

Intermediate between the polar opposites presentism and eternalism is the view, defended by C. D. Broad (1923, ch. II) and more recently by Michael Tooley (1997), that the past is real but the future is not. On this view reality consists of a growing four-dimensional manifold, the 'growing block universe'.

The status of tense is a second issue in the philosophy of time. Tensed sentences are those which presuppose a certain position or vantage point within the whole of time, for example:

It is *now* raining.

It *was* the case that there existed dinosaurs.

I *will* one day visit Utah.

Not all sentences involving time are tensed, for example:

It is raining on 28 June 2000.

World War 1 occurred after the American Civil War.

There existed dinosaurs before the appearance of this book.

Following McTaggart (1908), tensed and tenseless temporal judgments are often called A-judgments and B-judgments, respectively. The concepts *now*, *was*, *will*, and the like are called A-concepts, whereas the concepts *before*, *after*, and related concepts are called B-concepts. The mark of B-concepts is that they can be applied without knowing at what point in time they are being applied, whereas A-concepts require a vantage point. Relatedly, A-judgments typically change in truth value. A current utterance of 'It is now raining' is true, but future utterances will be false. In contrast, B-judgments are permanent: it is, always has been the case, and always will be the case that it rains on 28 June 2000. (If, as some say, the future is 'open', the permanence of B-judgments should instead be characterized as follows: once a B-judgment takes on a certain truth value, it forever after retains that truth value.)

---

[2] On presentism see Adams (1986); Bigelow (1996); Hinchliff (1996); Markosian (forthcoming); Merricks (1994*a*); Prior (1968*a*, 1968*b*, 1970); Zimmerman (1998*b*); and my (1999*b*); for a more complete list of references see Markosian (fothcoming, n. 3), and Bigelow (1996, bibliog.).

Do tensed judgments concern features of reality that are in some sense irreducibly tensed, or can their truth be reduced in some way to tenseless facts about time, those expressed by B-judgments? The leading idea for the reduction of tense is that *tokens* of tensed sentence types, whether uttered or thought, can be given tenseless truth conditions.[3] Consider a token, *o*, at some time, *t*, of the tensed sentence 'It is now raining'. This token may be given a tenseless truth condition: *o* is true iff it is raining at *t*. The truth condition is tenseless because 'raining at *t*' is a tenseless locution: if it is in fact raining at some particular time, *t*, then it always has been the case and it always will be the case that it is raining at *t*. The tenseless truth condition for a token at *t* of the tensed sentence 'There existed dinosaurs in the past' would be that there exist dinosaurs before *t*. Early reductionists set themselves the goal of *translating* tensed sentence types into synonymous tenseless sentence types, but contemporary reductionists content themselves with providing truth conditions for tensed tokens in the way described.

On this account, A-locutions like 'past', 'present', and 'future' may be usefully compared with indexical words like 'I' and 'here'. These indexical words make different contributions to the truth conditions of sentences depending on the *context* in which they are uttered. If Gore says 'I will win the election', what he says is true iff Gore wins; using the very same sentence, Bush makes a statement with different truth conditions—that Bush wins. Someone located at the North Pole will speak the truth by saying 'It is cold here', whereas the very same sentence expresses a falsehood when uttered at the equator. It is part of the semantics of 'I' that it refers to the person who utters it, and part of the semantics of 'here' that it refers to the place of utterance. The temporal reductionist claims that tensed locutions are similarly indexical. 'Present' applies to an event iff it occurs at the time of utterance, 'past' to an event iff it occurs before the utterance, and 'future' to events occurring after the utterance.

The reductionist goes on to give a general account of tensed language in this way, and concludes that nothing corresponding to tense need be admitted as a fundamental feature of the world. Anti-reductionists deny this reduction of tense, for one reason or another, and claim that tensed facts, for example the fact that dinosaurs existed in the *past* or that it is

---

[3] See esp. Mellor (1981). Revisions to this 'token-reflexive' theory along the lines of Kaplan (1989) are desirable; see e.g. Mellor (1998).

now raining, are ultimate features of reality. The pastness of dinosaurs is not simply the fact that dinosaurs are located before the time of this utterance. Anti-reductionism about tense is often called the 'A-theory' of time; its defenders are said to 'take tense seriously'. The traditional dispute over whether time 'flows' is perhaps this same dispute: A-theorists accept time's flow or movement, whereas reductionists are said to accept a 'static' account of time.[4]

The reductionist's account is called 'static' because B-judgments do not change in truth value. Since a B-description is claimed to capture all of the facts about time, in a sense the reductionist claims that the totality of temporal facts does not change. This is not to say that reductionists deny the existence of what is *ordinarily* thought of as change. Ordinary change, for the reductionist, emerges from the truth of B-judgments such as these:

The poker is hot on Thursday, 29 June 2000.

The poker is not hot on Friday, 30 June 2000.

Neither *judgment* changes in truth value; nevertheless, the temporal reductionist says, the *poker* changes, in virtue of the truth of this pair of statements. (This account of change is discussed further in Ch. 6, Sect. 2.)

Our two disputes—over the reality of past and future and over the status of tense—are intimately linked. The most obvious link is that only the eternalist seems to be in a position to offer the aforementioned reduction of tense. The alleged truth condition for a current token of 'there existed dinosaurs in the past' is that there exist dinosaurs before *t*, where *t* is the time of the token. But this truth condition says that *there exist* dinosaurs, albeit located before *t*, which no less commits one to dinosaurs than saying that there exist dinosaurs located on the moon. Reductionists about tense, then, are invariably eternalists. The combination of reductionism about tense and eternalism is commonly called the 'B-theory of time'.

Presentists reject the existence of merely past and future objects and so cannot make use of the reduction of the tenses. But no sensible presentist

---

[4] Contemporary discussion of the status of tense springs from the seminal McTaggart (1908, 1927, ch. 33). Reductionists about tense include Goodman (1951, ch. XI); Mellor (1981, 1998); Quine (1960, sect. 36); Russell (1915); Smart (1962); Williams (1951). A-theorists include Gale (1968); Prior (1957*a*, 1967, 1968*c*); and Schlesinger (1980). For further discussion and references see Le Poidevin (1991); Markosian (1992, 1993, 1995); Oaklander and Smith (1994); Smith (1993).

would flat-out reject all temporal talk. Presentists must therefore be anti-reductionists about tense; they must deny that tokens of 'there once existed dinosaurs' have truth conditions involving quantification over past dinosaurs. The usual move here is to regiment such sentences using sentential 'tense operators', analogous to the sentential modal operators of modal logic, and claim that these tense operators are primitive. The tense operators include 'WILL' and 'WAS', as well as the metrical tense operators 'it WILL be the case *n* units of time hence that' and 'it WAS the case *n* units of time ago that'. These tense operators combine with present tense sentences to form complex sentences, for example: 'WAS (there exist dinosaurs)'. For the presentist, such a sentence can be true despite the non-existence of a past containing dinosaurs; existential quantification within the scope of a tense operator like 'WAS' is not ontologically committing. (Note the parallel between the presentism/ eternalism and actualism/possibilism disputes. The possibilist analyzes the modal sentence '◊ (there exists a unicorn)' in terms that quantify over possibilia: 'there exists a unicorn located in some other possible world', whereas the actualist admits the truth of the modal claim while denying the existence of non-actual unicorns and thus denies the correctness of the analysis.)

Some say presentists and eternalists do not genuinely disagree since each side admits tensed talk. The alleged disagreement is over quantified sentences such as *'there exists* a dinosaur'. But the dispute would disappear if the presentist and eternalist meant different things by the quantifier. Suppose, for example, that what the eternalist means by 'there exists (atemporally) an *x* such that . . .' is what the presentist would express by a disjunction of combinations of tense operators and present tense quantifiers: 'WAS ($\exists x$ . . .) $\vee \exists x$ . . . $\vee$ WILL ($\exists x$ . . .)'.[5] Then, it might be claimed, the disagreement vanishes, for the presentist will *accept* the first disjunct of 'Either there was a dinosaur, or there is a dinosaur, or there will be a dinosaur'. However, this translation procedure will not dissipate all ontological disagreement between eternalists and presentists, for it sometimes maps claims the eternalist accepts to claims the presentist rejects. Since this translation procedure is the most likely strategy for reconciliation, genuine opposition is restored. An eternalist who believes in sets would accept the claim that *there*

[5] Compare Sellars (1962: 546–50, 566).

exists a set containing a dinosaur and a computer, but the presentist will reject the disjunction:

> WAS ($\exists x$ x is a set containing a dinosaur and a computer) or ($\exists x$ x is a set containing a dinosaur and a computer) or WILL ($\exists x$ x is a set containing a dinosaur and a computer)

One can think informally of $\lceil$WAS$(\varphi)\rceil$ as saying that at some past time, t, φ is true at t. (The presentist will not, of course, accept this as an analysis since it quantifies over merely past entities—times—but should accept it as a useful heuristic). The first disjunct, then, says (informally) that at some time in the past there existed a set containing a dinosaur and a computer; the second says that there exists such a set at the present time, and the final disjunct says that at some future time, some such set exists. Since at no one time did there exist *both* a dinosaur and a computer, it follows that at no time will there exist a set containing a dinosaur and a computer (assuming that a set exists only if its members do). Thus, from a presentist's perspective, each of the three disjuncts is false. The eternalist avoids this difficulty by avoiding the need to locate the set within any one time. Past, present, and future, for the eternalist, exists in its entirety as a single block universe, which contains both dinosaurs and computers as parts and thus contains sets with dinosaurs and computers as members.

Some will deny the existence of sets or the principle that a set exists only if its members do. We could consider instead a fusion of a dinosaur and a computer, but some will deny the existence of this thing or its dependence on its parts, just as with sets. However, I am inclined to think that even if these philosophers are correct, the argument still shows that presentists and eternalists genuinely differ. Even if I did not believe in entities like sets or fusions whose existence is contingent on their members or parts, I would regard the argument as showing that *if there were* any such things, presentists and eternalists would disagree about the truth of statements about them; and that would convince me that *in fact* presentists and eternalists have differing views about the world.

The idea that presentists and eternalists do not genuinely disagree is seductive, but it leads to claiming that too many other ontological disputes are not genuine, for example over whether numbers or merely possible entities exist. If the 'no-disagreement' position were correct for the eternalism/presentism dispute, it would likewise be correct for these other ontological disputes. Actualists and possibilists would not genuinely disagree, nor would mathematical Platonists disagree with nominalists. Applied to the mathematical case, the no-disagreement position would be that 'exists' could mean 'mathematically exists', in which case it is uncontroversially true to say that there are numbers, or it could mean something like 'physically exists', in which case it is uncontroversially true that there are no numbers. In the modal case, the view would be that if 'exists' expresses possible existence then there uncontroversially are merely possible things, but if it expresses actual existence then there uncontroversially are not. Philosophical ontology, on this view, is an impossible discipline. As discussed in the introduction, it is a premise of this book that the no-conflict view of ontology is incorrect. There is a single notion of existence relative to which there can be meaningful dispute. One can meaningfully ask: do numbers or merely possible objects exist—that is, exist *simpliciter*? Given this view of existence we can meaningfully ask: do dinosaurs exist *simpliciter*? The eternalist says they do, while the presentist disagrees.

We have seen that presentists are A-theorists, but some eternalists also reject the reduction of tense.[6] According to one such view, reality consists of the four-dimensional manifold accepted by the B-theorist, with an equally real past, present, and future. But one slice of the manifold enjoys a special metaphysical privilege: it is the *present*. Which slice is present of course varies over time; the picture of the present is that of a 'moving spotlight' successively highlighting different portions of reality.[7] Reductionism about tense fails on this view since an atemporal description of the world using B-concepts would leave out which slice of the block universe is present. The temporal reductionist has an 'indexical' notion of the present, on which any utterance of 'the present time' refers to the time of utterance. There is no metaphysical distinction to what I call the present; I truly call it present simply because it is when my utterance is located. The moving spotlight picture, on the other hand, is that of a 'metaphysical' notion of the present; the present is metaphysically privileged. The privilege is not existence, for that would collapse the view into presentism; presumably the exact sense in

---

[6] See Smith (1993, ch. 5) (though note that Smith calls his theory 'presentism'). For an interesting critical discussion see Zimmerman (1998*b*: 212).

[7] Compare Broad (1923: 59–60) (who does not support this view).

which the present is privileged is taken as an unexplained primitive. This anti-reductionist notion of the present then yields anti-reductionist notions of the past and future: the past is that which is earlier than the distinguished present; the future is that which is later than the distinguished present.

The problem with the moving spotlight view is that it is unmotivated. It is obvious why a presentist would resist the reduction of tense: the materials for the analysis do not exist.[8] But if you believe in the existence of past dinosaurs and future Mars outposts, why not employ them in a reduction of the tenses?

It will be seen in Chapter 4, Section 6 that the moving spotlight view can be used to solve the 'problem of temporary intrinsics'. That might be thought to be a reason to believe it. But it will be shown that the solution requires a particularly implausible version of the moving spotlight view.

Some think that Arthur Prior's 'thank goodness that's over' argument can be used to motivate the moving spotlight view. (Prior himself used it to argue for presentism.) Suppose after a painful experience I remark 'thank goodness that's over!' If tenseless facts exhausted reality, then the facts after the experience would be the same as the facts before the experience, so the argument goes; thus it would not be clear what I was thanking goodness for. I am clearly not thanking goodness for the fact that the painful experience is over on 20 October 1998, at 5.23 p.m., for I might know beforehand the exact date and time when the pain will cease, but I will not then thank goodness for anything. Himself a presentist, Prior takes the moral to be that we should not believe that past and future pains exist. I am thanking goodness for the fact that the pain is no more. However, the defender of the moving spotlight can draw a different moral: the relief is not misplaced since the world has changed in virtue of the pain ceasing to have the property of being *present*. The pain has become past, and anyone who has been in pain knows the difference between past and present pains.[9]

This argument for combining eternalism with irreducible tense is suspect. Compare John Perry's (1979) case of indexical belief. While

---

[8] Or are constructed from propositions and the tenses themselves, and so are unavailable for use in a reduction, as in Prior (1968*b*).

[9] See Prior (1959, 1970, 1996); for discussion see the essays in Oaklander and Smith (1994, part III).

shopping in a supermarket Perry follows a trail of sugar leaking from the cart of some shopper, and finally comes to realize that *he himself* is the person making a mess. In coming to this realization he does not come to recognize any new relevant impersonal facts, for he already knows all those. He already knows that *some shopper is making a mess*. He may even already know that *some philosopher is making a mess*. Indeed, he may even know already that *John Perry is making a mess*, for if he has amnesia he may not know that he himself is John Perry. What he comes to realize is that **he himself** *is making a mess*. What he comes to realize cannot be captured without using personal indexicals like 'I', as when Perry says 'I am making a mess', or 'he himself', as when we say 'Perry believes that he himself is making a mess'. But this should not drive us to claim that, in addition to all the facts describable in an impersonal language, a complete description of the world must acknowledge metaphysically new facts only expressible in language with indexicals. We should say instead that belief and related attitudes are not exhausted by relations to impersonal propositions. Our understanding of belief, not our understanding of the world, is what is challenged.[10]

What we learn from Perry's case, we can apply to Prior's. The cases are not perfectly analogous. For example, Perry's case crucially involves ignorance. But each concerns psychological attitudes involving expressions that are capable of being regarded as indexical: 'I', 'now'. This parallel points to a serious problem with Prior's argument, as well as towards a constructive response to Prior.

The problem is that there exist arguments parallel to Prior's for clearly incorrect conclusions. Suppose the right response to Prior's puzzle really were to postulate irreducibly tensed facts. We could then construct analogous spatial and personal cases that would force us to postulate irreducibly personal facts and irreducibly spatial facts. But surely we don't want to do *that*. Rather than populating the world with this menagerie of perspectival facts, we should instead revise our understanding of psychological attitudes. We have already seen the case pushing us towards irreducibly personal facts: Perry's messy shopper. And we can push Perry's case closer to Prior's by imagining the shopper saying 'thank goodness that's not *me* making the mess'. For the spatial case, imagine I am relieved that a forest fire has occurred over *there*, rather

[10] How exactly one cashes this out is a matter of controversy; see e.g. Chisholm (1979), Lewis (1979), and Perry (1979).

than over *here*. The object of my relief is not captured by sentences lacking spatial indexicals, for example 'the fire is in New Mexico, not in Syracuse' for I may not know where I am. If I am ignorant of my spatial surroundings, I may not know the location of the fire by any description other than 'it is there, not here'. If the right response to Prior's puzzle really were Prior's—past and future objects and events do not exist—then parallel examples would push us towards the apparently ludicrous position that other persons and distant places do not exist. And if the right response really were that of the moving spotlight theorist, parallel examples would lead us to postulate irreducible facts of *me-ness* and *here-ness*.

These parodies show that something is wrong with Prior's argument, but they do not tell us what that something is. What is wrong with Prior's argument is that it assumes an incorrect understanding of the nature of attitudes to time, and ignores a way of understanding those attitudes that blocks Prior's conclusion. The right response to Prior's example is, in a slogan, to build irreducible temporal perspective into psychological attitudes rather than the world. Relief is inherently perspectival, in that attitudes of relief do not reduce to attitudes towards eternal propositions. One way of developing this idea runs as follows.[11] Let us understand *propositions* atemporally, as being true or false *simpliciter*, not relative to time. Prior succeeds in showing that psychological attitudes are not simply relations to propositions, thus understood. A more appropriate object of the attitudes would be what one might call 'temporal propositions': functions from times to (atemporal) propositions. Temporal propositions may be thought of as the linguistic meanings of sentences expressed using temporal indexicals. For example, the sentence 'Ted's pain is just now over' would have as its linguistic meaning the temporal proposition, call it '*over*', that assigns to any time the atemporal proposition that Ted's painful experience ceases immediately before t.[12]

That temporal propositions are appropriate objects of psychological attitudes may be seen as follows. Psychological attitudes are relations between persons and temporal propositions at times. When at t I thank goodness that my pain is over, the object of my attitude at t is the temporal proposition *over*. Standing in the psychological attitude of relief

---

[11] Cf. Lewis (1979).

[12] Compare Kaplan's (1989) notion of character.

to *over* at *t* is *not* the same thing as being relieved, at *t*, that the *atemporal* proposition *over* (*t*) is true. For as Prior points out, where *t* is the time at which the pain is over, the person may have known ahead of time that the pain would be over at *t*. That relief is not reducible to relations to atemporal propositions is, after all, the moral of Prior's example. Think of the temporal argument *t* of the function *over* as corresponding to the indexical 'now' that we use to express *over*: 'Ted's pain is just now over.' A temporal proposition represents a 'perspective' within time; the temporal proposition *over* represents the perspective shared by the set of moments *t* at which Ted had a painful experience immediately before *t*—that is, the set of times, *t*, such that *over* (*t*) is true. To be relieved at a time that my pain is over is to be relieved that I am then in just such a perspective. Similarly, when I bear the relation of dread to the temporal proposition, *approaching*, that assigns to a time, *t*, the proposition that a pain will occur to me shortly after *t*, I could express this dread using the sentence 'a pain will occur to me shortly after *now*'. I am dreading at the time that my then-current perspective is that represented by *approaching*.

This conception of the attitudes does not require postulating irreducible tense. Temporal propositions were constructed from purely B-theoretic notions, as functions from times to eternal propositions. Thus, the phenomenon of temporally indexical belief does not require one to reject the reducibility of tense.[13]

It is natural, then, for an eternalist to be a reductionist about tense. As noted earlier, presentists must be anti-reductionists. The status of tense on the growing block universe, on the other hand, is rather delicate. On one hand it might seem that Broad and Tooley can accept the eternalist's reduction of tense. The past exists, on this view, and thus is available for providing truth conditions for tokens of past-tense statements. Since the future is absent, most future-tense statements would turn out uniformly false, or lacking in truth value, depending on the details of the account. But this consequence is at least intuitively palatable (unlike an analogous claim about the past), and may even be welcome, for it is part of one argument for the growing block universe view that truths about the future would rule out free will.[14] On the other hand, the reductive truth conditions for tokens of tensed sentences do not seem applicable to

---

[13] Compare Mellor (1981, ch. 5).

[14] I do not say I accept these arguments. For a critical discussion see Tooley (1997, ch. 3).

tensed sentences about the growing block universe itself. Broad and Tooley want to say that a current utterance of 'it once was the case that the entire four-dimensional reality contained only one world war' is true, since in 1935, for example, the growing block universe only contained what had occurred up until that point. However, if we evaluate the component sentence 'the entire four-dimensional reality contains only one world war' with respect to 1935 (let me stipulate that 'the entire four-dimensional reality' is to apply to *all* of reality), we obtain falsehood. The reason is that the component sentence concerns all of reality rather than just the 'time of evaluation', and hence evaluating the sentence with respect to 1935 is the same as evaluating the sentence for truth *simpliciter*. Since reality (now) contains a second world war, the sentence is false. A similar point can be made by invoking the notion of 'the crest of the wave', which is the present edge of reality, the portion of reality such that no events exist after it. The crest of the wave is, while I write this sentence, in 2000, but, Broad and Tooley want to say, it once was in 1935. The problem is that the proposed analysis of a current utterance of 'WAS-64-years-ago (the crest of the wave is present)' seems false, since when we inspect the 1935 slice of reality we find no crest.

These examples show that the defender of the growing block universe must accept *two* senses of the tenses. One sense is given an eternalist-style analysis in terms of the manifold; the other captures the *growth* in the manifold. (The defender of the moving spotlight must also accept two senses of the tenses, one reducible to B-facts, the other expressing the movement of the spotlight.) The latter seems not to be reducible to the former, for if it were, the actual growing block universe—a dynamic four-dimensional manifold whose crest is in 2000—could not be distinguished from a B-theoretic world in which time comes to an end in 2000. On the first sense, the tenses are in an important sense relative to times, since we need a reference point—the time of the token of a tensed sentence—to give an evaluation for truth. The tenses on the second reading are not relative in this way: it is true *simpliciter* that reality used to be smaller, and will be larger.

Michael Tooley appears to deny this (1997, chs. 1, 6, and 7). He defends the growing block universe theory of time, but holds that tenseless notions are analytically more basic than tensed ones. His core temporal notion is that of a state of affairs being *actual at a time*. Like the paradigmatic B-notion of having a property at a time, being actual at a time is a tenseless notion; whether a state of affairs is actual at a time does not change. He then uses this B-notion to give a reduction of various A-notions. The basic idea may be illustrated with an example. An utterance at t of 'there were dinosaurs', is true iff some time, t^*, is before t, and is such that some state of affairs involving dinosaurs existing is actual at t^*.

Tooley applies this account of tensed statements to statements expressing the growth of the block universe:[15]

... the states of affairs that are actual as of the year 1990 do not include any that involve purple sheep, whereas, given appropriate advances in genetic engineering, the states of affairs that are actual as of the year [3000] might very well do so. But such a difference is one that, on the face of it, can be described without using any tensed terms, since it is simply a matter of there being a spatiotemporal region in which various non-temporal properties, such as that of being purple, are instantiated, and which is actual as of the year [3000], but not as of the year 1990.

This passage is very confusing. Tooley appears to be saying *there are* states of affairs involving purple sheep, which are actual as of 3000 but not actual as of 1990. This seems to imply that there are states of affairs involving purple sheep; how then can he uphold the growing block universe view? Granted, he denies that these states of affairs are 'actual as of 1990', and would also deny that they are actual as of 2000, the current time. But they seem nevertheless to exist, on his view.

In interpreting Tooley's remarks in this way, I have implicitly construed his notion of actuality at a time as a binary relation between states of affairs and times. Given this construal, the statement that there is a state of affairs actual as of 3000 but not actual as of 1990 is parallel to saying there is a Democrat who voted for Clinton but not for Carter. It asserts the existence of a state of affairs, and goes on to describe its relations to the times 3000 and 1990. But Tooley may complain that I have not been fair to him. It was a slip, he might say, to make it sound as if *there are* states of affairs that are actual at 1990 but not 3000. It would be better to say: 'at 1990, it is not the case that there is a state of affairs of there being a purple sheep, whereas at 3000 it is the case that there is such a state of affairs'. On this alternate construal of actuality at a time, the binary predicate relating between states of affairs and times, $\lceil S$ is actual

---

[15] Tooley (1997: 19). I have changed his references to the year 2000 with a date safely guaranteed to be future whenever this book is read—the year 3000.

at $t^\rceil$, has been replaced by a sentential operator $\lceil$at $t, \varphi\rceil$, where t may be replaced with a name for a time and φ with a sentence. Moreover, this sentential operator shares the following feature with the presentist's operators WILL and WAS: $\lceil$at $t, \exists x\psi\rceil$ can be true even if $\exists x\psi$ is false— existential quantification inside the scope of the $\lceil$at $t\rceil$ operator is not ontologically committing.

This new position succeeds no better than the first. Tooley can now say that at 3000 there exists a state of affairs involving a purple cow without admitting that there exists any such state of affairs, just as a presentist can admit the truth of 'WAS (there exist dinosaurs)' without being committed to the existence of dinosaurs. The problem is that Tooley's statements about the past, for example 'in the Jurassic period, there exist states of affairs involving dinosaurs' are not ontologically committing either. So Tooley has no way to say that the past exists. For that matter, he has no way to say that the *present* exists. The quantification over states of affairs in the sentence 'in 2000, there exists a state of affairs involving Ted typing' remains inside the scope of the 'in 2000' operator, and hence is not ontologically committing. To commit to the existence of the past and present but not the future, Tooley would have to say one of two things, either of which reintroduces irreducibly tensed notions. One would be to say that quantification inside the scope of $\lceil$at $t\rceil$ *is* ontologically committing when t denotes a time at or before the *present* time. This use of 'present' would be irreducible to B-theoretic locutions, and thus would represent irreducible tense. The other would be to state his ontological commitments *without* using $\lceil$at $t\rceil$ operators. He could claim, without embedding this claim within an $\lceil$at $t\rceil$ operator, that *there exist states of affairs involving dinosaurs and computers, but not purple cows*. But this claim cannot be read as being eternally true— before there were computers it was false, and when there are purple cows it will be true—and thus represents an irreducibly tensed state of affairs. Thus, I continue to maintain that anyone who wants to defend the growing block universe theory must accept irreducible tense.

My discussion of Tooley has crucially employed a notion of existence that is not qualified or indexed in any way. In particular, I have assumed that in order to defend the thesis of the growing block universe Tooley must claim that dinosaurs and computers exist, and deny that purple cows exist. Whatever else he says about what exists or is actual *at times*, Tooley must make these claims about existence *simpliciter*. Compare what was said above about the genuineness of the dispute between presentists and eternalists. The difference between the views emerges when we ask: 'what exists'? Not 'exists at *t*'; rather, 'exists'! Likewise, the modal actualist and the possibilist disagree over what exists, not what exists at worlds; the mathematical Platonist and nominalist disagree over what exists, not over what 'mathematically exists' or what 'physically exists'. That questions about existence *simpliciter* are meaningful is central to the legitimacy of ontology.

In this book I will presuppose the B-theory—eternalism plus the reducibility of tense. It has already been argued that the moving spotlight view is unmotivated; that leaves two main competitors to the B-theory: presentism and the growing block universe. As a matter of fact, the growing block universe theory has pretty much the same bearing on the question of temporal parts as does the B-theory, so most of what I say while presupposing the B-theory could be easily rephrased if the growing block theory is correct. That leaves only presentism. Accordingly, for the remainder of this chapter I will set out the case against presentism.

2. CROSS-TIME SPATIAL RELATIONS

The typical presentist's tense operators include ⌜WAS φ⌝ and ⌜WILL φ⌝, as well as the metrical tense operators ⌜WAS, *n* units of time ago, φ⌝ and ⌜WILL, *n* units of time hence, φ⌝. These may be thought of, informally, as meaning, respectively, that φ is true at some past time, that φ is true at some future time, that φ is true at the time *n* units before the present, and that φ is true at the time *n* units after the present. These tense operators in a sense require talk of the past and future to proceed 'one time at a time', for in each case one can think of φ as asserted to be true at some one time. This fact was exploited above in demonstrating a genuine disagreement between presentists and eternalists, for the eternalist's claim that there exists a set containing a dinosaur and a computer could not be located within any one time. This fact also leads to an objection to presentism, that the presentist must deny the truth of everyday claims that concern multiple times taken together.

One example involves cross-time relations, for example the claim that some American philosophers admire some ancient Greek philosophers.

This claim is hard to capture in the presentist's tensed language. The present-tense sentence:

$\exists x \exists y$ (x is an American philosopher, and y is an ancient Greek philosopher, and x admires y)

is false because there do not (currently) exist any ancient Greek philosophers. The sentence:

WAS: $\exists x \exists y$ (x is an American philosopher, and y is an ancient Greek philosopher, and x admires y)

is no better, because at any time at which an ancient Greek philosopher exists, no American philosopher exists. The best bet would seem to be the following:

$\exists x$ [x is an American philosopher, and WAS: $\exists y$ (y is an ancient Greek philosopher, and x admires y)].

There is no longer a problem with existence, because only the quantifier over ancient Greek philosophers is embedded within the past-tense operator. However, there is still a problem: the predication 'x admires y' is within the scope of the 'WAS' operator, and is therefore required to be true at some one time in the past—a time at which ancient Greek philosophers existed. However, the admiration of an ancient Greek philosopher by a current American philosopher does not seem to be something that occurs at any one time in the past; it rather is a fact about two times at once. Thus, the claim that some American philosophers admire some ancient Greek philosophers is hard to capture in the presentist's tensed language. Similar issues are raised by David Lewis's (forthcoming) examples involving tensed plural quantifiers, for example the claim that there have been two kings of England named George.

It might be objected that the problem is due to overly narrow strictures on the sorts of tense operators the presentist is allowed to use. On the interpretation of the tense operators given above, WAS and WILL might be thought of as 'slice-operators': $\lceil$WAS $\varphi\rceil$ means that φ is true at some one instant—one slice of the past. The presentist might instead think of WAS and WILL as 'span-operators'. $\lceil$WAS $\varphi\rceil$ would then be regarded as true iff (as the eternalist would put it) φ is true in some extended region, or span, of the past. The problems then would be easy to solve. For example, Lewis's 'there have been two kings of England named George' could be represented as 'WAS $\exists x\ \exists y$ (x is a king of England named George and y is a king of England named George)'.

In fact the presentist cannot coherently make use of the span tense operators. Presentists do not think that it merely happens to be the case now that only currently existing objects exist. They think that it is *always* the case—indeed, that it *necessarily* is always the case—that only (then-) currently existing objects exist. (Compare: modal actualists do not think that it just happens to be the case that no non-actual things exist; they think that actualism is a necessary truth.) Presentists cannot admit, therefore, that there once were exceptions to presentism. But they would have to admit just this, if they accepted the span operators. For example, the sentence 'WAS $\exists x\ \exists y$ (x = Socrates and y = Kant)' comes out true, since its component sentence '$\exists x\ \exists y$ (x = Socrates and y = Kant)' is true of many spans of time in the past. And yet since there is no one instant at which Kant and Socrates exist, this component sentence '$\exists x\ \exists y$ (x = Socrates and y = Kant)' constitutes a violation of the presentist doctrine that there cannot exist non-present things—if two things never exist at the same instant then one or both must fail to exist at the present time.[16]

I will continue to assume, therefore, that the presentist must employ the slice tense operators. The problem remains how to represent sentences that concern multiple times taken together. Some presentists will attempt to paraphrase the problematic sentences into true sentences in their tensed language. Another strategy, which I discuss in Sider (1999*b*), is to admit the sentences are untrue but supply 'underlying truths', in virtue of which the sentences are in a sense grounded, and in virtue of which the utility of the sentences is explained.[17] But either strategy will have difficulty with certain fundamental cross-time relations that do not depend on facts expressible using the tenses. I have in

---

[16] The defender of span operators faces other difficulties as well. First, one worries that presentism thus construed is just eternalism in disguise. Secondly, as David Lewis pointed out (personal communication), the description of change using span operators is not straightforward. A situation where an enduring thing a is F yesterday and not-F the day before can be described with slice operators thus: WAS (a is F & WAS (a is not-F)). But with span operators we seem to have the apparently contradictory: WAS (a is F & a is not-F). This must somehow be dealt with.

[17] Yet another strategy is Ned Markosian's (forthcoming): admit the untruth of sentences ascribing cross-time relations but explain why they *seem* true to us.

mind spatial comparisons between objects at different times. Comparing the spatial positions of things at different times is crucial to science, for such comparisons are constitutive of notions like velocity and acceleration. The problem, roughly, is that these comparisons seem not to be captured by sentences formed from the presentist's tense operators since they involve comparing what happens at one time with what happens at a different time.

The problem evaporates if the presentist is willing to accept a Newtonian conception of substantival space, complete with the notion of absolute rest. On this picture there exist such things as *enduring places*, which have three important features. First, these places endure over time, unlike the momentary place-times of relativistic spacetime. Secondly, these places stand in the same spatial relations to each other at all times. Thirdly, material things *occupy* enduring places at times, and these facts about occupation ground all facts about the spatial relations between material things. I am currently 2 feet away from my computer screen because I currently occupy an enduring place that is 2 feet away from the place currently occupied by my computer screen.

If these enduring places are accepted, cross-time spatial comparisons could then be captured in the presentist's tensed language. For example, the claim that there used to be something with property *F* located at the very same place that object *a* currently occupies would be captured by the following sentence:

(*)   There is a place *p* occupied by object *a*, and WAS (there is something occupying *p* with property *F*).

The Newtonian theory of enduring places is known as a theory of 'absolute position' because the notion of remaining in one and the same place over time is well-defined on the theory—it is simply continuing to be located at one and the same enduring place. The problem is that there is no empirical basis for assuming that absolute comparisons of position make any sense. Such comparisons go far beyond the *relative* comparisons of position that are required for science, which are discussed below.

Newton, however, thought otherwise, because of his rotating bucket thought-experiment. In a world with nothing but a bucket of water there could still be a difference between a rotating and a stationary bucket, for only the water in the rotating bucket would produce a meniscus. These are empirically distinguishable scenarios, and hence any acceptable theory of space and time must allow them to be distinguished. Distinctions of rotation are distinctions of acceleration, but the rotating bucket does not accelerate with respect to any *other* objects since, by hypothesis, the world contains nothing other than the bucket. Acceleration is always acceleration *with respect to something*, Newton thought, and that something can only be an absolute space with enduring positions. However, as the subsequent development of spacetime geometry has shown, absolute position is not required to make sense of absolute acceleration. In both Minkowski spacetime and 'neo-Newtonian spacetime' absolute position is not well-defined, but certain classes of spacetime points correspond to the paths of unaccelerated particles. Absolute positions are not required to characterize these paths; the paths are simply the straight lines of the space's affine structure.

These ideas are described in detail in Lawrence Sklar's *Space, Time, and Spacetime* (1974: 202–9), but the basic idea is as follows. Think of constructing an abstract representation of the points of Newtonian spacetime in a familiar way, as ordered quadruples of real numbers, $<x, y, z, t>$, where x, y, and z represent spatial position and t represents the time (in some suitable units of measure). The square of the distance separating the points represented by $<x, y, z, t>$ and $<x', y', z', t'>$ is $(x - x')^2 + (y - y')^2 + (z - z')^2$. It is implicit in this representation that cross-time sameness of position is a meaningful notion, since the numbers representing spatial comparison are reused in points chosen from different times and figure in the calculation of distances between such points. But suppose we want to represent the structure of spacetime in such a way that cross-time sameness of position is *not* well-defined. We need, then, to find a representation of the structure of spacetime on which only notions that are empirically meaningful have corresponding components in the representation. We need to abstract away from cross-time sameness of position while retaining other meaningful comparisons.

To this end, let us construct an abstract representation of spacetime as a set of points, but in which these points are not quadruples of real numbers. Rather, the points are 'mere points'—for the moment they have no representational features beyond numerical distinctness from each other. These points are to be regarded as representing place-times— places at an instant. Now, a mere *set* of points represents nothing about spacetime beyond the number of points in spacetime. More structure must be introduced into the representation. Modern geometry has shown us various sorts of structure that can be introduced on a set of points; what is relevant here is what is called *affine structure*. The basic idea is to introduce notions which allow definition of the concept of a straight line. One way of doing this is to introduce a three-place relation on the points of the space, R (x, y, z), interpreted as meaning that point y is *linearly between* points x and z. Suitable axioms must be laid down constraining this relation R. Given how R holds over the points in the space, we can then categorize certain classes of points as *straight lines* (roughly: maximal classes such that any three distinct points in the class are such that one is linearly between the other two). But there will be no binary relation on points definable from R that would represent two place-times being *at the same position*.

Let us speak for the moment as eternalists. To say that an abstract representation of spacetime *represents* real-live physical spacetime is to say that there are physically meaningful relations whose distribution over physical spacetime points is isomorphic to the distribution of abstract relations (such as the betweenness relation R) over the points of the abstract spacetime, and that there are *no* physically meaningful spatiotemporal relations beyond those corresponding to the abstract relations built into the abstract space.

Finally we are in a position to relate these concepts to Newton's rotating bucket. The straight lines in an affine space may be physically interpreted as being the *paths of unaccelerated bodies*. In other words: in an abstract affine space, given how relation R holds, certain classes of points may be defined as abstract straight lines; any physical space represented by that abstract space will contain corresponding classes of physical points that may be thought of as physical straight lines; and these physical straight lines are the paths of unaccelerated bodies. In this sense, the notion of an unaccelerated path is meaningful in a physical affine space. In such a space, a stationary bucket of water is distinguished from a rotating bucket by its water molecules following straight paths through spacetime. Abstract Minkowski and neo-Newtonian spacetimes differ in important ways from each other, but each includes at least an affine structure. Thus, rotating and stationary buckets may be distinguished in physical Minkowski and neo-Newtonian spacetimes. But in neither Minkowski nor neo-Newtonian spacetime is *same-position-as* well-defined. That is to say, in abstract Minkowski and neo-Newtonian spacetimes there has not been introduced sufficient structure to define a binary relation of *same-position-as*, and hence there is no corresponding physically meaningful relation in the physical spacetimes they represent. The point, then, is that the physical considerations in Newton's rotating bucket thought-experiment do not support the claim that cross-time comparisons of position are meaningful, since Minkowski and neo-Newtonian spacetimes account for the thought-experiment (and are physically adequate in other ways as well).

The presentist cannot accept this argument, literally construed anyway. The notion of an abstract spacetime representing physical spacetime presupposed the existence of points of physical spacetime isomorphic to the abstract spacetimes, which contain points representing past and future place-times. Nevertheless, presentists should be moved by this argument not to presuppose absolute comparisons of position. *Philosophical* presentists, with whom this chapter is concerned, do not uphold presentism as a scientifically revisionary theory. While the typical scientist may speak as if eternalism is true in her talk of a single spacetime including past, present, and future, the presentist hopes such talk can be paraphrased (or at least regarded as quasi-true in the sense of Sider 1999b) using the tense operators. Since the scientists have given up on absolute comparisons of position, the philosophical presentist should not allow their analogs within his tensed statements, and so should disallow claims like (*) above.

Let us then set absolute rest aside. The presentist can still accept claims of *object-relative* spatial position over time, for example:

> It WAS/WILL BE the case *n* units of time ago/hence that: (Ted Sider is 5 feet from Bill Clinton).

Such claims specify my location at other times *relative to where Bill Clinton is located at those times*, but that is not good enough. Without a way of specifying Clinton's state of motion over time in some way that is not relative to the positions of other objects, these claims leave out certain kinds of information about my changing spatial position over time. The omitted information is not information about my absolute position, for as argued above there is no reason to suppose comparisons of absolute position to be meaningful. It is rather information about the affine and topological structure of my path through spacetime. As mentioned above, the notion of an unaccelerated path through spacetime is well-defined in both neo-Newtonian and Minkowski spacetime. Moreover, from the topological structure of both neo-Newtonian and Minkowski spacetime (a further level of structure even more fundamental than affine structure), the notion of a continuous curve through spacetime is also well-defined. Thus, there are three distinct possibilities for my state of motion over, say, the last five minutes:

(P1) I have moved along a continuous unaccelerated path.

(P2) I have moved along a continuous but accelerated path.

(P3) I have moved along a discontinuous path.

The problem for the presentist is that it is unclear how the possibilities can be distinguished. Recall that the facts about accelerated paths in an affine space flow from a three-place relation, R, of linear betweenness. This is a cross-time relation—the very sort of relation the presentist has difficulty capturing in his tensed language.

The presentist must describe the world using sentences of the form:

It WAS/WILL BE the case *n* units of time ago/hence that: φ.

The totality of such sentences specifies a series of 'snapshots' of the world at successive moments of time, complete with the order and temporal distance relations between the snapshots. (I here ignore relativity, and thus focus on neo-Newtonian spacetime; the Minkowski spacetime of special relativity introduces its own complications, explored in Sect. 4 below.) But the sentences do not specify how the snapshots line up with each other spatially, since such facts are not facts about what things are like at any one time. Any one of (P1) through (P3) is consistent with the totality of the sentences; the presentist's tensed facts do not fix which is true.

To simply accept this conclusion, that there is never any fact of the matter about the most basic dynamical physical facts, is just not an option. The only course open to the presentist would be to provide some sort of necessarily true 'bridge principles' that say: *if* the series of snapshots takes a certain form, *then* the snapshots 'automatically' line up in such and such a way. The bridge principles might, for example, line up the snapshots so as to maximize continuous unaccelerated motions. A little more carefully: consider constructing an eternalist model of the world, an abstract Neo-Newtonian spacetime with a selected time to serve as the present moment, based on the set **P** of the totality of the presentist's tensed truths. **P** constrains what goes on at the various times of the model, including single-time spatial relations between objects, but does not constrain cross-time spatial relations. Thus, **P** can be embedded in eternalist models in various ways. In any such model we can evaluate the degree to which motions are continuous and unaccelerated by comparing the distances between different particles at successive times, which **P** *does* fix. On one way of lining up the snapshots, the distance between a pair of particles might vary linearly with time, whereas on another it might vary non-linearly, or even discontinuously. Consider, now, the class **E** of eternalist models that are consistent with **P** and maximize continuous and unaccelerated motions. In any such model one can evaluate the truth value of a sentence (like (P1)–(P3)) that makes a cross-time spatial comparison. The presentist, then, can say that one of these sentences is true iff it is true in every member of **E**.

On this view, possibilities (P1) through (P3) can be distinguished in cases where the world is sufficiently rich. If the world is like the actual world, containing a vast number of things in motion, most of which are moving inertially (or nearly inertially), there will be only one way of lining up the 'snapshots' that maximizes continuity and unaccelerated paths. Relative to this way of lining up the snapshots, some particles may undergo non-inertial or discontinuous motion. But in simple cases possibilities (P2) and (P3) will disappear. If the world consists of just a solitary electron existing at all times, the theory has the result that the electron is moving inertially at all times; but, one might have thought, the electron could have been accelerating or even moving discontinuously. The presentist must deny these possible differences. The eternalist, of course, can accept them. Pre-analytically, the possibilities exist; the case of cross-time spatial relations therefore favors eternalism.

The argument has been that the presentist's tensed language contains the resources to specify a series of 'snapshots' capturing what the world is like at various instants, but not the resources to specify how to spatially line up the snapshots; the presentist cannot, therefore, capture certain facts about the states of motion of particles. But if states of motion are themselves specified by the snapshots, the objection fails. Which of (P1) through (P3) holds would then depend on which of the following groups of tensed claims is true:

(G1) I am not accelerating AND
      WAS-1-minute-ago (I am not accelerating) AND
      WAS-2-minutes-ago (I am not accelerating) AND
      etc.

(G2) I am accelerating AND
      WAS-1-minute-ago (I am accelerating) AND
      WAS-2-minutes-ago (I am accelerating) AND
      etc.

(G3) I am moving discontinuously OR
      WAS-1-minute-ago (I am moving discontinuously) OR
      WAS-2-minutes-ago (I am moving discontinuously) OR
      etc.

In fact I do not think that such claims would be legitimate for the presentist to invoke. The reason is that I, like many others, accept Bertrand Russell's (1903, ch. LIV) 'at-at' theory of motion and related dynamical quantities, according to which motion is simply the occupation of successive places at successive times. To have a velocity *at a time*, t, on this view, is to be appropriately located at moments of time immediately prior to and immediately following t. More carefully, to have an instantaneous velocity v at a time is for the derivative of one's position function $p(t)$ to have value v at that time. Given the familiar definition of the derivative in terms of limits of ratios, this means that velocity is not an intrinsic property of an object at a time; to have a velocity at a time is to be located at appropriate places in the 'infinitesimally immediate' past and future. The same goes for acceleration; to be accelerating at a time, t, is for the second derivative of one's position function to be non-zero, and therefore is a matter of the positions one occupies before and after t. Likewise for the state of moving continuously: one moves continuously depending on what one's positions are over time.

Given the Russellian theory, my instantaneous state of motion is a matter of my positions at various times. Claims like (G1) through (G3) are therefore not ultimate, but must be grounded in facts of location over time. But these facts are precisely what I have been arguing the presentist cannot capture. Given the Russellian theory of motion, then, the argument from cross-time relations stands.

There does exist an alternative to the Russellian theory of motion, according to which dynamical quantities are intrinsic to times. Whether and how an object is moving at a time is a fact about what that object is like *then*.

On this view velocity is independent in some sense of successive spatial position; but if the anti-Russellian introduces a quantity that is *entirely* unrelated to position it is hard to see what this quantity would have to do with *velocity*. This view's leading contemporary defender, Michael Tooley, therefore holds that velocities are irreducible 'first-order' properties that are *picked out* as those properties that are, in fact, nomically correlated with the first derivative of the position function. According to Tooley (1988, sect. 3), the term 'velocity' is to be given a theoretical definition of the Ramsey–Lewis style[18] in which the reference-fixing postulates are the laws of motion. Thus, Tooley picks out velocity as the property, v, that actually satisfies the following equation, among others:

$$\mathbf{T}_1: \ s(x,t_2) = s(x,t_1) + {}_{t1}\!\int^{t2} v(x,t)dt$$

I myself prefer the Russellian theory because of its simplicity and reductive nature. If it is true, no spatiotemporal facts beyond those of spatial and temporal distance need be postulated. It seems to me there are no good reasons to introduce Tooley's complications into the theory of space and time, and in the absence of such reasons the simpler Russellian theory is preferable. But even if I am wrong about the virtues of Tooley's theory, it is of no help to the presentist in solving the problem under discussion. According to Tooley we are to pick out velocity by its role in the laws of nature. This role concerns the relation between velocity and spatial position over time. But the latter is precisely what I have been arguing the presentist cannot capture in his tensed language. The presentist, therefore, has no way to pick out Tooley's non-Russellian velocities.

3.   THE TRUTH-MAKER OBJECTION

A second argument against presentism addresses the legitimacy of taking the tense operators as primitive.[19] The presentist claims that 'WAS

---

[18] See Lewis (1970).

[19] Another objection to primitive tense operators is McTaggart's (1908) infamous argument for the incoherence of the A-theory. It amazes me that this argument is still advanced. I sympathize with Broad (1938: 309–17) when he calls it a 'howler'; see also Prior (1967: 4–7).

(there exist some dinosaurs)' is true. But if there do not exist any past dinosaurs, what *grounds* the truth of this sentence?

The vague assumption that truths must be 'grounded' can be made precise in a couple of ways. One is the *truth-maker principle*: for every truth, T, there exists an entity—a 'truth-maker'—whose existence suffices for the truth of T.[20] These truth-makers are often called states of affairs or facts, and are thought of as concrete constituents of the world in the tradition of Russell (1918) and Wittgenstein (1961).

Many have objected to the requirement that negative existential sentences like 'there are no unicorns' must have truth-makers. It is comparatively easy to see how there could be an entity that necessitates the truth of 'there exists a cat'—for any cat, c, the fact of c's existence seems like the kind of entity one can bump up against and kick around. In contrast we never bump up against any fact whose existence entails that there are no unicorns. It is only the positive states of affairs whose inclusion in the concrete world seems unproblematic. And even very large positive states of affairs are not truth-makers for 'there are no unicorns', for given any such state of affairs, S, it would be possible for there to exist a unicorn *in addition to S*.

To avoid this sort of difficulty John Bigelow (1988: 130–3) and David Lewis (1992: 215–19) formulate the grounding principle instead as the claim that *truth is supervenient on being*: what is true supervenes on what objects exist, what properties those objects have, and what relations they stand in. This principle does not require the existence of a fact that there are no unicorns; it merely requires that since 'there are no unicorns' is true in the actual world, it must also be true in any world in which the same objects exist, those objects instantiate the same properties, and those objects stand in the same relations as they do in the actual world.

Either way the grounding principle is cashed out, the point is to rule out dubious ontologies that posit 'ungrounded' truths, for example 'brute counterfactuals' with no basis in the way things actually are. The thought is that it is illegitimate to postulate truths that 'float free' of the world. At first glance it would appear that the presentist's tensed truths float free of the world—they seem not to have truth-makers and not to supervene on being. For the presentist, all states of affairs are *currently* existing states of affairs, and the properties and relations of objects are

----

[20]   See Armstrong (1997, esp. ch. 8); Martin (1996); and Mulligan *et al.* (1984).

confined to those of *currently* existing objects. But surely the truth about the past is not fixed by such facts about the present.

Lewis invokes the principle that truth is supervenient on being in a discussion of something entirely different, but mentions in passing that presentism seems to be inconsistent with that principle (1992: 219). Bigelow, on the other hand, is himself a presentist, but wishes to uphold the principle that truth is supervenient on being. What he claims is that the world—the sum total of everything—instantiates properties like *previously containing dinosaurs*. Tensed truths then supervene on the instantiation of these properties (Bigelow 1996). The defender of the truth-maker principle could, in a similar vein, postulate tensed states of affairs such as *there once existing dinosaurs* as truth-makers. Clearly, the success of the truth-maker argument against presentism depends crucially on whether such moves are legitimate or whether they 'cheat'. In fact I think they do cheat, and I will say below in what sense I think they cheat. But first it must be argued that the presentist must indeed cheat in this way; it must be argued that no other truth-makers or super-venience base for tensed truths can be found in the present.

The presentist might try to ground tensed truths in facts about current objects and the laws of nature. On this approach, 'there once existed dinosaurs' is true because its truth is allegedly entailed by the laws of nature and the properties and relations instantiated at the present time by currently existing objects.

Note that no regularity theory of laws of nature could then be accepted. In its simplest form, a regularity theory says that a law of nature is simply a true statement of the form 'All *F*s are *G*s'—a 'regularity'. (Much modification is needed for this simple statement to approach adequacy; see Armstrong 1983, part I.) If tensed facts are to be grounded in the laws, the laws could not themselves be grounded in the tensed facts. The only regularities available for securing the laws would therefore be *current* regularities, and regularity theories are only plausible if the regularities are drawn from all of time. Some more robust account of laws of nature would appear to be required, some account allowing the presentist to say that what counts as a law of nature does not supervene on the distribution of non-nomic properties over currently existing objects.

The Armstrong (1983)/Tooley (1987)/Dretske (1977) view that laws of nature are relations between universals, for example, would better suit the presentist. On this view, nomic facts are facts over and above the totality of non-nomic facts. A law that all *F*s are *G*s involves the holding of a higher-order relation, the nomic necessitation relation, *N*, between the universals *F-ness* and *G-ness*. Whenever *N* holds between *F-ness* and *G-ness* then there is a regularity that all *F*s are *G*s, but the converse does not hold—it is possible for there to be a regularity without a corresponding law. Thus, two possible worlds alike in what regularities hold, and thus alike in the instantiation of first-order universals like *F-ness* and *G-ness*, might yet differ in how the higher-order relation *N* is instantiated, and thus might contain different laws of nature.

Appealing to this theory to reply to the truth-maker argument would represent an added commitment associated with presentism. Moreover, David Lewis (1986*b*, p. xii) and Bas van Fraassen (1989, ch. 5) have argued powerfully that Armstrong, Tooley, and Dretske cannot explain how *N*'s holding between *F-ness* and *G-ness* could possibly entail the regularity that all *F*s are *G*s.

More importantly, grounding the tenses in the present plus the laws of nature threatens to imply that the past is 'open', just as some have claimed that the future is open. If the laws of nature are present-to-past indeterministic, current facts plus the laws do not imply all the facts about the past; given presentism and either the truth-maker principle or the principle that truth supervenes on being, for many statements, φ, neither ⌜it was the case that φ⌝ nor ⌜it was the case that not-φ⌝ will be true. Jan Lukasiewicz (1967: 38–9) was one philosopher who was willing to accept the openness of the past, and in fact pointed out a welcome feature of this doctrine: 'There are hard moments of suffering and still harder ones of guilt in everyone's life. We should be glad to be able to erase them not only from our memory but also from existence.' But few, I suspect, would be willing to follow Lukasiewicz in this belief, however comforting it may be. (And of course it may well not be comforting, given that the good in the past would be erased along with the bad.) Perhaps we will never *know* what caused the dinosaurs to become extinct, but very few of us are so verificationist as to doubt there is a fact of the matter![21]

---

[21] The class of philosophers, as always, provides exceptions. Michael Dummett (1969) expresses sympathy for the verificationist position; see also Crispin Wright (1987, essays 3 and 5).

Even if the laws are deterministic, the problem of the open past still arises if the presentist accepts the Russellian theory of motion discussed in the previous section. If velocity is a matter of one's location in the past and future, fixing the properties and relations of present objects will not fix their velocities (I continue to set aside 'cheating' by allowing tensed properties or relations). And there is no hope whatsoever that the laws of nature plus *non-dynamical* properties of present objects will entail anything interesting at all about the past.

As before there is the possibility of rejecting Russell's theory of motion in favor of Tooley's. I continue to think this would detract from presentism's attraction since the Russellian theory is intrinsically preferable. But this issue need not be joined, for as in the previous section the presentist cannot make use of Tooley's theoretical definition of velocity as the property, v, that actually satisfies the following equation, among others:

$$\mathbf{T_1}: \quad s(x,t_2) = s(x,t_1) + {}_{t1}\!\int^{t2} v(x,t)dt$$

$\mathbf{T_1}$ is a law stated from an eternalist's point of view; the presentist's version must involve tensed properties of location. But now the velocities are being grounded in the tensed properties (via the Tooleyan theoretical definition that utilizes $\mathbf{T_1}$), while the tensed properties are being grounded in the velocities (to answer the challenge to presentism from the principle that truth supervenes on being or the truth-maker principle.) The worry can be brought out more carefully, as follows. Unless we 'cheat', the truth-maker principle or the principle that truth supervenes on being require truths to supervene on, or be made true by, facts about which non-tensed properties and relations are instantiated by which objects. A law of dynamics, for example $\mathbf{T_1}$, must then hold in virtue of these facts. But it can't, for once the tensed facts of location are left out, the law $\mathbf{T_1}$ can only involve the necessitation relation (remember that we are assuming the Armstrong/Dretske/Tooley view) and the primitive velocity properties, and thus cannot relate velocity to location.

I conclude, then, that if the presentist is to continue to uphold the principle that truth supervenes on being, or the truth-maker principle, she must 'cheat' by somehow incorporating tense into the properties or relations of present objects. She must stubbornly insist that, for example, it is a 'rock-bottom fact about the world' that the world has the property of *previously containing dinosaurs*. What should we make of this?

The point of the truth-maker principle and the principle that truth supervenes on being is to rule out dubious ontologies. Let us consider some. First, brute dispositions. Many would insist that the fragility of a wine glass—its disposition to shatter if dropped—must be grounded in the non-dispositional properties of the glass, plus perhaps the laws of nature. It would be illegitimate to claim that the glass's disposition to shatter is completely brute or ungrounded. Second example: brute counterfactuals. Most would say that when a counterfactual conditional is true, for example 'this match would light if struck', its truth must be grounded in the actual, occurrent properties of the match and its surroundings. Someone who postulates counterfactuals *not* grounded in this way is Alvin Plantinga (1974: 180). Imagine God deliberating whether to create a certain free creature, C. According to Plantinga this amounts to deciding whether to cause a certain individual essence to be instantiated; the essence exists whether or not instantiated. God must take into account certain true counterfactual conditionals specifying what free choices C would make if placed in certain circumstances. These counterfactuals hold even if God decides not to create C, and therefore seem objectionably ungrounded, since they depend in no way on what existing things are like. Third example: the theory that there is a law of nature that Fs are Gs iff each object in the world has a certain 'brute' property *being such that all* Fs *lawfully must be* Gs. Fourth example: imagine someone who believes in only one point in space, but introduces irreducible 'spatial tense operators', for example NORTH (φ), much like Prior's temporal tense operators. Final example: Prior himself (1968*b*) once investigated the possibility of introducing 'personal tense operators', which would be formally analogous to temporal tense operators. Instead of writing 'everyone taller than me is sitting', one would replace the quantifier over persons with an operator ALL-TALL, resulting in the sentence 'ALL-TALL (Sitting)'. Now imagine a solipsist claiming that the operators are primitive (Prior himself advocated no such thing). The solipsist claims to reject the existence of other people but reconstructs what the rest of us regard as talk of other persons using these personal tense operators.[22]

The argument against allowing the presentist to 'cheat' by invoking primitive properties like *previously containing dinosaurs*, or by invoking

---

[22] I thank Roy Sorensen for this example.

the tenses themselves as primitive, is that this cheat seems of a kind with the dubious ontological cheats of the previous paragraph. In each case the cheater is unwilling to accept an ontology robust enough to bear the weight of the truths he feels free to invoke.

What seems common to all the cheats is that irreducibly *hypothetical* properties are postulated, whereas a proper ontology should invoke only *categorical*, or occurrent, properties and relations. Categorical properties involve what objects are actually like, whereas hypothetical properties 'point beyond' their instances. The presentist's primitive tensed properties (or operators, or whatever) would be hypothetical. Whether the world has the property *previously containing dinosaurs* is not a matter of what the world itself is like, but points beyond itself, to the past. The distinction between categorical and hypothetical is admittedly elusive, though it seems to get at the core of what is wrong with the dubious ontologies. But note that the argument against presentism is not strictly tied to the hypothesis that non-categoricity is to blame. The argument without this claim would simply be that the presentist's primitive tenses share some unspecified negative feature with the rejected ontologies.

This argument against primitive tense would work just as well against taking modal operators as primitive, for modal notions are paradigmatically hypothetical. Here the argument hits close to home, since many philosophers do precisely this. I have been urging that we reject the presentist's primitive tense operators and instead accept the B-theoretic reduction of tense, which reduction requires postulating past objects. But only David Lewis pursues the analogous strategy in the philosophy of modality. In his infamous *On the Plurality of Worlds* (1986*a*), Lewis gives a reduction of modality analogous to the B-theoretic reduction of tense by interpreting modal operators as quantifiers over non-actual but existent possible worlds and individuals. Most philosophers, myself included, are unwilling to accept Lewis's modal realism, and instead are actualists. The question, then, is whether we actualists can consistently uphold the ban on primitive non-categorical notions.[23]

In fact we can, by reducing modality to categorical notions without invoking Lewisian possible worlds. Though this is not the place to pursue

---

[23] I thank Trenton Merricks for persistently pressing me on this issue.

this reduction in detail,[24] this is the place to show why one cannot equally well reduce the presentist's tenses. The crucial difference is that there is a hope for reducing modality to notions like logical consistency, analyticity, and so on, which (hopefully!) are themselves categorical notions, or at least reduce to categorical notions. Though the project faces obstacles, I believe they are surmountable. But there is no chance whatsoever of reducing the tense operators to anything like logical or analytical consistency. Beef up the notion of consistency any way you like; there will still remain consistent things that never happened. Thus, the symmetry between time and modality is broken. An actualist can object to the presentist's primitive tenses provided she is willing to forgo primitive modal operators.

4.   PRESENTISM AND SPECIAL RELATIVITY

I turn finally to what is often (justifiably, I think) considered to be the fatal blow to presentism: that it is inconsistent with special relativity. The notion of the *present* time that is so crucial to presentism is meaningless within Minkowski spacetime, in which there is no distinguished partition of spacetime into space and time, and no observer-independent notion of simultaneity.[25]

Some presentists have said: so much the worse for special relativity, at least in its Minkowskian formulation.[26] Perhaps future empirical research will bear out this position, but in cases of science versus metaphysics, historically the smart money has been on science.[27] At any rate, the present discussion will assume that consistency with something fairly close to current physics is a constraint that must be met by any adequate theory of time.

[24] For recent reductive theories of modality see Armstrong (1989), Peacocke (1999, ch. 4, 1997), and my unpublished 'Reducing Modality' (Sider 2000a).

[25] The literature on presentism and special relativity includes: Godfrey-Smith (1979); Hinchliff (1996); Prior (1970, 1996); Putnam (1967); Rietdijk (1966, 1976); Savitt (1994, 2000); Sklar (1981); Stein (1968, 1970); Weingard (1972).

[26] Prior (1970: 248): 'all physics has shown to be true or likely is that in some cases we can never *know*, we can never *physically find out*, whether something is actually happening or merely has happened or will happen'; see also Prior (1996).

[27] Note, however, that some recent work within physics has suggested a need for a distinguished simultaneity relation; see the end of Balashov (2000), who cites Cushing (1994, sect. 10.4.2).

I begin by describing informally the important differences between classical and Minkowski spacetime. Classical spacetime, whether in a Newtonian form that includes absolute rest or a neo-Newtonian form that does not, may be based on a four-dimensional manifold of space-time points that includes all that happens in the past, present, and future. In this spacetime, simultaneity is a well-defined, absolute concept. For any given point, p, the set of points simultaneous with p is called a hyperplane of simultaneity. Since classical simultaneity is an equivalence relation, the set of hyperplanes of simultaneity is a partition of classical spacetime. Think of any one of these hyperplanes as the 'present' and the rest of the spacetime divides into those points that are temporally after all the points in the hyperplane (the *future*), and all the points temporally before the points in the hyperplane (the *past*). These temporal relations of *simultaneity*, *before*, and *after*, are absolute, in the sense that they are intrinsic to the geometry of classical spacetime, and do not depend in any way on observers.

Minkowski spacetime also consists of a four-dimensional manifold of spacetime points that contains all of what happens in what we normally call the past, present, and future. But Minkowski spacetime does not include the classical notion of simultaneity. Just as the notion of absolute rest is not well defined in neo-Newtonian spacetime, the notion of simultaneity is not well defined in Minkowski spacetime. Thus, Minkowski spacetime is not partitioned into ordered hyperplanes of simultaneity. With any given point in spacetime, there cannot be associated a set of those points simultaneous with the given point. There are, however, three well-defined sets worth mentioning, relative to any given point p: (1) the *absolute future* of p: the set of points that could be reached from p by a signal traveling at or below the speed of light; (2) the *absolute past* of p: the set of points from which p may be reached by a signal traveling at or below the speed of light; and (3) the set of points *spacelike* separated from p: those points that cannot be connected to p by any signal traveling at or below the speed of light (see Fig. 2.1). These sets are well defined: although simultaneity is not well defined it is well defined which points can be reached from which by a signal traveling below the speed of light. The relation between points p_1 and p_2 when p_2 can be reached by a sub-luminal signal originating at p_1 is an intrinsic feature of the spacetime. Note that the relation of spacelike separation is intransitive, and therefore cannot be

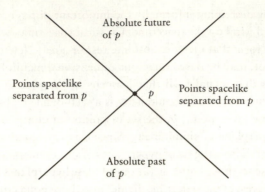

FIG. 2.1. Regions of Minkowski spacetime

used to partition Minkowski spacetime into anything like hyperplanes of simultaneity.

I have said that simultaneity is not well defined in Minkowski spacetime, but what is strictly speaking true is that absolute simultaneity is not well defined. A *relative* notion of simultaneity can be defined via the Einsteinian 'radar' definition of simultaneity for a given observer. Imagine an observer moving on some inertial (unaccelerated) path, F. Such a path is called a *frame of reference*. At a certain point, p_1, along path F, the observer sends out a light signal, which bounces off some other point, p, and intersects F at another point p_2. On the radar definition of simultaneity, point p is regarded as being *simultaneous relative to the observer's state of motion along path* F with the midpoint, m, between p_1 and p_2 on F. Simultaneity thus defined varies depending on the state of motion of the observer; points other than p will be regarded as simultaneous with m if the observer's path through m is something other than F. Given this definition of simultaneity relative to a frame of reference, one can also introduce frame-relative notions of past and future. Relative to any frame of reference F through point p, another point q may be defined as being in the past of p relative to F iff q is in the absolute past of some point simultaneous with p relative to F; q may be defined as future to p relative to F iff q is in the absolute future of some point simultaneous with p relative to F.

In what sense is Minkowski spacetime inconsistent with presentism? There is a superficial inconsistency right at the surface since Minkowski spacetime includes all of history's events in a single existent manifold.

But by this measure presentism is already inconsistent with classical spacetime, which also consists of a four-dimensional manifold. This is not surprising: scientific spatiotemporal theories are typically formulated under eternalist assumptions since the formulation is much easier, and since scientists do not typically share philosophers' scruples about the ontology of past and future objects.

The more interesting question is whether, despite the superficial inconsistency, there might yet be a consistent hybrid theory that departs in letter from presentism or special relativity (or both), but in some sense preserves the essential spirit of each. To give the idea of what is sought, return to classical spacetime. The presentist could replace the four-dimensional classical spacetime with a single hyperplane of simultaneity, the present. Assertions about other points in the spacetime would then be translated into tensed claims in which all quantifiers over non-present points or events or objects are inside the scope of tense operators. This is, in effect, what presentists who are not thinking about relativity usually do. This seems like a coherent view (although there are of course philosophical objections, for example those discussed above). The question is whether one can formulate this sort of presentism/Minkowskian hybrid.

My argument from relativity against presentism will be that no plausible presentism/Minkowskian hybrid exists. I will survey various possibilities for constructing a hybrid theory and raise objections in each case.

What would the hybrid look like? The presentist wants to deny existence to some of the events and objects accepted by the eternalist. The classical presentist wanted to banish *past* and *future* events and objects, but the notions of present, past, and future look very different in Minkowski spacetime. Each hybrid theory I will examine will be a claim that only a certain proper subset of the eternalist's Minkowski spacetime is real. Talk of the rest of spacetime must be captured in some way by primitive tense operators. The hybrids differ by selecting different portions of spacetime as the real portions.

Hybrid 1: here-now-ism. First, the presentist might banish all of spacetime other than a single point.[28] (A related proposal would be to banish

---

[28] See Hinchliff (1996), Savitt (2000), Sklar (1981), and Stein (1968: 15).

all of spacetime other than a single point plus its past light cone.)[29] Thus construed, presentism is more rightly called 'here-now-ism'. Note that the right way to assert here-now-ism is to say that only a single point of spacetime is real, that there exist no spatiotemporally distant events. The wrong way is to say that *at any point in spacetime, only a single point of spacetime is real*. This suggests a misleading picture, that there *are* multiple points in spacetime, but somehow, from the perspective of one of them, the others are not real. Unless the presentist is indulging in a Meinongian distinction between being and existence, this can only be a confusion.

The first problem for here-now-ism involves the tense operators that must be postulated. The here-now-ist cannot simply take over the classical presentist's WAS and WILL, since those presuppose that there are absolute facts about what is before, simultaneous, or after a given point-event. What WAS the case or what WILL be the case should depend on the states of motion of observers. The natural way to incorporate this in a relativistic context would be to relativize the tense operators to frames of reference. The sentence 'WAS (*F*, There exist dinosaurs)' might be thought of as expressing a relation between a frame of reference, *F*, and the proposition that there exist dinosaurs. The eternalist would say that this sentence, as uttered at point *p*, is true iff there exists some dinosaur located in the past of *p* relative to frame of reference *F*, though of course the presentist takes the tense operator as primitive. But the problem for the here-now-ist is that the tense operators cannot be relations to frames of reference, since the here-now-ist's ontology contains no frames of reference. A frame of reference is a path extending through spacetime, whereas the here-now-ist's ontology consists only of a point.

Secondly, the truth-maker objection to presentism becomes more acute than ever. Reality has shrunk to a single point, and seems to contain few truth-makers and little Being on which Truth might supervene.

Finally, here-now-ism is solipsistic in a way that presentism was not. While the presentist denied reality to all times other than a single one, multiple objects within the present time were equally real. Not so for the here-now-ist. ('Solipsistic' is in fact a bit of a misnomer, for there may be no person located at the sole point that is real. One might worry that persons and other macro-objects would *never* exist given here-now-ism

---

[29] See Godfrey-Smith (1979) and Hinchliff (1996).

since no macroscopic object could fit into a single point. But the here-now-ist might claim that a person can exist without *fitting into* reality, just as the standard non-relativistic presentist claims that I exist despite not temporally fitting into the present moment.)

Hybrid 2: retain an arbitrary 'hyperplane'. A second possibility would be to banish all of Minkowski spacetime save a single 'hyperplane' of simultaneity relative to some frame of reference. From the eternalist's point of view the idea can be put as follows: for some frame of reference, F, and some point, p, the presentist accepts the reality of all and only points simultaneous with p relative to F. I call this accepting an 'arbitrary' hyperplane because, from the eternalist's point of view, the presentist's selection of the frame of reference, F, which is used to pick out the set of points deemed real, is arbitrary—no suitable frame of reference is distinguished by the intrinsic geometry of Minkowski spacetime.

Hybrid 2 improves on here-now-ism by eliminating the solipsistic element—spatially distant planets, for example, become real. In this way it is closer to the spirit of traditional presentism. Being, moreover, includes a bit more on which Truth might be thought to supervene. The tenses must still presumably be taken as primitive, but at least *some* statements, for example present-tense statements about Mars, may be grounded in Being.

The main problem with Hybrid 2 is that it is scientifically revisionary, for it in essence recognizes a distinguished relation of distant simultaneity. According to the eternalist Minkowskian, if I snap my finger there are events such that there is no fact of the matter whether they are simultaneous with the snapping. But according to Hybrid 2 this is not the case, for one may define simultaneity with the snap as *coexistence*. If you snap your finger across the room and your snap and my snap equally exist, there surely is an affirmative answer to the question whether they occur at the same time. No such answer can be given by the eternalist Minkowskian.

So, the defender of Hybrid 2 must admit the existence of an absolute simultaneity relation. It would be natural to be even more scientifically revisionary and admit all the other spatiotemporal comparisons of classical (or at least neo-Newtonian) spacetime, including absolute comparisons of temporal and spatial distance. From the eternalist's point of view, admitting absolute simultaneity is in effect choosing an arbitrary frame of reference, *F*, to pick out a distinguished relation of simultaneity. The admission of absolute comparisons of temporal and spatial distance in addition seems to be of a piece with the admission of absolute simultaneity: absolute spatial and temporal comparisons would be, from the eternalist's point of view, temporal and spatial distance comparisons relative to this same frame *F*. Moreover, suppose the defender of Hybrid 2 resisted admitting absolute comparisons of spatial and temporal distance. She would then need to relativize the metrical tense operators ⌜WAS *n* units ago⌝ and ⌜WILL *n* units hence⌝ to frames of reference. But since reality according to Hybrid 2 consists only of a plane, frames of reference do not exist.

Hybrids 3 to 5: retaining four-dimensional regions. A different reaction to special relativity would be to retain a four-dimensional region rather than merely a point (or hypersurface), of Minkowski spacetime. Three possibilities present themselves (see Fig. 2.2.): (1) retain a past light cone—a point *p* plus every point in *p*'s absolute past; (2) retain a future light cone—a point *p* plus every point in *p*'s absolute future; (3) retain some point, *p*, plus every point spacelike separated from *p*—a 'bowtie'. The ontology of each of Hybrids 3 to 5 is a four-dimensional region, and hence includes inertial paths through spacetime—frames of reference— to which tense operators may be relativized. This is a great improvement on Hybrids 1 and 2. Another improvement is that reality contains more truth-makers and more Being; fewer truths must float on nothing. None of Hybrids 3 to 5 is scientifically revisionary in the way Hybrid 2 is. Each of the three sorts of region (a past light cone, a future light cone, and a bowtie) are regions definable within Minkowski spacetime, once point *p* is chosen. None of these hybrids resurrects absolute simultaneity. Of course, the eternalist will deny that any point *p* within Minkowski spacetime is distinguished in the way required by these hybrids. But this just represents the core disagreement between presentists and eternalists. Even in classical or neo-Newtonian spacetime the presentist chooses a single hyperplane of simultaneity as the solely existing present; the choice of *p* is analogous.

However, new difficulties emerge. A serious problem with Hybrids 3 and 4 is that they are quite distant from the intuitive picture with which presentists began. Reality contains dinosaurs according to the first, and (perhaps) Martian outposts according to the second. Gone is the intuition

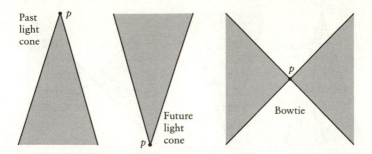

FIG. 2.2. Hybrids 3 to 5

that the past is no more, and the future is yet to be. These were the intuitions motivating the presentist to adopt his theory in the first place. If
they must be sacrificed, why be a presentist? (As Steven Savitt (2000)
points out, similar remarks apply to the view mentioned parenthetically
above, that reality consists of a point plus all the points on the surface of
its past light cone.)

Moreover, all three hybrids lack certain theoretical features that have
been claimed to be distinctive of presentism. First, it has been argued
(Hinchliff 1996; Merricks 1994*a*) that presentism is to be accepted
because only the presentist can acceptably account for the phenomenon
of change without relativizing property instantiation. This argument
will be discussed fully in Chapter 4, Section 6, but the quick version runs
as follows. A changing thing apparently exemplifies contradictory
properties *F* and not-*F*. Any adequate theory of change must resolve the
apparent contradiction. One way is to relativize property instantiation
to times: a changing thing is *F* relative to one time but not relative to
another. This is argued by some to be objectionable, since it makes all
properties relational. But Merricks and Hinchliff argue that the presentist can account for change without relativizing property instantiation.
Suppose *x* used to be *F* but is not any longer. Reality consists only of the
present, and so we can say that *x* lacks *F* *simpliciter*, and capture the fact
that *x* changed by saying that it WAS the case that *x* instantiated *F* (*simpliciter*). This is a nice solution, but it is ruined by the acceptance of any
of Hybrids 3 to 5. On any of these views, if *x* is appropriately situated,
reality contains multiple points along *x*'s worldline (see Fig. 2.3).
To avoid contradiction, instantiation will need to be relativized to
points in spacetime—*x* is *F* *at* certain points of spacetime but not others.

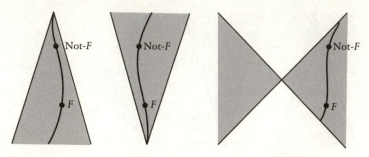

<small>FIG. 2.3. Change for hybrid presentists</small>

The presentist's distinctive solution to the problem of change would thereby vanish.

Other common arguments for presentism are similarly undermined. The 'thank goodness that's over' argument for presentism is clearly undermined by the past-light-cone formulation (Hybrid 3), since for any point q on any worldline, any earlier point on that worldline is equally part of reality—pains never 'go away'. As can be seen from the diagram, it is also true on the other two formulations that reality contains both pains (F) and subsequent painless states (not-F) as equally existing events along a single worldline. However, it is hard to say whether this undermines the argument in those cases. As with Broad's growing-block-universe view, on any of these three versions of 'presentism' we must distinguish two senses of the tenses (now relativized to frames of reference), one given by an eternalist style analysis in terms of four-dimensional reality, the other irreducible sense describing the change in that reality.[30] On the second sense, it WILL be the case (with respect to some chosen frame of reference) that the relief exists but the pain does not (on either Hybrid 4 or Hybrid 5). What is unclear is whether this supplies the explanation of relief that the argument requires, for despite

---

[30] This second sense of the tenses is of course primitive, but it may help to give the picture by seeing how an eternalist would view this sense (just as the gloss 'WILL (φ) is true iff φ is true at some future time' clarifies, though does not provide an analysis for, the non-relativistic presentist's tense operator). Let p be the 'generator point' of reality, in the sense discussed in the text below. A truth, φ, about changing four-dimensional reality WILL be true, relative to F, iff there is (in the eternalist's spacetime) another point p', such that (1) relative to F, p' is in the future of p, and (2) φ is true of the segment of spacetime 'generated by' p'.

the truth of this tensed claim the relief and the past pain are equally parts of reality.

There is also the argument that the reality of the future must be denied to make room for free will (this argument of course does not favor presentism over Broad's growing-block-universe view). Like the thank-goodness-that's-over argument, this argument is clearly undermined by one of our three formulations, and has an unclear status on the other two. On the future-light-cone formulation, from any point q in reality all points in the absolute future of q are themselves parts of reality; thus, if the existence of the future undermines free will, the defender of this formulation is in no better shape than the eternalist. As for the other two formulations, suppose reality contains a case of agent S deliberating whether to do a certain action, as well as containing the commission of this action A. When S deliberated whether to do A, was S free? Using the tense operator 'WAS' in its irreducible sense, the defender of Hybrids 3 and 5 can say truly that it WAS the case (relative to some frame of reference) that the deliberation existed but act A itself did not. Nevertheless, the deliberation and action are equally part of reality, which (according to the defender of the argument) undermines S's freedom while deliberating.

A final critical problem is that each of Hybrids 3 to 5 grants a special privilege to a single point in reality. On each view there exists a 'generator point', a point p such that all other points in reality are: (1) in the absolute past of p (Hybrid 3); (2) in the absolute future of p (Hybrid 4); or (3) spacelike separated from p (Hybrid 5). The rest of the points in spacetime are equally part of reality, but are not generator points. According to non-relativistic presentism, no particular point (or event, or object) is granted any such status—given that classical simultaneity is an equivalence relation, each point (or event, or object) is a generator point of reality (in the sense that all other points are simultaneous with it). Nor does Hybrid 2 postulate any such privileged point; and even here-now-ism grants no point any special status at the expense of others (since only one point is real).

Notice that in Broad's (non-relativistic) growing-block universe there is a privileged *class* of points. The points on the crest of the wave generate reality (in the sense that spacetime consists of the class of points before the members of this class), whereas other points in spacetime are not generators in this sense. This inegalitarianism is related to the (not unintuitive) conviction on the part of the view's defenders that time and space are importantly disanalogous. While it *would* be implausible to say that one region of space is ontologically privileged, it is not implausible, Broad could claim, to say that one region of time is ontologically privileged. This defense of inegalitarianism could perhaps be extended to Hybrids 3 and 4, since the generator point in each case enjoys a purely temporal distinction: it is time-like related to all other points. But the defense utterly fails for Hybrid 5, the bowtie view, since on that view the generator point is simultaneous, relative to suitably chosen frames of reference, with other points in reality. This asymmetry is important. As noted above, Hybrids 3 and 4 do not retain much of the original spirit of presentism, since reality contains dinosaurs on Hybrid 3 and Martian outposts on Hybrid 4, but Hybrid 5 seems closer to the original spirit of presentism. The additional argument against it is therefore welcome: Hybrid 5 implies the existence of an implausibly distinguished point. Located at the generator point, I could say truly that reality consists of all points with spacelike separation from me. An utterance by you, located across the room, would be wrong.[31]

We have considered five hybrid theories combining elements of presentism and special relativity. None avoids being scientifically revisionary or otherwise unbelievable while retaining the alleged virtues of traditional presentism. Only Hybrid 2 really preserved the spirit of traditional presentism, but it was Hybrid 2 that was the most scientifically revisionary. I conclude that presentism can be upheld only by those willing to revise their science because of their metaphysical views on the nature of time. A physical theory of time other than special relativity must be constructed which is statable using the usual (classical) presentist's tense operators, but which is consistent with the observed experimental data that has led scientists to special relativity.[32] For all I know this may be possible. And I do not say that philosophical argumentation can never push us to revise science. Berkeley's objections to infinitesimals were a valuable gadfly prodding mathematicians to develop foundations for the calculus, to which Prior (1996) compares his defense of presentism. But given the other arguments of this chapter, presentism is in independent philosophical trouble. Moreover, there is an alternative theory, the B-theory, which is consistent 'as-is' with contemporary science and suffers no apparent philosophical defects. At the least, tentative rejection of presentism seems in order.

---

[31] Compare Putnam's rejection of 'Privileged Observers' (1967: 241).
[32] See Tooley (1997, ch. 11).

Three- and Four-Dimensionalism Stated

The four-dimensional picture is that of a world spread out in time populated by spacetime worms, sums of instantaneous stages from different times. The opposing three-dimensional picture is equally vivid: a world with objects wholly present at multiple times, sweeping in their entirety through, rather than being spread throughout, spacetime regions.

In addition to pictures we have a battery of synonyms. Four-dimensionalists say that things have *temporal parts*, that they *perdure*, and that they are spread out over time. Three-dimensionalists say that things *endure*, that they have no temporal parts, that they are *wholly present* at every moment of their careers.

These pictures and phrases are suggestive, but fall short of precise theses. So before engaging in debate about which is correct, I want to get clearer about what exactly three- and four-dimensionalism amount to. This will both focus the debate and clarify its relationship to related debates in ontology and the philosophy of time.

1. WHY FUSS OVER FORMULATION?

The value of tidy formulations can be overestimated. A theory begins as a picture, to which any proposed formalization must conform. It is difficult to use the formalization to resolve controversy over what the theory entails, for the controversy then becomes whether the picture behind the theory has been misrepresented. Nevertheless formalization has its point. If no precise statements whatsoever can be gleaned from a picture, the picture may be a mirage, based on confusion. Conversely, someone skeptical that a picture has any content can be answered by formulating theses that flow from the picture. Certain arguments may be made rigorous only if the theory is rigorously articulated. Finally, different strands in the theory may be disentangled and their conceptual relations investigated.

Another reason for precise formulation is that our doctrines have often been misleadingly or obscurely formulated. If saying that an object is four-dimensional means that it has extension in all four dimensions, then on one natural reading of 'has extension in' (namely as meaning 'is present at more than one point of') nearly everyone is a four-dimensionalist, because nearly everyone agrees that objects persist through time. That is not controversial; what is controversial is *how* they do so. Perhaps the saying has a richer meaning, but then we would need to know what that richer meaning is; the saying itself does not suffice. Another example: David Wiggins rejects four-dimensionalism by saying that continuants do not *occupy* time, but rather persist *through* time (1980: 25 n. 12). If persisting through is different from occupying, we need some account of the difference. Wiggins goes on to claim that continuants persist through time '. . .gaining and losing parts'. But no sane four-dimensionalist would deny that continuants persist, or that they gain and lose parts (see the discussion of temporary parthood below). For Mark Heller, enduring objects are *spatial* and exist *at* different times; whereas four-dimensional things are *spatiotemporal* and exist *from* one time *until* another (1990: 4–5). In a similar vein, Peter van Inwagen, an opponent of four-dimensionalism, says that a perduring object would have 'temporal extent', whereas the concept of temporal extent does not apply to enduring objects (1990: 252). These distinctions are no less obscure than the distinction between three- and four-dimensionalism to be clarified.

Yet another poor characterization one sometimes hears is that enduring objects are 'strictly identical' over time.[1] *Everyone* who accepts the basic phenomenon of persistence over time accepts 'strict' identity over time in this sense, three- and four-dimensionalists alike.[2] A spacetime

---

[1] See for example Carter and Hestevold (1994: 269), and Merricks (1994*a*).

[2] Even a defender of the stage view (see Ch. 5, Sect. 8) will accept one reading on which this is true, on which 'exists at future time *t*' is given a counterpart-theoretic interpretation.

worm with temporal parts today and tomorrow exists today, and also tomorrow. It, like everything else, is strictly identical with itself. So it exists today and is strictly identical with something that exists tomorrow.

A final reason to have a clear statement is that it is sometimes said that the dispute is meaningless, or even merely verbal! Peter van Inwagen, for example, has said of temporal parts: 'I simply do not understand what these things are supposed to be, and I do not think this is my fault. I think that no one understands what they are supposed to be, though of course plenty of philosophers think they do' (1981: 133). And Eli Hirsch (1982: 188 ff.) and Storrs McCall (1994: 214–16) have claimed that the dispute is merely verbal.

2. FOUR-DIMENSIONALISM STATED

Given the obscurity in typical formulations and the skepticism of van Inwagen, Hirsch, and McCall, one might worry that there is less to the 3D/4D controversy than meets the eye. Perhaps the suggestive pictures cannot survive serious scrutiny. This worry can be answered by giving a clear statement of four-dimensionalism.[3] That statement will be phrased in terms that are clear and acceptable to the *opponents* of four-dimensionalism. These opponents will then not be able to claim that four-dimensionalism is unintelligible. Moreover, the formulation will make it clear that the dispute is not merely verbal. In giving this statement I presuppose the B-theory of time, in particular eternalism. (Whether this presupposition is strictly required will be discussed in Section 4 below.) To rule out the possibility of obscurity, I will restrict myself to a meager set of primitive notions: the mereological notion of a part at a time and the spatiotemporal notion of existing at a time. Each requires comment.[4]

Having a part at a time is familiar. The end of my fingernail is part of me today but is not part of me tomorrow if I clip it off; a plank is part of a ship at one time but not another. Familiar as this notion is, it is *not* the notion of parthood usually discussed by four-dimensionalists.

---

[3] Cf. Haslanger (1994: 340–1).
[4] See Fine (1994) for a way of thinking about parthood very different from that about to be discussed.

Following Leonard and Goodman's (1940) 'Calculus of Individuals',[5] four-dimensionalists tend to speak of the parts of an object *simpliciter*, rather than the parts it has at this time or that. This is actually a special case of a more general fact: four-dimensionalists tend to employ an atemporal notion of exemplification of properties and relations. Thus, a four-dimensionalist will say that my current temporal part is, atemporally, sitting, 69 inches tall, and wearing a (temporal part of a) hat. Likewise, the four-dimensionalist will say that my current temporal part is, atemporally, part of the larger spacetime worm that is me. This is not to say that four-dimensionalists reject change. Intrinsic change is difference between successive temporal parts. I change from sitting to standing by having a temporal part that sits and a later one that stands. Change in relations is analogous: I sit in a chair at one time but not another because my earlier temporal part sits (*simpliciter*, atemporally) in a temporal part of the chair whereas one of my later temporal parts fails to sit in the corresponding later temporal part of the chair. Mereological change is a special case of relational change: my fingernail end ceases to be a part of me because its later temporal parts are not part of my later temporal parts.

We can think of the four-dimensionalist's notions of atemporal parthood, and atemporal exemplification generally, as being those we employ when we take an 'atemporal perspective' and contemplate the whole of time. (Even some three-dimensionalists admit that 'part of' is sometimes used atemporally, when talking about events, times themselves—'the 1960s are part of the 20th century'—or allegedly atemporal things—'arithmetic is part of mathematics'.) But when discussing objects in time, we typically do not take this atemporal perspective. Suppose I will clip off my fingernail end tomorrow. My fingernail end is therefore not part of me in the atemporal sense, for it has parts that are not part of me (namely, its future temporal parts after the clipping). Despite this, today before I have clipped my fingernails we will say 'the end of my fingernail is part of me now'. The everyday notion of parthood is temporary, rather than atemporal: the fingernail end is part of me *now*. This is not to say that there is something wrong with the atemporal notion of parthood. A four-dimensionalist can take it as basic, and then use it to define the temporary notion:

---

[5] See also Simons (1987: 5–100) on classical mereology.

(P@T) x is part of y at t iff x and y each exist at t, and x's instantaneous temporal part at t is part of y's instantaneous tem-
poral part at t.

(Thus, the four-dimensionalist can reply to the complaint of Judith
Jarvis Thomson (1983: 210) and Ali Akhtar Kazmi (1990: 231 n. 3) that
four-dimensionalism implies that, for example, my fingernail end is not
part of me—the reply is that my fingernail end is part of me *now*, in the
sense of (P@T).)

The *three*-dimensionalist theory of temporary parthood (in its eternalist version) will be very different. (P@T) must be rejected since it presupposes temporal parts. Instead, parthood-at-t must be primitive, and
the four-dimensionalist notion of atemporal parthood must be rejected
(at least as applied to mereologically inconstant continuants). Of
course, everyday *uses* of 'part' could be missing a temporal qualifier, but
in such cases 'part of' implicitly means 'part of now'. As it is with parthood, so it is with predication generally. For the four-dimensionalist,
temporary properties like *being 5 feet tall* are had *simpliciter* (by temporal parts), whereas the three-dimensionalist insists that such 'properties' are had only relative to times (see Ch. 4, Sects. 6 and 7).[6]

Throughout much of this book I will happily speak of atemporal parthood. But when I am trying to convince my opponents that four-
dimensionalism is intelligible I had better not speak of atemporal
parthood. By a three-dimensionalist's lights, talk of atemporal parthood is incomplete in something like the way 'John is 10 feet from' is
incomplete. Thus, the three- dimensionalist would regard a formulation
of four-dimensionalism in terms of atemporal parthood as being
ill-formed. Moreover, it is sometimes useful to formulate arguments for
four-dimensionalism in the language of parts at times. Any argument
for four-dimensionalism that uses 'part of' without temporal qualification in its premises faces the charge of begging the question since it
is central to many versions of three-dimensionalism that 'part of'
requires temporal qualification. So I will qualify the part-whole relation
to times in my formulation of four-dimensionalism. Note that

---

[6] I do not mean to suggest that a four-dimensionalist must accept in its full generality
the schema ⌜x is F at t iff x's temporal part at t is F⌝; examples like 'Ted is 33 years old in
2000' raise problems. A four-dimensionalist *qua* four-dimensionalist is under no obligation to produce a general analysis of English in terms of temporal parts. See Ch. 6, Sect. 1.

four-dimensionalists will also be able to accept the formulation since talk of temporary parthood can be analyzed via (P@T).

If parthood is temporally relative then so must be certain other mereological notions that can be defined in terms of parthood. Four-dimensionalists speak of objects overlapping (sharing a part in common), and of the mereological fusion, or sum, of a class of objects: an object that contains every member of the class as a part and is such that each of its parts overlaps some member of the class. In the temporal framework we must speak of objects overlapping *at* a given time, and of an object being a fusion of a class *at* a specified time.

The basic undefined notion of temporal mereology can be *parthood-at-t*. I follow standard practice in using the term 'part', whether temporally qualified or no, in such a way that a thing counts as a part of itself. Parts of a thing other than itself are called its *proper* parts; the thing itself is an *improper* part of itself.

Two objects *overlap* at a time iff something is part of each then. x is a *fusion at* t of class S iff (1) every member of S is part of x at t, and (2) every part of x at t overlaps-at-t some member of S. Parthood-at-t is transitive; everything that exists at t is a part of itself then; x is part of y at t only if x and y both exist at t. Moreover, the following principle seems correct:

(PO)   If x and y exist at t, but x is not part of y at t, then x has some part at t that does not overlap y at t.

(This is the temporal analog of a theorem of the Calculus of Individuals; see theorem SCT13 from Simons 1987: 38.) See also Thomson (1983: 213–20), and Simons (1987: 175 ff.).

We should *not* assume that the 'identity principle' carries over from atemporal mereology. This principle would state that no two objects can be parts of each other at a time. But given four-dimensionalism (and assuming (P@T)), two spacetime worms sharing a temporal part would be parts of each other at the time. Moreover, some three-dimensionalists distinguish coinciding statues and lumps of clay, which would be (as argued in the next section, and in Ch. 5, Sect. 3) parts of each other at the time of coincidence.

In addition to parthood-at-t, I need a temporal notion of *existence-at*. The notion is familiar: I exist at the present time but not times before 1967; Socrates existed in the distant past but does not exist at the present time. As with temporary parthood there is a principle governing existence-at that is accepted by the four-dimensionalist but not by the three-dimensionalist: an object exists *at* a time iff it has a temporal part that exists at that time. (There is a distinct notion that a four-dimensionalist might legitimately call 'existence at' (cf. Heller 1984: 328–9), on which I exist only at intervals that contain all my temporal parts. I choose my usage so that three- and four-dimensionalists can accept the same notion of existence-at and speak of non-instantaneous objects as existing at instants.) Existence-at must be distinguished from quantification. By 'there is', I intend atemporal quantification over all objects, not just those located at any particular time (this of course continues my presupposition of eternalism). 'Exists-at' is analogous to the spatial predicate 'is located at', not the logician's '∃'.

'Temporal part' may now be defined. The temporal part of x at time t is sometimes defined as the part of x that exists only at t and has the same spatial location as x, but I distrust the appeal to spatial location. The idea is to insure that the temporal part of x is a 'big enough' part of x, but the definition fails for an object without spatial location, and for an object sharing spatial location with one of its proper parts (for example a 'trope' for its shape). I therefore prefer a purely mereological definition:

> x is an *instantaneous temporal part* of y at instant $t =_{df}$ (1) x exists at, but only at, t; (2) x is part of y at t; and (3) x overlaps at t everything that is part of y at t.

This captures the idea that my current temporal part should be a part of me now that exists only now but is as big as I am now. It should overlap my arms, legs—everything that is part of me now. Four-dimensionalism may then be formulated as the claim that, necessarily, each spatiotemporal object has a temporal part at every moment at which it exists.[7]

This all could be made relativistically acceptable by relativizing the definition of a temporal part to a frame of reference, and then stating four-dimensionalism as the claim that for any chosen frame of reference, every spatiotemporal object has a temporal part at every moment of time at which it exists.

---

[7] Four-dimensionalists who think that spatiotemporal objects have some enduring parts, for example immanent universals, must revise the definition somehow. Other accounts include Heller (1984: 325–9); Lewis (1983*a*, postscript B); Thomson (1983: 206–10); van Inwagen (1981: 133, 1990*b*: 245–8). Some may wish to restrict the necessity in some way (see Lewis 1986*b*, p. x, and Haslanger 1994: 340). Sider (1997) gives a more general formulation, from which the present formulation follows.

Some may wish to avoid commitment to instantaneous parts.[8] An *extended* temporal part of x during interval T may be defined as an object that exists at, but only at, times in T, is part of x at every time during T, and at every moment in T overlaps everything that is part of x at that moment. Four-dimensionalism may then be reformulated as the claim that spatiotemporal objects have temporal parts during intervals of certain sorts, perhaps extended continuous intervals. But unless otherwise noted I will think of temporal parts as being instantaneous.

'Temporal part' can also be defined using the atemporal part-whole relation of the Calculus of Individuals:

x is an *instantaneous temporal part* of y at instant t $=_{df}$ (1) x is a part of y; (2) x exists at, but only at, t; and (3) x overlaps every part of y that exists at t.

This definition is more perspicuous for a four-dimensionalist since it is stated using atemporal parthood, but as noted it is sometimes better to have a definition that the three-dimensionalist can accept as intelligible.

Four-dimensionalism as I have stated it merely implies the existence of temporal parts. It does not imply that temporal parts are in any sense prior to or more fundamental than the objects of which they are parts. Nor does it imply that objects are 'constructed' from their temporal parts. Nor does it imply that identity over time is reducible to temporal parts. Nor does it presuppose David Lewis's Humean Supervenience (although see Ch. 6, Sect. 5 for a defense of Humean Supervenience against the Kripke/Armstrong rotating homogeneous disk/sphere). These questions of priority and reducibility are important questions about temporal parts, but they must be separated from the more basic question of whether temporal parts exist at all, which is my primary concern.

My statement is likewise neutral about the relationship between temporal parts and ordinary language. A four-dimensionalist is free to accept any of a number of possible views about this relationship. On the *worm view*, it is spacetime worms that are *continuants*—the referents of ordinary terms, members of ordinary domains of quantification, subjects of ordinary predications, and so on. This is the usual view adopted by four-dimensionalists. On the *stage view*, on the other hand, which I

---

[8] See e.g. Zimmerman (1996, sect. 4).

defend in Chapter 5, Section 8, it is instantaneous stages rather than worms that play this role. Other views are possible: Mark Heller (1990) argues that although the true ontology is the four-dimensional one, *none* of the objects in this ontology are referred to by everyday terms. As I stated it, four-dimensionalism is the thesis that spatiotemporal objects have temporal parts. This leaves open which spatiotemporal objects (if any) are continuants.

On my definition, a temporal part of x at t must literally be part of x at t. Temporal parts thus defined must be distinguished from various surrogates. First there are what we might call 'ersatz temporal parts', ordered pairs of objects and times. Secondly, there are slices of the *histories* of continuants accepted by some three-dimensionalists. These three-dimensionalists say that for each enduring object there is an event that comprises all that (intrinsically) happens to that object; unlike continuants these histories have temporal parts. Ersatz temporal parts and slices of histories are, in fact, suitable to play *part* of the role that temporal parts are supposed by four-dimensionalists to play. For example, as John Perry (1975, introd.) shows, it is convenient to represent the search for the proper criterion of personal identity over time as the search for the relation that holds between two person stages iff they are part of the same continuing person; but here person stages can be ersatz temporal parts, or slices of histories (as Perry takes them to be). Another example, discussed in Chapter 4, Section 2, is Quine's use of temporal parts in giving a logical analysis of tensed talk in natural language. But many philosophical uses of temporal parts require that temporal parts literally be parts of objects. This is particularly clear in the use of temporal parts to solve the traditional paradoxes of co-located objects. Temporal parts theorists often say it is possible for a statue and the lump of clay from which it is made to share spatial location because they overlap by sharing a single temporal part. But ersatz temporal parts and slices of histories are not genuine parts of continuants, and so the overlap between the statue and lump would not be secured. Moreover, if the temporal part of x at t were simply $<x, t>$, no two numerically distinct objects could share a temporal part, for whenever x and y are distinct, so are $<x, t>$ and $<y, t>$. Ersatz temporal parts are also powerless to help solve the problem of temporary intrinsics (Ch. 4, Sect. 4). Four-dimensionalism is supposed to allow an account of property instantiation that avoids both presentism and the need for relativizing property instantiation to times: instantaneous stages instantiate temporary intrinsics *simpliciter*. But ersatz temporal parts instantiate properties only in a derivative sense: '<x, t> is F' just means 'x is F at t'. Instantiation would remain fundamentally relative to times.

There is a kind of skeptic who would say that there can be no genuine disagreement over whether four-dimensionalism is true. After all, one can introduce a 'linguistic framework' in which, for example, one is permitted to say 'x has a short temporal part followed by a tall temporal part' whenever x is first short and later tall. Not even my opponents deny this is a possible linguistic framework; but then, the skeptic will ask, in what sense is four-dimensionalism a controversial thesis? My first reply would be that four-dimensionalism requires that temporal parts *genuinely* be parts, but the skeptic will roll his eyes at this use of 'genuine'. After all, an appropriate linguistic framework can be introduced for 'genuine' as well.

My answer to this sort of skeptic was given in the introduction to this book. The answer consisted of a model of the nature of claims of existence on which meaningful ontological disagreement is possible. Note in particular that whether four-dimensionalism is true affects how *many* things there are. It may well be that the number of subatomic particles (from all of time) is finite, in which case, if three-dimensionalism is true, there is some finite number, n, of concrete things (understand 'concrete' things as spatiotemporal things other than events, points of spacetime, immanent universals, and so on). That there are exactly n concrete things can be expressed in the language of predicate logic with identity plus a single predicate 'C' for concreteness (for $n = 2$ one can say '$\exists x\, \exists y$ [Cx & Cy & $x \neq y$ & $\forall z$ ($Cz \rightarrow [x = z \lor y = z]$)]'). On the other hand, if four-dimensionalism is true there will be infinitely many concrete things, if time is dense; and so the sentence will be false. We here have a statement that is phrased only in the language of first-order logic, plus a predicate for a very basic ontological category, that of a concrete thing. The skeptic must therefore carry his doubts over to such austere language. Even quantification, identity, and fundamental predicates 'have no autonomy outside linguistic frameworks'; even with such vocabulary, if sentences can be incorporated into a linguistic practice, there is no further question of their truth. As argued in the introduction, questions about what there is and how many things there are have more objective answers than this.

3.   WHAT IS THREE-DIMENSIONALISM?

The precise formulation of four-dimensionalism in the previous section answers van Inwagen's charge that temporal parts are unintelligible. Ironically, it is far from clear that three-dimensionalism can be adequately formulated.

Friends and foes alike often characterize that doctrine as the view that a continuant is 'wholly present' at every moment of its existence. We have D. H. Mellor (1981: 104): 'things are wholly present throughout their lifetimes'; Peter Simons (1987: 175): 'At any time at which it exists, a continuant is wholly present'; George Graham (1977: 309), who though he rejects three-dimensionalism thinks it our 'everyday' view: '. . . we usually think . . . that at any time at which a person exists the whole or entire person exists at that time . . .'; Lawrence Lombard (1986: 69–70): '. . . if a thing persists, say, from a time, t, to a time, t′, then at any time between t and t′ during which it exists it has *all* of its parts'; Paolo Dau (1986: 464): 'On the three-dimensional conception, the entire object is to be found at each instant that it exists'; David Wiggins (1980: 25):

. . . questions of continuity and persistence that perplex our habitual modes of thought about identity and difference . . . [need] answers given in language that speaks as simply and directly as natural languages speak of proper three-dimensional continuants—things with spatial parts and no temporal parts, which are conceptualized in our experience as occupying space but not time, and as persisting whole *through* time.

And finally David Lewis (1986a: 202, 210):[9]

Let us say that something *persists* iff, somehow or other, it exists at various times; this is the neutral word. . . . [Something] *endures* iff it persists by being wholly present at more than one time. . . . many would favor the view that [a person, e.g. Hume] endures, wholly present at every time of his life, so that those times . . . overlap by having him as a shared part.

The suggestion in these quotations seems to be that for any (continuant), x, and any time, t, if x exists at t then x is 'wholly present' at t. (The

___

[9] Lewis has not made the mistake of forgetting the temporal qualifier, but rather is stating three-dimensionalism within his own framework, and therefore with the unfriendly presupposition that the part-whole relation is atemporal.

restriction to continuants—ordinary things like persons, planets, protons, medium-sized dry goods, and so on—is necessary since some three-dimensionalists admit that some entities, events for example, do have temporal parts.)

What is it for x to be 'wholly present' at t? The idea is presumably that every part of x exists at t. But every part at what time? For three-dimensionalists, the parthood relation is temporally relative, and so 'every part of x exists at t' is incomplete since 'part of' is temporally unqualified.

We might take 'x is wholly present at t' to mean that everything that is part of x *at* t exists at t. But then the claim that objects are always wholly present whenever they exist becomes utterly trivial, and not the controversial doctrine we thought it was, for no one would deny that a part of an object at a given time must exist then. Note further that a four-dimensionalist who defined temporary parthood via (P@T) would *accept* that objects are wholly present in this sense.

Another sense of 'wholly present' might be defined as follows:

x is *strongly wholly present* throughout interval T $=_{df}$ everything that is at *any* time in T part of x exists and is part of x at *every* time in T.

But the claim that objects are always *strongly* wholly present throughout their careers is too strong a formulation of three-dimensionalism, for it entails the impossibility of gain or loss of parts. Granted, *some* three-dimensionalists would accept this consequence, most notably Roderick Chisholm (1976, app. B). But Chisholm's mereological essentialism should not be *built into* the statement of three-dimensionalism, for most three-dimensionalists reject it.

What, then, is three-dimensionalism? It cannot be the denial of the possibility of temporal parts, for many three-dimensionalists will admit the possibility of instantaneous objects, objects which appear only for an instant and then disappear. Such objects would be temporal parts of themselves, given the present definition of 'temporal part'. Nor can it be the denial of the possibility of *proper* temporal parts. Imagine a lump of clay that gets made into a statue-shape for only an instant (by a god, say). Some three-dimensionalists might want to say that in that instant a statue comes into being but immediately goes out of existence. After all, many three-dimensionalists say that when a lump of clay becomes statue-shaped for some extended period of time and then gets squashed, a statue comes into being for that period of time; the instantaneous statue would be a limiting case. I am not claiming that instantaneous statues are possible, only that they are not inconsistent with the picture three-dimensionalists seem to accept, and so should not be ruled out automatically by a canonical formulation of three-dimensionalism. But the statue would be a proper temporal part of the lump. As defined above, a temporal part of the lump at t is anything that (1) is part of the lump at t, (2) exists only at t, and (3) overlaps at t everything that is part of the lump at t. Condition (2) is clearly satisfied. As for condition (3), at the time in question, the lump and the statue are made up of the same subatomic particles; thus, anything that is part of the lump then will share subatomic particles with the statue. Finally, that condition (1) is satisfied may be established as follows. The following is a temporally relativized analog of a principle from the Calculus of Individuals (see p. 58) and is surely correct:

> (PO) If x and y exist at t, but x is not part of y at t, then x has some part at t that does not overlap y at t.

Since the statue and the lump are made up of the same subatomic particles at the time in question, every part of the statue at that time will share subatomic particles with, and thus overlap at that time, the lump. By (PO), (1) then follows.[10]

Friends of constitution (Ch. 5, Sect. 3) might deny my claim that a statue and its constituting lump share subatomic particles as common parts. Perhaps parts of statues are never identical to parts of lumps, but are merely constituted by them.[11] The defender of this response faces some awkward questions. Any given subatomic particle, P, could be part of only one of the statue and the lump. If P is part of the statue then presumably P must be constituted by some thing X which is part of the lump; if P is part of the lump then some X must be constituted by P, and must be part of the statue. Either way, what is this thing X, and what are

---

[10] A variant formulation of three-dimensionalism would be: necessarily, nothing that exists for more than an instant ever has a temporal part at every moment of its existence. But imagine a certain lump of clay with a radically discontinuous shape throughout its entire career: at every instant, t, of its life, (1) the lump has some statuesque shape S at t, and (2) there is an interval of time about t, such that at every moment in the interval, if the lump exists at that moment, the lump has at that moment a shape that is quite different from S. A three-dimensionalist might well claim that the lump constitutes a different statue at each instant. These statues would count as temporal parts of the lump.

[11] I thank an anonymous referee for drawing this possibility to my attention.

its persistence conditions? There seems to be no ordinary sortal term under which it falls; the 'statue'/'lump' duality has no analog at the subatomic level. The friends of constitution will not want to be committed to the likes of X.

Some more likely candidates for the formulation of three-dimensionalism include:

(3D-1) In the *actual* world, small particles (e.g. electrons) are strongly wholly present throughout their careers.

(3D-2) It is possible that some continuant is strongly wholly present over some extended interval.

(3D-3) Necessarily, every continuant is *possibly* strongly wholly present throughout some extended interval.

But (3D-1) seems too empirically bold to count as a formulation of three-dimensionalism. If scientists discovered that subatomic particles are constantly in flux, exchanging parts at every moment, would those who accept the intuitive three-dimensionalist picture change their minds? The impression one gets from reading Wiggins, van Inwagen, Mellor, and company, is that three-dimensionalism would not be falsified by such empirical research. No doubt most three-dimensionalists, having no reason to accept this empirical thesis of flux, will conjecture that (3D-1) is probably true. They might also conjecture that there are no actual (instantaneous) temporal parts, whether proper or otherwise. But no such thesis confined to actuality is a conceptual thesis about the essential nature of identity over time. Moreover, three-dimensionalists seldom confine their remarks to subatomic particles; they say that macroscopic objects such as persons are wholly present over time. For both of these reasons, (3D-1) seems to leave out part of the three-dimensional picture.

(3D-2) will be accepted as an a priori truth by all three-dimensionalists, for three-dimensionalists will accept that while persons *in fact* gain and lose parts, they might not have; and even if subatomic particles are in fact constantly in mereological flux, they might not have been. But there is a nagging feeling that something is missing. Like (3D-1), (3D-2) does not contain a universally applicable, positive claim about the essential nature of identity over time. One gets the feeling from three-dimensionalists that they have some such claim in mind, but the claim is hard to pin down.

A positive thesis about the essential nature of persistence might be sought in the *potentialities* of persisting objects. The suggestion that three-dimensionalism is the denial of proper temporal parts was rejected because of the possibility of a lump instantaneously constituting a statue. But it might be objected that the problem is with my definition of 'temporal part' rather than the proposed formulation of three-dimensionalism. I define temporal parts as (mereologically) large enough parts that are instantaneous, but perhaps the definition should require that temporal parts be *essentially* instantaneous. The instantaneous statue *could* have lasted longer than an instant, it might be argued, and so should not count as a temporal part of the lump. Under the revised definition of 'temporal part' three-dimensionalists would generally reject the possibility of temporal parts. In fact, a strengthened view might be defensible, based on the idea that the difference between perduring and enduring objects is *de re* modal: while perduring objects are composed of *essentially* instantaneous parts, every enduring object is at least *capable* of being strongly wholly present over time. This suggests formulation (3D-3) of three-dimensionalism. Now we have a universally applicable thesis about persisting objects, for the claim is that *every* possible continuant has a certain kind of capability.

The modal claim presupposed here will not be acceptable to all. Some four-dimensionalists might reject the assumption that temporal parts are essentially instantaneous. (I discuss essentiality of temporal extent in Ch. 6, Sect. 4. Given a 'flexible' account of *de re* modality, for example a counterpart-theoretic account on which the modal properties of an individual can vary depending on how that individual is conceptualized, denying the essentiality of temporal extent is at least an open possibility.) And some three-dimensionalists might think that *some* continuants are essentially in mereological flux. But the most important problem with (3D-3) is that it locates our dispute in the realm of potentiality, whereas the dispute should be in the realm of the actual. Three-dimensionalists have a vivid picture of an object persisting 'wholly', 'identically' through time, 'sweeping through spacetime' rather than being spread out in spacetime. This is a picture of what objects actually do, not what they are capable of doing.

A three-dimensionalist might give up on the attempt to give a mereological account of an object's being wholly present and characterize that notion in some other way. One wonders whether 'wholly present' would then be an apt term. Moreover, attempts like this tend towards the obscure (recall Wiggins's distinction between occupying a region of time and persisting through that region).

A core, positive thesis behind the three-dimensional picture has proved elusive. But this does not mean that we cannot proceed, nor does it mean that our discussion must be inherently vague. For three-dimensionalists are united in their opposition to *four*-dimensionalism, which has been precisely stated. If there is anything else to three-dimensionalism beyond this opposition, I challenge its defenders to say what it is.

4. PERDURANCE, ENDURANCE, PRESENTISM, AND ETERNALISM

So far I have presupposed eternalism in characterizing the 3D/4D dispute. I wish now to examine how, if at all, this dispute might be characterized assuming presentism, and more generally the relationship between the 3D/4D controversy and ontological status of the past and future.

The term 'four-dimensionalism' actually obscures the distinction between these debates. Does it mean that *objects* are *mereologically* four-dimensional in the sense of having temporal as well as spatial parts, or does it mean that *reality* is *ontologically* four-dimensional in the sense of other times as well as other places being real? In the former sense it signifies perdurance, in the latter, eternalism. As mentioned in the introduction, I use the term in the sense of perdurance, saving 'eternalism' for the thesis about time. Terminology, then, leaves open any of the four possible combinations: eternalism + perdurance, eternalism + endurance, presentism + endurance, presentism + perdurance.

Only the first three combinations have seen defenders in the contemporary literature; no contemporary philosopher defends the combination of presentism and perdurance.[12] Moreover, many early writers seemed to think of eternalism and perdurance interchangeably, thus ignoring the possibility of combining eternalism with endurance. But

---

[12] It seems, though, that this may have been the view of the Buddhist school of the Sautrantikas. See Stcherbatsky (1970, app. I, and also ch. XI); see also Stcherbatsky (1992, part II, ch. I).

are there, in fact, conceptual difficulties with upholding any of these four combinations? For the most part, there are not; each of the combinations is a coherent view.

I say these combinations are coherent, not difficulty-free. A given objection to a metaphysics of persistence might be aided by, or even totally dependent on, a philosophy of time. For example, Trenton Merricks (1995) and William Carter and H. Scott Hestevold (1994) have argued that eternalism and endurance are incompatible, since an eternalist who embraces endurance must relativize property instantiation to times and thereby fall prey to David Lewis's argument from temporary intrinsics. Whether Lewis's argument is indeed successful is a difficult question. In Chapter 4, Section 6 I argue that although Lewis's argument has some force it is far from being conclusive. But the success of the argument is beside the point. The eternalist endurantist may need to embrace some controversial philosophical theses, but there is no hidden internal inconsistency or patent absurdity concealed within the view, as for example there was in naive set theory.

Eternalism + perdurance and presentism + endurance are clearly coherent (modulo, in the second case, obscurity about what endurance itself amounts to). The former may be called the 'manifold theory'. It is the picture sketched in Chapter 1, and is certainly the view that most philosophers have in mind by perdurance. The metaphor of a world of spacetime worms is most apt assuming eternalism, for past and future worms, as well as past and future segments of current worms, are equally real, inhabiting the manifold of reality. The latter view has also been defended by many, and is certainly a live option.

But the other positions seem coherent as well. This is clearly true for the combination of endurance and eternalism, which has been defended in a number of places.[13] On this view, reality consists of 'wholly present entities' which sweep through spacetime without being spread out in spacetime. In the previous section I formulated a definition of what it is for *x* to be strongly wholly present throughout an interval (it is for *x* to contain as a part, at every moment in that interval, any object which at *any* moment in the interval is a part of *x*), and it is evidently coherent for an eternalist to claim that there are objects that are strongly wholly present in this sense over extended intervals of time. This merely requires

---

[13] See e.g. Haslanger (1994, 1989*a*); Johnston (1987); Lowe (1987, 1988*a*); Mellor (1981, 1998); van Inwagen (1990*b*); Wiggins (1968 and 1980).

that the occupation relation between persisting things and points of spacetime be a one–many relation. Even mereological simples (such as fundamental particles) are *bi-located*, much as 'immanent universals' are supposed to be, occupying multiple points in spacetime.[14]

A worry about the combination of endurance and eternalism is that the general formulation of endurance, given eternalism, is in trouble, as was discussed in the previous section.[15] But despite the difficulty of articulating a general thesis capturing the three-dimensional picture, it was shown that there are coherent theses in the neighborhood that many who share the picture may well want to defend. There was, for example, the claim that it is possible that an object be strongly wholly present over an extended interval, the claim that subatomic particles are *actually* strongly wholly present throughout their careers, and the claim that no actual entity has an instantaneous temporal part. Each is a coherent claim, each is consistent with eternalism, and each seems to flow from the three-dimensional picture.

The problem of formulating endurance is not particular to eternalists. Below, I state a presentist analog of the doctrine of perdurance. Presentist defenders of endurance will want to resist this thesis, and will want to claim some tensed version of the doctrine that objects are wholly present. But what does that claim amount to? Is it the claim that all of an object's parts exist? No, that is trivial. Is it the claim that anything that is ever part of an object is (now) part of that object? More carefully, is the claim that x endures the claim that: ALWAYS (for all y, if y is part of x, then NOW: y is part of x)? No—that rules out temporary parts. We are back in our earlier quandary. Even for presentists, the claim that objects endure is difficult to coherently formulate.

---

[14] See Armstrong (1978*a*, 1978*b*) and Lewis (1986*a*: 63–9), on immanent universals.

[15] Merricks (1999) defines 'endurance' thus: 'For any presently existing object, O, O *endures* if and only if O persists and *all* of O's parts *simpliciter* exist at the present time', and argues that endurance is therefore inconsistent with eternalism, since eternalist endurantists (at least, those who do not want to be mereological essentialists) could not accept the notion of parts *simpliciter*. To my mind, this formulation of endurance is unacceptable in a context where the relationship between eternalism and endurance is under dispute, since the incompatibility with eternalism is built directly into the definition. Moreover, since *any* sentence of the form 'all Fs exist at the present time' is a trivial consequence of presentism, the sentence 'all of O's parts *simpliciter* exist at the present time' is a trivial consequence of presentism; therefore, if presentism is true, Merricks's definition simply equates endurance with persistence, and so rules out by definition the possibility of combining presentism with perdurance.

The case of the final combination, that of presentism and perdurance, is more delicate. As noted in Merricks (1995), the claim that objects have (merely) past and future temporal parts is inconsistent with presentism since it entails that there are objects that do not currently exist. And yet that claim seems central to four-dimensionalism.[16]

It is certainly true that most if not all four-dimensionalists *presuppose* eternalism. As a consequence the four-dimensional position is usually stated in a tenseless language that is hostile to presentism; it is said that an object *has* temporal parts located in the past and future. But it is far from clear that four-dimensionalists *must* state their position in this way. When one becomes a presentist one must reword many assertions about the past. Instead of saying that there are dinosaurs located in the past, one must speak with tense operators and say that it WAS the case that there existed dinosaurs. Similarly, instead of saying that an object *has* (timelessly) past and future temporal parts, a presentist must say that it WAS or WILL be the case that it has these temporal parts. Talk of temporal parts, then, will have the same status as talk of anything else in the past or future.

More carefully, a presentist could offer the following *tensed* definition of a temporal part:

> *x* is an *instantaneous temporal part* of *y* =$_{df}$ (1) *x* is part of *y*; (2) *x* overlaps every part of *y*; (3) it is not the case that WILL (*x* exists); (4) it is not the case that WAS (*x* exists)

and then defend the following version of the doctrine of temporal parts:

> **Presentist perdurance:** Necessarily, ALWAYS (every object has a temporal part).

Several points about the definition and thesis. First, note the interplay between the tense operators and the quantifiers. The combination of 'ALWAYS' and the universal quantifier in the thesis of presentist perdurance instructs us, intuitively, to consider any time and any object that exists at that time. Secondly, note the nested tense operators: the operator 'WILL' in clause (3) of the definition instructs us to consider points in time that are future relative to points introduced by the operator 'ALWAYS' at the beginning of the thesis. Thirdly, notice the temporally

---

[16] See also Carter and Hestevold (1994, sect. IV).

unqualified ascriptions of properties and relations, which when inside the scope of tense operators can be thought of, intuitively, as being relative to the time of evaluation. Clause (1), for example, says that x is part of y at a given point in time introduced by 'ALWAYS' at the beginning of the thesis.

While there is no question that this thesis is a coherent view that is consistent with presentism, some may hesitate to call it a thesis of genuine *perdurance*.[17] A bad reason for this hesitation would be that presentist perdurance expresses a proposition that is numerically distinct from the proposition expressed by its eternalist analog simply because the one is tensed and the other is not. Nearly every thesis that involves time requires reformulation depending on one's philosophy of time; that does not mean that all such views are importantly tied to presentism. A presentist utilitarian must say 'ALWAYS (for any action, A, A is right iff A maximizes utility)' rather than 'for any action, A, at any time, A is right iff A maximizes utility', but the ethical import is the same.

In what sense, if any, are the presentist and eternalist versions of perdurance the 'same view'? First, the eternalist's version is the result of applying a certain translation procedure to the presentist's version. This procedure takes a tense-logical sentence as input and produces as output its truth condition within a familiar possible worlds style model of tense logic in which the 'worlds' of the model are thought of as times.[18] 'ALWAYS' becomes 'at all times, t, . . .', tensed predications within the scope of tense operators become predications relative to times, and so on. This procedure maps 'ALWAYS $\forall x$ (if x is a bachelor, then x is unmarried)' to 'For all x, for all t, if x is a bachelor at t, then x is unmarried at t', maps the presentist utilitarian doctrine to the eternalist version, and maps presentist perdurance onto its eternalist counterpart. Judging from the first two examples the procedure seems generally to map presentist claims onto eternalist claims that feel, in an elusive sense, analogous. If there were no close relation between eternalist claims and their tense-logical counterparts, it would be a mystery why possible worlds semantics offers insight into tense logic, and why explicit quantification over times in natural language is so natural and intuitive. Yet the exact relationship between tensed sentences and their eternalist translations is difficult to specify. Perhaps some progress may be made

---

[17] Here and elsewhere in this section I am indebted to Trenton Merricks.

[18] See Burgess (1984) for an overview of this sort of semantical treatment of tense logic.

as follows. Ordinary folks speak of past and future objects heedless of their ontological status. A presentist might claim that a charitable semantics would associate tensed propositions with these utterances rendering them capable of truth; such a semantics must presumably make use of something like the translation procedure to which I have gestured.[19] Thus, the translation procedure results in sentences that express propositions that would count as those *ordinarily meant* by utterances of the input sentences.

The second point about the relationship between presentist and eternalist four-dimensionalism is that they play similar, though not identical, theoretical roles. Part of our sense that presentist and eternalist utilitarianism count as 'the same' or 'analogous' is that ethical considerations that favor one will favor the other, and ethical objections that tell against one equally tell against the other. So, do arguments for or against perdurance distinguish between the presentist and eternalist versions?

Some do not. Each version is subject to Judith Jarvis Thomson's 'crazy metaphysic' objection (Ch. 6, Sect. 3) that the doctrine of temporal parts has a high degree of intrinsic implausibility because it implies (for example) that there are person-like things popping into and going out of existence at every instant. Each version is subject to the modal argument against perdurance (Ch. 6, Sect. 4). Each is equally favored by my argument from vagueness (Ch. 4, Sect. 9). However, other considerations impact the two versions differently. Arguments for perdurance based on analogies between space and time are undercut by the assumption of presentism (Ch. 4, Sect. 5). Likewise for the argument from timeless worlds (Ch. 4, Sect. 7) and Lewis's argument from temporary intrinsics (Ch. 4, Sect. 6).

---

[19] I would resist, however, the view that such a translation procedure always results in presentist truths wherever the input is something taken by the eternalist to be true, as well as the view that presentism is acceptable only if this translation procedure can be extended to all everyday discourse about the past and future. See Sider (1999*b*).

CHAPTER 4

In Favor of Four-Dimensionalism
Part 1

> ... The theory of the manifold is the very paradigm of philosophic
> understanding. This is so with respect to its content, since it grasps
> with a strong but delicate logic the most crucial and richest facts.
>   Donald C. Williams, 'The Myth of Passage', 471–2

It is easy to feel, with Williams, an intellectual joy in contemplating a
theory so elegant and beautiful as four-dimensionalism, and it is tempting to accept the theory simply on this basis, utilizing arguments to
rationalize more than justify. Despite this temptation it is to arguments
that I now turn. One will occupy the whole of the next chapter: temporal
parts are needed to solve puzzles in which distinct objects appear to
share the same parts and spatial location. In the present chapter I discuss
the rest.[1] The first few are familiar, while the arguments in Sections 7, 8,
and 9 are, as far as I know, new. The arguments are not uniformly
strong. While some are compelling, others have only limited persuasive
power; still others I flatly reject. I regard none as knock-down; that
would be too good to be true. In each case my goal will be to set out the
strengths and weaknesses of the argument as accurately as possible. The
reader must then judge for him or herself. I proceed roughly in order of
increasing plausibility-to-me. Note that some of the arguments presuppose the B-theory of time, or at least the falsity of presentism, and thus
rest on Chapter 2.

---

[1] The survey is not intended to be exhaustive. For example, I do not discuss the interesting argument of Lewis (1983a, postscript B), since I have nothing to add. I do note, however, that while the argument from vagueness of Section 9 shares some of its assumptions, it
does not assume that causal relations supervene on local qualities.

I.   RUSSELL'S ARGUMENT FROM PARSIMONY

Early defenders of temporal parts include C. D. Broad, Jonathan Edwards, David Hume, Hermann Lotze, J. M. E. McTaggart, Bertrand Russell, and A. N. Whitehead.[2] Their arguments were sometimes familiar from a contemporary perspective, but sometimes not. Russell's defense of temporal parts, for example, is tied up with the program of constructing the world of physical objects from sense-data. Sense-data have temporal parts; physical objects, being sequences or sums of sense-data, therefore themselves have temporal parts (Russell 1914: 109 ff.).

I will leave a detailed historical survey of these figures to those more able. I will, however, mention one other Russellian argument, since it remains tempting to this day but is, as I see it, unsuccessful. The argument is that the postulation of anything *more* than temporal parts would be empirically unjustified. In perception, all that is immediately given is a sequence of objects. Belief in a single enduring object accounting for the sequence is, according to Russell, unwarranted metaphysical speculation.[3] This comes in two versions, depending on whether the objects of perception are sense-data or physical things. In the first case, the metaphysical speculation would be twofold: that there exists anything other than sense-data, and that there is a single such thing. Set the first aside; of the second Russell says:

> . . . the physical object, as inferred from perception, is a group of events arranged about a centre. There *may* be a substance in the centre, but there can be no reason to think so, since the group of events will produce exactly the same percepts; therefore the substance at the centre, if there is one, is irrelevant to science, and belongs to the realm of mere abstract possibility . . . (1927: 244).

Suppose I infer, from a sequence of perceptions, a sequence of objects $o_1, o_2, \ldots$. Grant Russell for the sake of argument that it goes beyond

---

[2] See Broad (1923: 54–5, 63, 1933: 141–66, esp. 166), in which he defends the view that we can 'dispense with' things in favor of processes; Edwards (1758, part 4, ch. 2); Hume (1978, book 1, part 4, sects. 2, 6), though it is perhaps questionable to place him in the temporal parts camp; Lotze (1887, chs. 1–4); McTaggart (1921: 176–7) (who does not really defend temporal parts since he does not really believe in time!); Russell (1914: 112 ff., 1927: 243 ff., 284–9); and Whitehead (1920).

[3] Russell (1914: 112). This sort of argument can perhaps also be regarded as Hume's; see the *Treatise* (1978, book 1, part 4, sect. 2).

the evidence to claim that the observations are of a single thing, that $o_1 = o_2 = o_3$ . . . . It would likewise go beyond the evidence to claim that $o_1 \neq o_2$ . . . . At best, the conclusion can be that we should be neutral, so far as observation and science are concerned, about whether objects endure or perdure; the question must be resolved on philosophical grounds. (It is a separate question whether the observed objects must be distinct because they differ qualitatively; see Sect. 6 below. Russell's argument is not based on change, for he applies it even in the case of electrons (ibid. 246–7).)

2. THE ARGUMENT FROM LOGIC

In *Word and Object* (1960: 170–6), Quine points out that tensed sentences of English may be symbolized using tenseless quantifiers and predicates if one utilizes quantifiers over times and relativizes temporary predicates to times. Thus, 'A mammal was once trampled by a dinosaur' becomes '$\exists x \,\exists y \,\exists t \,(t < n \,\&\, Dx \,\&\, My \,\&\, Txyt)$' ('n' is a name for the current time, *now*; '$t < n$' means that time t is earlier than time n; '$Txyt$' means that x trampled y at t) . Elsewhere he claims that this is the only workable treatment of tense (1953: 442–3):

The only tenable attitude toward quantifiers and other notations of modern logic is to construe them always, in all contexts, as timeless. This does not mean that the values of 'x' may not themselves be thing-events, four-dimensional beings in space-time; it means only that date is to be treated on a par with location, colour, specific gravity, etc.—hence not as a qualification on '$\exists$', but merely as one of sundry attributes of the thing-events which are values of 'x'.

The four-dimensional view of space-time is part and parcel of the use of modern formal logic, and in particular the use of quantification theory, in application to temporal affairs.

. . . I do not see how, failing to appreciate the tenselessness of quantification over temporal entities, one could reasonably take modern logic very seriously.

To partake of the wonders of modern logic one must accept the 'four-dimensional view of spacetime'.

What Quine seems to be calling the four-dimensional view of spacetime actually has two components. There is first the B-theory of time. (The B-theory, recall, also has two components: eternalism—the thesis that past and future entities are real—and the thesis of the reducibility of tense.) Secondly, there is the thesis that things perdure, are composed of temporal parts. Call the combination of these two views the *manifold theory*.

To some extent Quine's argument is simply outdated, for there subsequently occurred the invention of tense logic by Arthur Prior and others.[4] Prior gives a rigorous treatment of tense that is very different from Quine's, and which does not presuppose the manifold theory. But the real problem is that Quine's argument at best supports the B-theory. The second component of the manifold theory, namely perdurance, is by no means required for the logical systems developed by Quine himself and others, for example Carnap (1967) and J. H. Woodger (1937, 1952). Only the B-theory is needed.[5] Even if past dinosaurs endure, a B-theorist can still quantify over them and relativize their temporary predicates to times. Quine (1960: 172–4) later extended the above treatment of tense by introducing the phrase 'x at t' (which denotes x's segment during time interval t) and interpreting tensed locutions as concerning temporal segments. But the temporal parts here could be ersatz, not genuine (see Ch. 3, Sect. 2). Assertions about ersatz temporal parts may be translated as assertions about enduring entities as follows:

$$
\begin{array}{lll}
x\text{-at-}t & \Rightarrow & <x, t> \text{ (where } x \text{ exists at } t) \\
<x, t> \text{ is F} & \Rightarrow & x \text{ is F at } t \\
R\,(<x, t>,<x', t>) & \Rightarrow & R\,(x, x') \text{ at } t \\
R\,(<x, t>,<x', t'>) & \Rightarrow & R\,(x, x') \text{ at } t, t'
\end{array}
$$

The final two cases give the translations for synchronic and diachronic ascriptions of relations between temporal parts, respectively. The phrase '$R\,(x, x')$ at t, t''' is to be read 'x, as it is at t, bears R to x', as it is at t'''. Similar remarks apply to other uses of temporal parts by these authors. Woodger, for example, is primarily interested in axiomatizing biology to clarify the logical relations between different biological claims. No use is made of the fact that temporal parts are supposed to be literally parts; their only use is in an account of the logical form of biological sentences. This use is preserved if *further* analysis of talk of temporal parts is subsequently given, which treats the temporal parts as ersatz and which ultimately rests on a foundation of endurance.

---

[4] See the bibliography in Copeland (1996), and Burgess (1984).

[5] For this sort of point see also Wilson (1955), Geach (1972*b*: 303), and Butterfield (1984).

Related arguments, if we can call them that, are based on the fact that temporal parts make possible a neat statement of this theory or that. In any such case we must look to see whether the temporal parts are really indispensable. Often they are not.

3. THE A-THEORY OF TIME IS INCOHERENT

Another argument from around the same time was that endurance must be rejected because it is part of an untenable philosophy of time. In chapter 7 of *Philosophy and Scientific Realism*, J. J. C. Smart argues against what he calls an 'anthropocentric' account of time, according to which 'the notions of past, present, and future apply objectively to the universe' (1963: 132). This is the 'A-theory' of time. Against this account, Smart puts forward a view which is in essence what I am calling the manifold theory. A similar argument is contained in D. C. Williams's classic paper 'The Myth of Passage'.

Smart has three objections to the A-theory. First, he claims but does not argue that the manifold theory fits better with contemporary science.[6] Presumably Smart is thinking about special relativity, and he may well be correct that the B-theory half of the manifold theory may be thus supported (see Sect. 4 of Ch. 2). But, as will be argued in Section 4 of this chapter, it is less clear that special relativity supports temporal parts. Like Quine, Smart (and Williams as well) seems to lump the two components of the manifold theory together and assume that considerations in favor of one must invariably favor the other. It is vital to distinguish these components. I suspect that temporal parts have gained undeserved credibility by tagging along in this way with the B-theory.

Matters are similar with Smart's second and third objections to the A-theory, which are that (1) the A-theory is anthropocentric and (2) that it introduces 'unnecessary mystification' (1963: 140). Argument (1): distinctions of past, present, and future are those that human *thinkers* make from particular perspectives, and should not be exalted into objective metaphysical distinctions in the world. Argument (2): the mys-

---

[6] Smart says on p. 130 that 'a four-dimensional spacetime framework' has been 'forced on physicists by the theory of relativity'; and on p. 140 he says that 'I advocate my way [of analyzing temporal discourse], because it fits our ordinary way of talking much more closely to our scientific way of looking at the world . . .'.

teries resulting from the A-account stem from its claim that time flows. How fast does time flow? Must there be a hyper-time in which the flow takes place? (Williams says in this connection that 'Most of the effect of the prophets of passage . . . is to melt back into the primitive magma of confusion and plurality the best and sharpest instruments which the mind has forged' (1951: 472).) Moreover, there is McTaggart's famous 'proof' of the unreality of time, in which the incoherence of the A-theory is allegedly demonstrated. Against such claims A-theorists have responded,[7] but this debate is not my concern here, for it is evident that the arguments at best support the B-theory; they do not support the temporal parts component of the manifold theory. (Of course, if one could argue that the combination of the B-theory and endurance is untenable then this gap in the arguments of Smart and Williams would be bridged; see Sects. 6, 7, and 8.)

4. FOUR-DIMENSIONALISM AND SPECIAL RELATIVITY[8]

It is often claimed with little argument that the special theory of relativity requires perdurance. Russell (1927: 286), for example, says 'The old notion of substance had a certain appropriateness so long as we could believe in one cosmic time and one cosmic space; but it does not fit in so easily when we adopt the four-dimensional space-time framework'.[9] In fact, however, the support for temporal parts here is weak; one can accept special relativity and endurance alike. (At any rate, provided one is not a presentist; presentism itself is in tension with special relativity (Ch. 2, Sect. 4).)

There is no doubt that the language of Minkowski spacetime at least suggests four-dimensionalism. The world is typically described as a

---

[7] See Prior (1968a) and Markosian (1993) on the seeming paradoxes of claiming that time flows; Prior (1959) in essence confronts the anthropocentricity objection. On McTaggart's argument see Broad (1938: 309–17) and Prior (1967: 4–7).

[8] I thank Phillip Bricker, Yuri Balashov, John Hawthorne, and Dean Zimmerman for helpful comments on this section. See also Balashov (1999, 2000); Mellor (1981: 128 ff.); Oderberg (1993, ch. 4); Rea (1998); and Smart (1972) on this topic.

[9] See also Armstrong (1980: 74) and Quine (1960: 172) (though it is not completely clear whether Quine has in mind primarily the B-theory or perdurance).

world of events; point particles are construed as the sum total of events along their worldlines; extended objects are described by worm-like sections of spacetime, which have time-slices; and so on. Moreover, many descriptions of endurance are couched in terms hostile to relativity. Friends of endurance say that an object is wholly present at every moment of time at which it exists, and they speak of properties instantiated relative to times. This talk of times appears to conflict with the denial in special relativity of a privileged separation of spacetime into space and time. But endurantists may just be ignoring relativistic considerations. (We four-dimensionalists commit the same sin when speaking of *temporal* parts.) The question is whether the endurance theory *can* be stated in a relativistically acceptable way. In this section I will show that this can indeed be done. (I ignore general relativity, since it appears to present no new obstacles for three-dimensionalism.)[10]

Begin by assuming a four-dimensional Minkowski spacetime, as described in Chapter 2, Section 2. Reality thus contains a four-dimensional manifold of points of spacetime. In addition to the spacetime, let us also suppose that there exist continuants—fundamental particles, tables and chairs, people, and so on—which inhabit the spacetime.[11] This 'inhabiting' may be characterized by means of a binary relation of *occupation* holding between continuants and points of the spacetime.

The three-dimensionalist wants to say that these continuants endure, that they have no temporal parts. This is easiest to characterize in the case of a fundamental particle. Such a particle would have two crucial features. First, it would have no proper parts whatsoever (no parts, that is, with respect to any points of spacetime—see below). Secondly, the occupation relation between it and points of spacetime would be one-many: it would occupy all the points that comprise its worldline.

This way of viewing things may be contrasted with that of the four-dimensionalist. The four-dimensionalist would agree that the occupation relation between the particle and points of spacetime is one-many, but she would deny that the particle is mereologically simple. Rather, at each

---

[10] Although see Mellor (1981: 130–1).

[11] The combination of endurance and special relativity I am presenting here faces pressure from my argument in Section 8 below that substantivalists about spacetime should identify continuants with regions of spacetime. In the present section I am only trying to show that endurance is *consistent* with special relativity; my overall position is of course that perdurance is the more attractive view.

point along its worldline, the particle has a *spatiotemporal point-part*—an object that (1) is part of the particle, (2) is located at that point, and (3) is not located at any other point. For the four-dimensionalist, the occupation relation between mereologically simple things and points of spacetime can never be one-many.

We also want to know how to talk about the properties and relations of fundamental particles. Let us first discuss spatiotemporal relations. Here the endurantist should say that spatiotemporal relations hold primarily between points of the spacetime. Fundamental particles then stand in spatiotemporal relations derivatively by occupying points of the spacetime that stand in those relations. Let us first get clear about the spatiotemporal relations that hold between points in Minkowski spacetime. Just as observer-independent simultaneity is not a well-defined notion in Minkowski spacetime, neither are observer-independent spatial or temporal distance. However, relative to any frame of reference—that is, unaccelerated path through spacetime—not only are simultaneity relations well defined, but temporal and spatial distance relations between points are also well defined. Relative to a frame of reference, F, any two points x and y are separated by some definite temporal and spatial distance. These frame-relative distances flow from facts about the intrinsic geometry of the spacetime (they may be derived from information about the 'interval', which is an absolute (frame-invariant) quantity defined for any two points in spacetime).

We therefore proceed as follows. Since simultaneity is well defined relative to any frame of reference, F, relative to F we can divide the points of spacetime into equivalence classes of simultaneous points. These equivalence classes may be thought of as times, so long as we remember that the division of points into times is valid only relative to the chosen frame, F. So now, relative to F, consider any time, t, and any two fundamental particles x and y. We may first say that one of these particles *exists at t* iff it occupies some point of spacetime that is contained in t.[12] And given that x and y both exist at t, the spatial distance between x and y at t (relative to F) may be defined as the spatial distance relative to F between the points of spacetime in t that are occupied by x and y, respectively.

The defender of endurance must account for the qualities of fundamental particles as well as their spatiotemporal relations. When an

---

[12] This notion of *exists-at* is a spatiotemporal, not quantificational, notion (Ch. 3, Sect. 2).

endurantist is not thinking of relativity she typically construes property instantiation as being in some way relative to time, to account for change (see Sect. 6 below). Given relativity, instantiation must be indexed instead to points of spacetime.[13] Thus, an electron will have unit negative charge, spin $1/2$, and so on, relative to the points of space-time that it occupies. (The *four*-dimensionalist will regard point-relative property instantiation as being definable from property instantiation *simpliciter* as follows: a particle x has property P at point p iff the spatiotemporal point-part of x that occupies p has P *simpliciter*. The three-dimensionalist will reject this definition since it presupposes spatiotemporal point-parts.) We can then define a frame-relative notion of instantiation at a time: relative to any chosen reference frame F, and given any time t in the partition of spacetime for frame F, x has P at t iff x has P at the spacetime point in t that x occupies.

So far we have formulated a theory of enduring fundamental particles in which properties of and spatiotemporal relations between these particles may be characterized. The relativistic physics of the small, at any rate, is consistent with endurance.

But a relativistic theory of macro-entities must be formulated as well, and here we encounter new difficulties. One problem is due to Yuri Balashov (1999). One and the same macroscopic object will have different shapes relative to observers traveling at different velocities, even as observed from the same point in spacetime (allow as an idealization that the observers coincide spatiotemporally at the point of observation). What *explains* the fact that one and the same object has these different shapes for different observers? Balashov puts the point as follows (p. 653):

The same object has different 3D shapes. There are strong reasons to believe that the difference is due neither to intrinsic change (shapes are observed at the same time) nor to the variation of a merely spatial perspective (shapes are observed from the same place; furthermore, even if they were not, it is hard to see how a variation of a merely spatial perspective could affect the three-dimensional shape of an object) . . .

[The three-dimensionalist] will have a hard time explaining how 'separate and loose' 3D shapes come together in a remarkable unity, by lending themselves to

---

[13] Or must it? At present we are only presenting an endurance theory for fundamental particles, which apparently have their *intrinsic* properties, anyway, permanently; one might take such properties to be instantiated *simpliciter*. But I do not wish to base the relativistic theory of endurance on this assumption, which may well only hold contingently.

an arrangement in a compact and smooth 4D volume. Where the four-dimensionalist has a ready and natural explanation of this fact: different 3D shapes are cross-sections of a single 4D entity, the three-dimensionalist must regard it as a brute fact, indeed, as a complete mystery.

According to Balashov, only the *four*-dimensionalist has a ready answer of why the object has different shapes for different observers, and why those shapes fill up a compact and smooth 4D volume. The three-dimensionalist allegedly cannot provide a unifying explanation of the different shapes, but must rather postulate a brute fact that a plenitude of 'perspective-indexed' 3D shapes all belong to a single enduring thing, and fit into a compact and smooth 4D volume.

But assuming the account of enduring fundamental particles given above, the three-dimensionalist can reply as follows. To have a shape at a time is just to have *parts* that are spatially related in a certain way at that time. As we have seen, relative to a chosen reference frame we can account for spatial relations between fundamental particles at times. Provided the three-dimensionalist can make sense of the part-whole relation in a relativistic context, then, she can account for the shapes of macroscopic objects in various reference frames.[14] All of the perspective-indexed shapes are the result of a single set of facts about the enduring object, which include (1) the holding of the part-whole relation, and (2) the holding of the occupation relation between fundamental particles and points of spacetime.[15] This also explains also why the shapes fit into the 4D volume that they do. The volume is generated as the sum of all the points occupied by the parts of the object; the shapes are slices of this volume.

---

[14] For full generality, the explanation should not presuppose atomism about matter. Suppose a macroscopic object is 'gunky', containing no simples as parts. Facts about its shape in different reference frames would be generated by the facts about the points occupied by the infinitely many objects that overlap it at various points in spacetime.

[15] Lowe (1987) made a similar response to Lewis on the problem of temporary intrinsics. In reply, Lewis (1988a) claimed that since the three-dimensionalist denies that composition is identity, facts about the spatial relations between the parts of a thing are not the same as facts about the thing itself; thus, shapes cannot be the same thing as spatial relations between the parts of a thing. As I see it, Lowe should reply that although composition is not identity, still an object's shape at a time supervenes on the spatial relations at that time between its parts. Thus an adequate ontology need only explicitly address the latter. *Mutatis mutandis* for the relativistic case.

This presupposes a relativistically acceptable mereology. Relativistic mereology for the *four*-dimensionalist is easy. Since the four-dimensionalist's part-whole relation is atemporal, the theory of that relation is unaffected by relativistic considerations. (Of course, which parts of a spacetime worm count as *temporal* parts is a matter affected by relativity, but that is different.) As we saw in Chapter 3, Section 2, the eternalist three-dimensionalist rejects atemporal mereology. The strategy discussed there of indexing the part-whole relation to times can no longer be pursued without modification in the relativistic case since there are no such things as times. The natural course is to relativize the fundamental mereological locutions to points of spacetime instead; frame-relative facts about parts at times may then be derived.

On behalf of the three-dimensionalist, let us take as primitive a three-place relation of *overlap* at a point: one continuant overlaps another at a point of spacetime. The idea may be made vivid by thinking of the histories of the relata: the picture is that objects overlap one another at p when their histories both include p (though this should not be thought of as definitional since a three-dimensionalist might not want to rule out, a priori, the possibility of two mereologically disjoint objects sharing the same spacetime location). The primitive of overlap should be assumed to obey the law that if objects overlap at a point then they both occupy that point (though the converse should not be assumed if spatio-temporal co-location is not to be ruled out a priori.)

(Notice that the four-dimensionalist would define overlap-at-a-point in terms of two-place mereological locutions and occupation: x overlaps y at p iff some z is part (*simpliciter*) of both x and y, and z occupies p. For the three-dimensionalist overlap-at-a-point remains primitive.)

A frame-relative notion of overlap at a time can now be introduced:

> x *and* y *overlap at time* t (relative to some chosen frame, F) iff there is some point in t at which x and y overlap.

We can then use familiar methods from the Calculus of Individuals to define other temporally qualified mereological notions, for example parthood-at-t:

> x *is part of* y *at time* t (relative to some chosen frame, F) iff x and y both exist at t, and everything that overlaps x at t also overlaps y at t.

In sum, the three-dimensionalist may appeal to the following sorts of facts holding within Minkowski spacetime:

- facts about overlap-at-spacetime-points for enduring objects;
- facts about the occupation relation between enduring objects and spacetime points;
- facts about properties of enduring fundamental particles at space-time points;
- facts about the intrinsic geometry of spacetime (for example facts about the interval).

The three-dimensionalist could plausibly go on to claim that all of what we say in science and everyday life supervenes on these facts. In this sense, then, endurance can be reconciled with special relativity.

There remains the issue of how to formulate the central three-dimensionalist thesis itself, that objects are wholly present whenever they exist, within this framework. As we saw in Chapter 3, Section 3 above, even leaving aside relativity there are serious problems in arriving at an acceptable formulation of three-dimensionalism. We *can* give a relativistic analog of the definition of being strongly wholly present throughout a temporal interval:

> Definition: Given a choice of frame, F, in the partition of spacetime relative to F, x is *strongly wholly present* throughout region T iff anything that is at any time in T part of x is, at every time in T, part of x.

But what will be the central claim of three-dimensionalism? We do not want to claim that, with respect to every (or even any) reference frames, every object is strongly wholly present at every moment at which it exists, because this would rule out mereologically inconstant objects. As we saw, the proposition that *it is possible for there to be an object strongly wholly present throughout an extended interval* will be accepted by all three-dimensionalists; and most three-dimensionalists will at least conjecture that *every fundamental particle is strongly wholly present throughout its career*. This much we already knew from Chapter 3, Section 3. Relativity now raises the additional question of which reference frames the claim and conjecture will be made from. The natural course seems to be to relativize to *all* (inertial) reference frames. The claim would then be that it is possible for there to be an object that is, with respect to every reference frame, strongly wholly present throughout some extended interval with respect to that reference frame. The conjecture would be that, with respect to every reference frame, every fundamental particle is strongly wholly present throughout its career. I see no obstacle to the coherence of these things. It therefore appears that relativistic three-dimensionalism is a coherent position.

One final worry must be faced by three-dimensionalists who combine their rejection of temporal parts with the acceptance of 'arbitrary spatial parts'. Might something count as a spatial part with respect to one reference frame and a temporal part with respect to another? In fact this cannot happen.[16] Consider, for example, a fundamental particle e that is strongly wholly present throughout its career with respect to some reference frame, and let p_1 and p_2 be two points along its worldline. The worry now involves a second reference frame with respect to which p_1 and p_2 are simultaneous. Since e is strongly wholly present throughout its career in the first frame, we would appear to have a violation of the doctrine of arbitrary spatial parts in the second frame, for there is an object—e—which occupies two points in space—p_1 and p_2—without containing parts that are confined (at that time) to those points in space. The error in this argument is, of course, the assumption that there is any reference frame in which p_1 and p_2 are simultaneous: since the points are each on the worldline of a particle, one must be in the absolute future of the other.

The relativistic account of endurance presented in this section has assumed substantivalism about spacetime. As argued in Section 8 below, there are difficulties in combining relationalism about classical spacetime with endurance; relationalism about Minkowski spacetime would presumably inherit the same difficulties. Moreover, published developments of relationalism about Minkowski spacetime of which I am aware have presupposed perdurance.[17] But a detailed investigation of combining endurance with relationalism about Minkowski spacetime is beyond my technical competence.

The account also assumes two kinds of atomism, first that spacetime is made of points, and secondly that continuants are ultimately made up of simples. Though it is beyond my technical competence to explore dropping the first assumption, dropping the second assumption by

[16] See also Mellor (1981: 129).
[17] See Mundy (1983) and Friedman (1983, ch. VI).

allowing 'gunky' inhabitants of spacetime may require only a little modification. Assuming spacetime itself is not gunky, we can still utilize overlap-at-a-point as our fundamental mereological relation, and we can still take occupation to be a relation between things and points of spacetime. (Any gunky thing will of course occupy many points.) Property instantiation can presumably also remain relative to points of spacetime, although it is difficult to anticipate obstacles since I have never seen any detailed theory of the properties of gunk constructed, never mind a relativistic one.

5. SPACE AND TIME ARE ANALOGOUS

A common argument in favor of temporal parts is based on the analogy between space and time. We observe an analogy between these dimensions in many respects. All physical objects are represented in our experience as located in both space and time. There is a common topological and metrical structure between any given spatial dimension and the temporal dimension (at least relative to any given reference frame). Objects move in both space and time. Other times are as real as the present, just as other places are as real as here. (The argument from analogy here depends on eternalism.) The more this analogy holds, the more entitled we are to expect it to hold in new areas. We thereby should expect the part–whole relation to behave with respect to time as it does with respect to space. But objects are spread out in space; few think that everyday particulars are 'wholly present' at more than one place. By analogy, therefore, objects are spread out in time as well: four-dimensionalism is true.[18]

One way of challenging the argument is to point out disanalogies between time and space that even the four-dimensionalist will accept. Unlike time, space has three dimensions and lacks a distinguished direction; unlike space, time seems to be specially connected with causation. A second challenge would be this: why should similarity in one respect, for example, metricality, persuade us of similarity in a quite different respect, namely, parthood? This weakness surfaces in the literature on

---

[18] See e.g. Armstrong (1980). For critical discussion see Chisholm (1971: 15–16; and 1976, app. A); Rea (1998); and Thomson (1983, sect. V). For extended discussion of space/time analogies see Schlesinger (1980, ch. 1) and Taylor (1955).

this argument in various ways. Chisholm (1971: 15–16; and 1976 app. A) for example, criticizes the argument by alleging the following disanalogy between time and space:

Possibly, there exists an x such that every part x ever has exists at more than one time at the same place.

NOT: possibly, there exists an x such that every part x ever has exists at more than one place at the same time.

The former statement will be denied by a four-dimensionalist: existing at multiple times requires distinct parts confined to those times. The analogy would then be reinstated. Chisholm realizes this, but claims that it would be circular to base the argument on this sort of consideration, premised as it is on temporal parts. No more circular, I think, than Chisholm's argument that time and space are *not* analogous, since Chisholm's opponent accepts temporal parts. Nevertheless, the argument *for* temporal parts is dialectically weak. The three-dimensionalist need not feel awkward in claiming that three-dimensionalism itself constitutes a breakdown of an analogy that was limited to begin with. Similarly, in his classic article 'Spatial and Temporal Analogies and the Concept of Identity' (1955), Richard Taylor argues for a pervasive analogy between space and time, but many of the arguments simply assume the doctrine of temporal parts.[19] This sort of dialectical impasse is typical.

The traditional argument from analogy, then, is weak. Some improvement may be possible, however. Why do we think that a desk, say, has spatial parts? Why do we not think that the desk is mereologically simple, 'wholly present' at multiple places? We *do* take the desk to have parts, justifiably I think. But various *arguments* for spatial parts have plausible temporal analogs in favor of temporal parts.

One argument is that the desk is spatially extended. But if spatial extension implies the existence of spatial parts, would not temporal extension imply the existence of temporal parts? It is true that we are dealing with different sorts of extension in the different cases, but (assuming the B-theory, anyway) there seems to be nothing distinctive about spatial extension that makes the argument succeed only in the spatial case.

Another argument appeals to qualitative variation within objects. If the desk is smooth at one place and rough at another, by Leibniz's Law

---

[19] Cf. Oderberg (1993: 98 ff.).

we naturally conclude that the thing that is smooth is distinct from the thing that is rough, and thus that the desk has proper parts. (The argument of the previous paragraph may be regarded as an instance of this argument: the differing properties are properties of location. But perhaps the argument is more plausible when the selected properties are intrinsic.) This argument, too, has a temporal analog: the well-known argument from temporary intrinsics, to be discussed in Section 6 below. When I change from sitting to standing, Leibniz's Law seems to imply that the thing that is sitting is distinct from the thing that is standing. These distinct things would be my temporal parts. It is common to resist the argument by indexing properties to times—one and the same enduring thing is alleged to be sitting *at* one time while standing *at* another time. This is indeed consistent with Leibniz's Law; but an analogous move could render spatially wholly present objects consistent with Leibniz's Law. The desk might be asserted to be smooth *at* one place and rough *at* another.

A third reason for postulating spatial parts is modal. Call the left half of the region of space occupied by the desk 'R'. R and its material contents might have been, intrinsically, exactly as they actually are even if the rest of the world had been eliminated. In that case an object exactly occupying R would have existed. But then we should postulate an object in actuality that exactly occupies R. For surely the elimination of the rest of the world outside of region R would not bring a *new* object into existence; but what other actual object could this object be, other than a part of the desk that actually occupies region R? (Some—for example Peter van Inwagen; see Ch. 5, Sect. 6—would deny the premise that an object exactly occupying R would exist in the world where everything else was eliminated. But even van Inwagen might accept a version of the argument when R is required to be a point-sized region of space.)

It is clear that the modal argument for spatial parts has a temporal analog. Note, though, that the plausibility of either the spatial or temporal version of the argument may depend on the particular region, R, chosen. In the spatial case, if R is chosen to be a very large part of the entire region occupied by the desk it is tempting to say that the resulting isolated object is the original desk itself, in truncated form. This would undermine the argument's final step, that the isolated object can only be identified with an actual proper part of the desk. In the temporal analog of this argument, if the isolated region is chosen as an initial segment of the life of a thing (even a short one), it is tempting to identify the isolated object with the original object itself, similarly undermining the argument. Nevertheless, certain cases of each argument fare better, cases in which we are not tempted to make these identifications. When a small spatial region of the desk is selected, the resulting isolated object seems not to be the original desk, and when a small *final* temporal segment of a thing's life is isolated, it is much less tempting to identify the result with the original thing. And perhaps if the modal argument succeeds in generating parts of a thing in certain of the regions of space or time that it occupies, perhaps considerations of symmetry would justify postulating parts in the rest of those regions, regions for which the modal argument is implausible.

A related argument involves division. Suppose the desk is divided into halves. (Followers of van Inwagen may substitute division of a living thing into point-sized parts.) Since the halves are spatially separated, they are distinct objects. These objects were presumably not created by division, so they must have existed before division.[20] But surely it does not matter whether the division ever *actually* occurs, so anything *potentially* divisible must actually have parts.

One might think the division argument has no temporal analog, until Taylor-style spatial and temporal analogies are recalled. Begin by examining the spatial division argument more closely, in terms of the total region of spacetime involved. At time t_1 the desk is intact; by time t_2 it has been divided in two halves, which occupy spatial regions R_1 and R_2, as in Figure 4.1. The argument is that since R_1 and R_2 are spatially separated, they must contain distinct objects, although notice that R_1 and R_2 are spatiotemporally connected, via the 'V-shaped' path.

But now consider Figure 4.2, in which the temporal and spatial axes are reversed (assume, for simplicity, that the regions R_1 and R_2 are point-sized). We now have a case in which an object is 'separated into its temporal parts', only now the dimension of separation between the temporal parts is temporal, and the 'dynamic' dimension along which the separation takes place is spatial. Less cryptically, the figure now represents a point particle that begins at place p_2 at time t_1, moves to place p_1 at time t_2, and then moves back to place p_2 at time t_3. The temporal analog of the

---

[20] In some cases this is not clearly correct. Some say that when an amoeba divides, two new amoebae come into existence. The division argument for parts should not be applied to such cases.

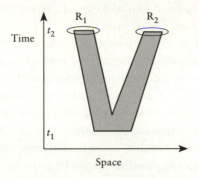

FIG. 4.1. Division into spatial parts

argument for parts now runs as follows. Regions R_1 and R_2 are separated in time (though connected by a 'V-shaped' spatiotemporal path). Thus, we must posit distinct objects occupying those regions. These distinct objects can only be temporal parts. But then, the temporal parts ought to be posited even when the spacetime path does not take such a V-shape.

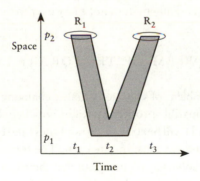

FIG. 4.2. Division into temporal parts

Those who wish to resist temporal parts face a double challenge. It is not enough to show why the temporal arguments just discussed fail, for the opponents of temporal parts typically accept spatial parts and so must show why their objections to the temporal arguments do not carry over, invariably, to their spatial counterparts. Of course, it can be admitted that *some* of the spatial arguments fail as well. But at least one must succeed if the belief in spatial parts is to be justified, and then we can ask why its temporal analog fails.

The response will presumably be a particularly stubborn version of the response to the original argument from analogy. Some spatial argument succeeds where its temporal counterpart fails because it involves space, not time. The first argument assumes that spatial extension implies spatial parts, the second that properties should not be indexed to places, the third that spatial isolation cannot 'create' a new entity, and the fourth that spatially disjoint (though spatiotemporally connected) regions must be occupied by distinct things. Perhaps the analogous principles assumed in the temporal arguments are less plausible: that temporal extension implies temporal parts, that properties should not be indexed to times, that temporal isolation cannot create a new entity, and that temporally disjoint (though spatiotemporally connected) regions must be occupied by distinct things. Perhaps. In a sense, we have returned to our starting-point: the friend of temporal parts upholds a spacetime analogy that the opponent resists. But now there is more pressure on the opponent of temporal parts, for she must positively *commit* to an argument for parts in the spatial case, and so has the burden of explaining why that argument does not carry over to the temporal case.

6.   THE PROBLEM OF TEMPORARY INTRINSICS

The traditional problem of change is that a changing object appears to exemplify incompatible properties. Right now I am bent, since I am sitting. When I stand I will be straight. Straightness and bentness seem to be incompatible, and yet I instantiate each. The formal contradiction can, of course, be resolved by pointing out that these incompatible properties are had *at* different times, but some are not satisfied with this glib response. Hermann Lotze dismissed similar glib responses to the problem of change as follows:

In what sense can that at different moments remain identical with itself, which yet in one of these moments is not identically like itself as it was in the other? It is scarcely necessary to remark how entirely unprofitable the answers are which in the ordinary course of thought are commonly given to this question; such as, The essence always remains the same with itself, only the phenomenon changes; the matter remains the same, the form alters; essential properties persist, but many unessential ones come and go; the Thing itself abides, only its states are variable. All these expressions presuppose what we want to know. (Lotze, 1887: 62–3)

My guess is that he would have as little patience for the present response as for the ones he considered.

The glib response is not entirely useless. The problem of change is sometimes put forth by a *skeptic* as showing that no object persists through change. The glib reply is then that *being bent now*, and *being straight in 30 minutes* are not incompatible. This will not convince the skeptic that I *do* persist over time, since it presupposes that I have the property *being straight in 30 minutes*, and therefore that I persist. But it is familiar that convincing the skeptic and remaining unconvinced by the skeptic are two very different things.

It is likewise familiar, however, that the skeptic plays a valuable role even if we remain sure she is wrong, for discovering exactly where her arguments fail may teach us something valuable about the concepts contained therein.[21] The glib response to the problem of change is unsatisfying, for the skeptic about persistence will ask: what is it for objects to have properties at different times? A more satisfying answer requires constructing a metaphysics of change.

The temporal parts account of change is that incompatible properties are had by different objects, different temporal parts of the whole. Change is therefore no more remarkable than the variation of a road with some bumpy stretches and some smooth stretches.

The question then is whether endurantist accounts of change are possible. David Lewis's discussion of 'the problem of temporary intrinsics' (1986a: 202–4) consists primarily of a negative answer to this question. Lewis presents three models of change and argues that the only acceptable one invokes temporal parts. The three models are these:

(1) An eternalist-endurantist model according to which so-called properties are in fact relations to times. This model in effect elevates what I called the glib response into serious metaphysics. I bear the bent-at relation to the present time, and the straight-at relation to another.[22]

---

[21] Cf. Pollock (1986, ch. 1, sect. 1).

[22] This view is explicitly held by Mellor (1981: 110–14). Variations are defended by Haslanger (1989a); Johnston (1987); Lowe (1987, 1988a); van Inwagen (1990b); whether these variations differ importantly from Mellor's view is controversial; see below.

(2) A presentist model. On this model, the only properties a changing object has are its present properties, because only the present time is real. All facts are facts about what objects are like *now*. On this view, the apparent contradiction between incompatible properties vanishes with the banished past and future. Since I am presently bent, I am bent *simpliciter*, and in no way straight, since there is no future in which to locate my straightness.

(3) A temporal parts model, according to which the incompatible properties involved in change are really had, not by the persisting object itself, but rather by its temporal parts. Change is heterogeneity of temporal parts.

Lewis provides reasons to reject models (1) and (2), leaving us with model (3) and temporal parts.

Given Chapter 2, the presentist model may be set aside. Note, however, that there is a worry here that Lewis's trilemma is not exhaustive. The attraction of the presentist's account of change is that it allows us to claim that I am bent *simpliciter*, rather than bent with respect to some time. But this virtue might be thought to flow just from taking tense seriously, without requiring the additional claim that only the present is real. As mentioned in Chapter 2, it is possible to combine eternalism with irreducible tense. The defender of this combination might claim that objects have temporary intrinsics *simpliciter*, which change over time in the sense that irreducibly tensed propositions about the instantiation *simpliciter* of temporary intrinsics are true. An object that exists currently has the property of being bent, objects located in the past have the property of being formerly bent, and so on. This view might appear to have the virtues of presentism while lacking its defects.

Suppose someone accepts the existence of past and future objects while denying that tenseless facts about these objects exhaust the facts about reality. Of any such person we must ask what exactly is missing from a tenseless description of reality. One answer is that of the moving spotlight view discussed in Chapter 2: the B-theoretic description of the world is completely adequate except that it leaves out information about which time is *present*. But information about the properties of objects at various times is part of the tenseless information regarded as unproblematic by the moving spotlight theorist; the moving spotlight theorist, therefore, cannot deliver an alternative to the three models of change listed above.

For a distinctive solution to the problem of change we would need to go further and claim that more is wrong with a B-theoretic description of reality beyond its omission of facts about presentness. Irreducibly tensed facts must include facts about property instantiation in addition to facts about presentness. All that can be accurately reported from a tenseless point of view is *which* objects exist from the past, present, and future; to report the *features* of these objects—their properties and relations—requires irreducible tense. But now we have a very strange combination of views. What properties does Socrates have? The standard B-theorist's answer is that all talk of property instantiation is fundamentally tenseless. One can then say that Socrates has the property of sitting at various times at which he existed, has the property of standing at other times at which he existed, and so on. Once tenseless property attribution is rejected in favor of taking tense seriously, any properties attributed to Socrates would need to be properties he has *now*. This turns Socrates into a very shadowy figure: he has properties like *formerly sitting*, *formerly being wise*, and so on, but for no 'manifest' or categorical property, F, can we say that Socrates is F. We got ourselves into this sorry position by accepting an element of the B-theory—atemporal quantification—while rejecting too much else of the picture, namely tenseless property exemplification. This fourth model of change, therefore, is unattractive. It seems, therefore, not to be a viable alternative to Lewis's three models of change.[23]

The most important part of Lewis's argument is his argument against model (1). According to this model, what we ordinarily think of as properties are in fact relations to times. But this is an implausible view, according to Lewis, given that change sometimes involves *intrinsic* properties. *Being bent* is intrinsic; its instantiation by me cannot, therefore, involve my relations to other things, not even times. Surely I am just plain bent, not bent with respect to something else.

It is worth distinguishing two objections Lewis gives to this view, though I think that the bottom line is the same. The first is that the eternalist-endurantist model would obliterate the distinction between intrinsic and relational properties; all properties would turn out relational. As Sally Haslanger points out (1989a: 123–4), the eternalist-endurantist could respond with an understanding of 'intrinsic' that

---

[23] Dean Zimmerman (1998b) makes similar points.

would allow for a distinction to be drawn, despite the fact that instantiation of properties is temporally relative:

> P is *intrinsic* iff for every time at which an object has P, it has it then solely in virtue of the way it is then.

This is in contrast to Lewis's gloss on intrinsic properties as those instantiated by an object in virtue of the way that object is, considered in itself (1983*b*: 197). Lewis anticipates such a response:

[a defender of properties had *at* times can draw a distinction] he will *call* the distinction between matters of one's own intrinsic character and matters of one's relationships . . . [but] his account reveals that really he treats shape, no less than unclehood, as a matter of relations. In this account, nothing just has a shape *simpliciter*. (1988*a*: 65)

Lewis is insisting on the following as a datum: some things have shapes *simpliciter*.

The second version of the objection is this: 'If we know what shape is, we know that it is a property, not a relation' (Lewis 1986*a*: 204). Some have responded by defending theories of property instantiation that allow shapes to be properties but which relativize the instantiation relation to times in some way. Property instantiation for van Inwagen (1990*b*) and Mark Johnston (1987) is a three-place relation between a thing, property, and time; for Sally Haslanger (1985, 1989*a*), things and one-place properties combine to form propositions, which are then true or false relative to times. On all of these views, shapes are properties but are nevertheless had relative to times; they are 'relativized properties'. I agree with Lewis (1988*a*: 65–6 note 1) and Mark Hinchliff that such circumvention accomplishes little. Hinchliff puts this well: 'As appealing as the relativization strategy is, it fails to accommodate our intuition that shapes are properties. Relativized properties are not properties, because a thing cannot just have them. So what are they? They are nothing new; they are relations in disguise' (1996: 122). We have arrived at the same place as above: Lewis's argument against model (1) rests on the alleged datum that some objects are 'just plain straight', that shapes can be ascribed to objects without qualification or relativity of any kind.

Can any progress be made here, or must the datum be baldly asserted as intuition? As discussed in Section 5 above, one might press the defender of eternalist endurance on the analogy between space and time. If the argument from temporary intrinsics for temporal parts is to be resisted by indexing to times, why not also resist the analogous argument for spatial parts, index properties to places, and claim that objects are wholly present across space as well as time? Of course, this move inherits the weakness of the other arguments from analogy considered above: the eternalist can admit some analogies between time and space while denying a general analogy.

The argument, then, seems only as strong as the claim on which it is based, that some objects are 'just plain straight'. It is unclear how strong this basis is. There is indeed something odd about relativizing shapes: 'One and the same enduring thing may bear the bent-shape relation to some times, and the straight-shape relation to others. In itself, considered apart from its relations to other things, it has no shape at all' (Lewis 1986a: 204). But, it might be asked, when we are clear that *time* is the source of the relativity, what is wrong with denying that objects are ever just plain straight? We ordinarily speak as if objects are just plain straight, but present tense is normally implicit. It is therefore easy to forget that '*x* is straight' means '*x* is straight *now*'. Once this is made clear, Lewis faces E. J. Lowe's (1988a: 73) question: 'why can't we just happily deny that changeable, persisting physical objects can ever correctly be described as "just plain being straight"?' (As Lowe immediately observes, Lewis would say we *can* deny this, since it is not changeable persisting objects—spacetime worms—that are just plain straight, but rather temporal parts. But what Lowe seems to be saying in the following sentences is that we can happily deny that *anything* is just plain straight.) Nothing is simply straight or bent, since things change.[24]

At this point it is hard to evaluate the argument. The main premise of the argument, that some things are just plain straight, is accepted by the argument's proponents, and denied by its targets. The argument does, I think, favor four-dimensionalism, but not strongly so. We do have some initial attachment to the main premise, but the rejection of that premise is certainly not rationally unacceptable.

It is worth noting that the version of four-dimensionalism that is *best* supported by the argument from temporary intrinsics is not actually the view that ordinary continuants are spacetime worms, but rather the

[24] Might something that happens to be permanently straight be just plain straight? No: surely such a thing would be straight in exactly the same way as is a temporarily straight thing.

view (to be defended in Ch. 5, Sect. 8) that ordinary continuants are to be identified with instantaneous stages. As noted, Lewis himself cannot claim that ordinary continuants are just plain straight since for him continuants are sums of stages, some straight, others not. Lewis's objection to model (1) must be carefully qualified: it is that model (1) implies that *no* objects are just plain straight. But here Lewis's critics have pounced. How can Lewis lay claim to ordinary intuitions if his claim does not involve continuants—the objects of our everyday ontology? Moreover, Lewis's theory of change has its own counterintuitive consequence: it violates a plausible principle about change, that an object that changes shape must *itself* have a shape *simpliciter*.[25] As Hinchliff (1996: 120) puts it, discussing a changing candle, 'If the candle never has the shapes itself, it cannot change *its* shape'. However, this rejoinder to Lewis only applies to the worm view. According to the stage view, I myself have the property *being straight*, for I am a stage, not a spacetime worm. Thus, the stage view allows both that temporary intrinsics are instantiated *simpliciter* and that they are instantiated by ordinary continuants such as persons and candles.[26]

7.   ARGUMENTS FROM EXOTICA

Assume the B-theory of time (see Ch. 2), that past and future objects exist in addition to presently existing ones, and that tensed notions reduce to tenseless ones. (Or, for that matter, assume either the moving-spotlight or the growing block universe theory of time; in this section it will not matter.) Then either the subjects of momentary property instantiation are stages, or we must index instantiation to times.[27] So any argument against indexing is an argument for temporal parts. Lewis's argument against indexing has been discussed; in this section I consider two others. The first is based on the possibility of a timeless world. Some may consider this possibility too bizarre to be useful in argumentation. Fortunately, while the second argument is also based on a rather exotic possibility (time travel), there are powerful reasons to

---

[25] Haslanger (1989a: 119–20); Hinchliff (1996, 120–1); Lowe (1988a: 73–4).

[26] See also Sider (2000c).

[27] Assuming substantivalism about time, that is. At the very end of the next section I discuss how the arguments of the present section apply to a spacetime relationalist.

take that possibility seriously—that argument cannot be so lightly dismissed.

7.1.   *The argument from timeless worlds*

If being straight-shaped is a relation to times, nothing would remain straight-shaped if you cut away all the times from a world. And yet surely objects in a timeless world *could* be straight-shaped.

More carefully, consider two worlds: first, a non-relativistic world with a Euclidean space and separable time dimension, and secondly, a world without any time dimension at all. It seems plausible that a persisting object in the first world could be straight-shaped in exactly the same way as a timeless object in the second. Since time and space are separable, shape seems to be a purely spatial property, and thus should remain if the time dimension is removed. Given four-dimensionalism this is straightforward: *straightness* is a property that can be instantiated by instantaneous stages and alien timeless objects alike. But in one way or another, the three-dimensionalist will need to treat the straightnesses of the timeless and temporal objects differently. If *straightness* is a relation to times, there is no time in the timeless world for the object to be related to. At best, the timeless object could instantiate some closely related property. But what would this *property* have to do with the straightness *relation*? Similar but more complicated remarks apply to endurance theories that postulate three-place instantiation relations, or states of affairs true at times: the timeless object cannot instantiate *straightness* in the same way as the temporal object since a different relation of property instantiation or truth of states of affairs will be involved in the different cases.

The claim that timeless and temporal objects could be straight in the same way is not so plausible when applied to a relativistic world. There, shapes are not purely spatial since no dimension is purely spatial. However, an analogous argument will hold for non-spatial intrinsic properties: it should be possible for an electron to have unit negative charge in a purely spatial world without time in the same way that a persisting electron in the actual, relativistic, spatiotemporal world has unit negative charge. A three-dimensionalist must say that actual charge is a relation to points in spacetime, which cannot be instantiated in a timeless world. It might be responded that electrons have their charge permanently, and so charge is had absolutely, not relative to points in spacetime. However, it is unlikely that the three-dimensionalist would want to rest the case on this; for all we know, we might discover tomorrow that some subatomic particles have their charges temporarily.

It might be argued that a single abstract entity, *straightness*, is a relation to times in the temporal world and a property in the timeless world. Thus the temporal and timeless objects could each instantiate *straightness*. This reply strains our conception of the modal properties of abstract entities. But even if we grant the objector that *straightness* is involved in both worlds, the timeless object still is not straight in exactly the same way as is the persisting object since straightness is in one case a property and in the other case a relation.

Timeless worlds are admittedly quite distant from ordinary concerns; denying my claims about them, or denying their possibility, would not count too terribly heavily against the three-dimensionalist. My own feeling is that we do have *some* opinions about such exotic possibilities; hence the argument retains *some* weight.

Furthermore, a more mundane version of the argument can be advanced against certain versions of three-dimensionalism.[28] Three-dimensionalists deny that continuants perdure, but some—call them dualists—believe that in addition to continuants there exist events, or facts, which *do* perdure.[29] My life history, for example, is an event that is in many ways exactly like me, except that it, being an event, has temporal parts. It is present everywhere that I am present, is straight-shaped when I am, and bent when I am. However, its being straight is importantly different from my being straight, for when I am straight I bear a relation to a time, whereas it is straight by having a temporal part at the time that is straight *simpliciter*. This relationship between straightness-at-a-time and straightness *simpliciter* is mysterious—why does each count as a kind of straightness? Moreover, why is it a necessary truth (as it must be) that I bear the straightness *relation* to a time iff the temporal part of my life at that time instantiates the straightness *property*? Relatedly, the dualists say that my life history has parts; but these parts would be parts *simpliciter*, and what does the two-place relation of parthood *simpliciter* have to do with the three-place relation of having a part at a time? (Yet another related argument: some three-dimensionalists

[28]   I owe this observation to David Lewis. See the section on Mellor in Lewis (2000).
[29]   See e.g. Mellor (1998, ch. 8, 1981: 104–7); and Wiggins (1980: 25 n. 12).

want to apply parthood in other cases where temporal relativization is inappropriate: to abstract entities, or to sets, or to intervals of time. But parthood could not hold between such entities in the same way it holds between continuants, if parthood for the latter must always be temporally relativized.)

A three-dimensionalist might accept the existence of events but construct them in such a way as to render this argument ineffective. The event *x's being* F *at* t might be identified with the ordered triple $<x, F, t>$; such an event might be said to instantiate property F *simpliciter* iff *x* instantiates F at *t*. Property instantiation by events would thus be analyzed in terms of continuants bearing relations to times, and the argument would not apply. It is towards those dualists like D. H. Mellor (1981, 1998), according to whom events are *sui generis* entities that genuinely perdure, that the argument is directed.

7.2. The argument from time travel

A second argument from exotica, to my mind more compelling, may be based on time travel. Three-dimensionalism, I will argue, is inconsistent with the possibility of traveling back in time to meet one's former self. Since there are philosophical and physical reasons to believe in the possibility of time travel, this inflexibility of three-dimensionalism is unwelcome.

Suppose I travel back in time and stand in a room with my sitting 10-year-old self. I seem to be both sitting and standing, but how can that be? The four-dimensionalist's answer is that there are two distinct person stages, one standing, the other sitting.[30] (Given the Chapter 3 definition of a temporal part, the fusion of these two stages counts as my temporal part at the time in question, so let us understand 'person stage' to refer to 'person-like' parts of temporal parts. Ordinarily my temporal part at any time is a person stage, but not in cases of time travel.) If three-dimensionalism is true, on the other hand, the case involves only a single 'wholly present' person, which seems to be both sitting and standing.

---

[30] According to the worm theory, these are two stages of a single person, a spacetime worm that has 'doubled back on itself'. According to the stage view (Ch. 5, Sect. 8), there are actually two persons involved, since each person stage is a person. One of these can say that he *will* be the other; the other can say that he *was* the first, provided the stage-theoretic truth condition for '*x* will be F' is modified to read: '*x* has a counterpart in his *personal future* that is F'. See Lewis (1976) on the distinction between external and personal time.

This might be denied. Perhaps the object that sits and the object that stands are two distinct spatial parts of me at the time. These spatial parts cannot both be identical to me; otherwise they would be identical to each other. Indeed, the three-dimensionalist will probably want to say that *neither* is identical to me; rather, I have two person-like proper parts at the time. (Anyway, remarks similar to those I am about to make would apply if one of the spatial parts is me.)

Where did these spatial parts come from? Presumably they popped into existence upon arrival of the time machine; there seem to be no future or past objects with which they could be identified. But then 'a meeting of my former self and me' no longer seems an apt description of the event. Rather, it seems to be an event in which two wholly *new* persons meet each other. The later self who looks at what he takes to be himself and thinks 'I wonder what I was thinking at this moment' is *not* me, and is *not* in fact looking at himself. He is a person who just came into existence and mistakenly thinks he is a time traveler. It might be argued that it is really the composite of the two spatial parts who is looking and thinking, though of course it is doing so through one of its spatial parts. If this is correct, then since I am the composite, I really would be looking at myself and thinking about myself. But this is a distortion of the concept of a person. The correct description is quite clearly that the spatial parts are the persons, and that the case is not one of a person meeting his former self.

It seems, then, that to genuinely accommodate time travel, the three-dimensionalist must describe the case as involving only a single wholly present person. This leads to trouble. The most immediate oddity is that the person appears to have incompatible properties: *standing-at-*t and *sitting-at-*t, where *t* is the time in question. (Similar remarks apply to the sophisticated variants of the relations-to-times theory, for example that instantiation is three-place.)

The three-dimensionalist may be willing to live with this oddity, that something can stand and sit at a single time. After all, it is not as if the thing is standing and also not standing. Standing and sitting turn out not to be incompatible in the bizarre case of time travel.

There is a further objection that cuts deeper. In the story I told, I am standing while my former self is sitting. But our roles might have been reversed—I might have sat where he sits while he stood where I actually stand. We have here what appear to be two distinct possibilities. When

I meet my former self I think: 'I am standing and he is sitting, but it could have been the case that I sat and he stood.' The problem is that the three-dimensionalist cannot distinguish these possibilities. The *four*-dimensionalist can easily distinguish them. Each case involves two person stages, T_1 and T_2. In one case T_1 stands and T_2 sits, whereas in the other case T_2 stands and T_1 sits. But the three-dimensionalist can only speak of what properties *I* have at *t*. In the first possibility, I am standing at *t*, and also sitting at *t*. Exactly the same is true in the second possibility. (Relatedly, the three-dimensionalist will have trouble distinguishing the case where 'each' sits from the case in which 'just one' sits.[31])

The cases could be distinguished after all if I and my former self were qualitatively different. If I were taller than my former self, for example, then in the case where I stand a certain point in space would be occupied by me—namely, the point occupied by the top of my head—but would not be occupied by me in the case where it is my shorter former self that is standing. So let us stipulate that I and my former self do not differ in ways that would thus distinguish the cases.

The three-dimensionalist might try to distinguish the possible worlds in which these cases occur by differences at times other than the time of the meeting. To get around this sort of problem, let us stipulate that my time machine transports me 'instantaneously' into the room with my earlier self, and that my later self is then immediately annihilated after the meeting. But might not whether my later self sits or stands be caused by whether I am sitting or standing while entering the time machine? Given any such causal dependence of the later self's state on my state while entering the time machine, the cases might be distinguishable after all. I cannot get around this problem by stipulating that my emergence in the past is entirely causally unconnected to my entering the time machine since I accept that causation is a prerequisite of personal identity. What I need to do instead is, roughly, stipulate that my entry into the time machine causally determines that I emerge at the time of the meeting, but does not cause whether I am sitting or standing then. More carefully, I stipulate the following. First, in each case, I am standing when I enter the time machine. Secondly, in each case I am standing shortly before the time at which my former and later selves meet. Thirdly, the laws of nature in the two cases are identical, and are indeterministic. As applied

---

[31] Thanks to John Hawthorne for this point and also for help with the next paragraph.

to my entry into the time machine, they determine that I will emerge at a certain spatial location in the past, but they leave it open whether I am sitting or standing at the time. As applied to me immediately before the meeting of my former and later selves, the laws determine that I will remain in a certain spatial location, but leave it open whether I will be sitting or standing at that time. Given these stipulations, it can be argued that the cases cannot be distinguished by causal means. Given stipulations one and two, the cases do not differ in non-causal ways at times other than the time of the meeting. And given three-dimensionalism, the two cases do not differ in non-causal ways at the time of the meeting (in each case I am sitting at the time and standing at the time). Given stipulation three, the laws of nature are common to the two cases. But any differences in causation between the cases would need to be due to differences in the laws of nature or non-causal differences. Thus, the worlds do not differ causally.

('Singularists' about causation reject the principle that differences in causation must be due to differences in the laws of nature or non-causal differences. But even they may be willing to allow me to stipulate that the causal relation holds between *my entering the time machine* and *my emergence at a certain place at the time of the meeting*, and between *my being located at a certain place at times before the meeting* and *my being located at that place at the time of the meeting*, but that the causal relation does *not* hold between any event after or before the meeting and any event specifying whether I sit or stand at the time of the meeting.)

Suppose my 'later self' is located at place P, whereas my 'earlier self' is located at place P'. We might try to distinguish the possibilities by saying that in the first case I have the property *standing (at* t*) at* P, but not the property *standing (at* t*) at* P', whereas in the second case I have the latter property but not the former.

This response appears unsuccessful. What is it to have a property *at a certain place* (at a given time)? One of two things, I would have thought: (1) to be both located at the place (at the time) *and* to have the property (at the time), as when we say that I have the property of typing in my office at 3.15 p.m., EST, on 5 November 2000; (2) to have a part (at the time) that has the property (at the time) and is located at the place (at the time), as when we say that a road is bumpy at a place. Neither helps the defender of endurance. The second reading may be set aside, since the three-dimensionalist denies I have temporal parts. As for the first reading, in each possibility I am located at P (at t), and also at P' (at t). And in each case I am standing (at t). Thus, in each case, I have *both standing (at* t*) at P and standing (at* t*) at P'*. The possibilities still have not been distinguished.

The defender of endurance might claim that the relativity of instantiation to places is irreducible. For that matter, as we saw in Section 4 above, special relativity requires relativizing property instantiation to spacetime points anyway. The latter difficulty may be circumvented by stipulating that the case in question is to take place in a non-relativistic world. Still, the endurance theorist might insist that even in non-relativistic worlds, property instantiation is to be irreducibly relative to both places and times. But there is no independent motivation for this claim. Moreover, if all properties are relativized to places, one important argument for spatial parts goes away, namely the problem of 'local' intrinsics (Sect. 5); why not then claim that objects are wholly present across space as well as time?[32]

I have granted relativization to times for the sake of argument and then complained about relativization to places. Interestingly, something like this complaint can be made even under special relativity: one can insist that point-particles, anyway, can differ with respect to a property at a pair of points only when the points are time-like related. This is probably just what the defender of endurance wants, since it allows intrinsic change yet preserves the argument from local intrinsics for spatial parts. But now imagine a time-traveling electron meeting its former self, where the former self is F and the later self is F'. Since the spacetime points at which F and F' are instantiated are space-like related, the time travel argument goes through.

I note finally that the argument could appeal to time-traveling objects that lack spatial location, in which case the relativization response is unavailable. A desperate reply would be to appeal to differences in which properties are co-instantiated with which. The reply is desperate because it depends on rejecting what is surely a correct account of co-instantiation, namely that F and G are co-instantiated by x at t iff x instantiates F at t *and* x instantiates G at t. For the reply to work,

---

[32] Relativizing to places would be even more unpalatable to a presentist, who normally would not even relativize to times. Indeed, this ability to avoid relativization is the basis for a currently popular argument for presentism—see Hinchliff (1996) and Merricks (1994*a*).

property instantiation would need to be irreducibly relative, not only to time and to place, but also to other properties.

One might try to distinguish the possibilities by relativizing property instantiation to 'personal time' (as in Lewis 1976) rather than external time. Personal time is time experienced by the time traveler, whereas external time is time *simpliciter*, time according to the public ordering of events. If I travel back to the time of the dinosaurs, my arrival is located before my departure in external time, but after it in my personal time. Now imagine I travel back in time and meet myself in 1977. Though I am both sitting and standing at a single moment of external time, there are two moments of my personal time involved, call them pt_1 and pt_2. The cases may then be distinguished by claiming that in one case I stand at pt_1, whereas in the other I stand at pt_2.

The problem is that personal time, as construed by Lewis anyway, is not an additional fundamental physical element of the world, but is rather a defined quantity. Roughly, experiencing one minute of personal time is defined as undergoing the amount of change that would normally occur to a person during one minute of external time. Since personal time is a defined quantity, all facts about personal time must be capable of being stated in vocabulary that just mentions external time. But it has already been argued that the possibilities in question cannot be distinguished in this vocabulary by the defender of endurance. One might consider instead cases of time travel in which personal time is not a defined quantity, but rather a second physically real temporal dimension. I do not deny that two-dimensional time is one way to make sense of time travel, but I also think that time travel is intelligible in worlds with a single temporal dimension, and I am free to stipulate that the case of time travel I am considering is in such a world.

The argument from time travel is only as powerful as its assumption that time travel is possible. Some may wish to deny that claim. Some might even regard inconsistency with time travel as an *advantage* of three-dimensionalism, as a vindication of a prior belief that time travel is impossible! I see no merit in these claims. Arguments that time travel involves some sort of inconsistency fail.[33] And there are two good reasons to think that time travel is possible. First, the fact that physicists take the physical possibility of time travel seriously suggests that time

---

[33] See Lewis (1976) for an excellent discussion.

travel may well be physically possible. This will be discussed below. Secondly, time travel is conceivable or imaginable, which creates a presumption in favor of its possibility. The presumption is defeasible. It would certainly be defeated if time travel could be shown to involve some hidden inconsistency, but as I have said, arguments attempting to demonstrate such an inconsistency do not succeed. Presumptions of possibility can also be defeated if the possibility of the proposition in question would conflict with other things reasonably believed. Whether this is the case for time travel depends on an assessment of all the issues discussed in this book. But so long as time travel is presumptively possible, the argument from time travel provides a prima-facie reason to reject three-dimensionalism, and can take its place in the cumulative case I am amassing in favor of four-dimensionalism.

A priori arguments about possibility are sometimes thought to be threatened by the phenomenon of the necessary a posteriori (Putnam 1975; Kripke 1972). Once it was perfectly conceivable that water was not H_2O and that heat was not the motion of molecules; nevertheless, it is argued, these things have turned out to be metaphysically impossible. Perhaps time travel and timeless objects are also conceivable but impossible.

My arguments do not directly assume that conceivability *entails* possibility. So long as conceivability provides a defeasible reason in favor of possibility, the arguments have some force. I admit, though, that if the analogy with familiar cases of the necessary a posteriori is correct then my arguments would be undermined. They would be like arguing against the identity of Hesperus and Phosphorus because of the conceivability of discovering its falsity.

Fortunately the analogy is bad. Take a typical case of the necessary a posteriori: that water is H_2O. It is crucial to the standard Kripkean explanation of the divergence between conceivability and possibility in this case that there *is* a possible world in which our conventional activity concerning the term 'water' is just the same as it actually is, but in which 'water is H_2O' expresses a falsehood. Such a world might be one in which XYZ, rather than H_2O, is in rivers and oceans. We *think* that water might not have been H_2O because we see that a certain scenario is indeed possible—a scenario in which everything is 'qualitatively' exactly as it actually is but in which 'water is H_2O' expresses a falsehood—and we then confuse the possibility of this scenario with the possibility of water's failing to be H_2O. The world in which XYZ fills our rivers and oceans is not a world in which water fails to be H_2O. Why not? Why doesn't the existence of the XYZ world imply the truth of 'possibly, water is not H_2O'? Because it is part of the semantics of 'water' that an utterance of 'water' in a world w rigidly refers to whatever stuff plays the 'water role' in w. That is, 'possibly, water is F' is true, as uttered in w, iff for some world, v, the stuff that plays the water role *in* w is F in v; 'necessarily, water is F' is true, as uttered in w, iff in every world, v, the stuff that plays the water role *in* w is F in v. So the inhabitants of the XYZ world could say, truly, 'water is not H_2O' (and indeed, 'necessarily, water is not H_2O'). Nevertheless, *we* speak truly when we say 'necessarily, water *is* H_2O'.

But in the cases of time travel and timeless worlds, there is no term involved in the description of the relevant possibilities to play the role 'water' plays in the case just considered. 'Water' is a natural kind term that rigidly refers to different substances depending on what substance happens to play the 'water-role' in the world of utterance. In David Chalmers's (1996: 56–71) terminology, 'water' is two-dimensionally inconstant, in that it has different secondary intensions relative to different worlds of utterance. That is how there can be a world in which 'water is not H_2O' could be truly uttered (while remaining governed by the same conventions that actually govern that sentence) without rendering actual utterances of 'possibly, water is not H_2O' true. But persistence words presumably have constant two-dimensional intensions. Relative to any world of utterance, in any world of evaluation, persistence words pick out whatever plays the 'persistence-role' in that world. For example, if our world is non-relativistic, relativistic worlds should count as worlds in which things persist; persistence words would not rigidly designate actual, non-relativistic persistence. Similarly for four-dimensional persistence: if there are four-dimensional worlds in which inhabitants using our same linguistic conventions could say truly 'time travel has occurred', then the sentence 'it is possible that time travel occur' would be actually true.[34]

The phenomenon of the necessary a posteriori, then, gives us no reason to distrust our modal intuitions about time travel and timeless worlds. There might be other reasons to distrust those intuitions. One

[34] George Bealer (1996, sect. 4) gives a similar defense of a priori philosophical reasoning from the challenge of the necessary a posteriori.

might, for example, be some sort of modal skeptic (see e.g. van Inwagen 1998). Or one might have a view of modality on which the facts of modality, even facts expressible in two-dimensionally constant terms, depend crucially on what happens to be actual. The a priori part of the defense of the possibility of time travel is therefore dependent on a modal epistemology on which intuitions about possibility supply genuine, even if defeasible, evidence.

A three-dimensionalist might grant that time travel is possible, and that its possibility requires temporal parts, and thus concede that temporal parts are *possible*, while denying that they are actual. Three-dimensionalism would then be a contingent thesis. I note that three-dimensionalists seem not to have this attitude. They tend to regard three-dimensionalism as a necessary truth, perhaps because they take it to be a conceptual truth that perdurance would not be genuine persistence, that four-dimensional change would not be genuine change, and so on. Moreover, even if a three-dimensionalist were to admit that four-dimensionalism is *metaphysically* possible, she would presumably want to claim that it is impossible in some sense. Four-dimensional worlds would be very distant possibilities, worlds unlike our own in fundamental ways. At the very least, the three-dimensionalist will not want to admit that four-dimensional worlds are *physically* possible.

This brings us to the second reason for believing that time travel is possible: the fact that physicists take its possibility seriously. This is not just a fringe movement: time travel is currently discussed in major physics journals.[35] It would be rash to rule out, a priori, the possibility of a physical hypothesis that is taken seriously by physicists. Even defenders of contingent three-dimensionalism, then, should be moved by the time travel argument. So should skeptics who doubt conceivability arguments for possibility. So should anyone who doubts my defense against the challenge of the necessary a posteriori. Anyone reluctant to tread on the toes of physicists should reject metaphysical theories like three-dimensionalism that preclude time travel.

---

[35] For extensive references and an illuminating discussion see Earman (1995).

8.   THE ARGUMENT FROM SPACETIME

Given eternalism, which I continue to presuppose, spatiotemporal reality apparently consists of a spacetime in which past, present, and future
objects are located. Concerning spacetime itself one can be either a substantivalist or a relationalist. The substantivalist takes the physicist's
talk of spacetime at face value: points and regions of spacetime are genuine entities. The relationalist, on the other hand, rejects the genuine
existence of points or regions of spacetime and reduces all talk of spacetime to talk of spatiotemporal relations between entities she is willing to
accept. Either substantivalism or relationalism is true; I will argue in
each case that the four-dimensional ontology is favored. In brief: if we
are substantivalists then we should identify objects with regions of
spacetime, which perdure; on the other hand, relationalism is tenable
only if the relata of spatiotemporal relations perdure; either way, the
result is a metaphysics of perduring objects.

First, assume that substantivalism is true, that there are such things as
points and regions of spacetime. There is then the question of whether
there is anything else, whether spatiotemporal objects *occupy*, but are
distinct from, regions of spacetime, or whether they simply *are* regions
of spacetime.

There is considerable pressure to give the latter answer, for otherwise
we seem to gratuitously add a category of entities to our ontology.[36] All
the properties apparently had by an occupant of spacetime can be
understood as being instantiated by the region of spacetime itself. The
identification of spatiotemporal objects with the regions is just crying
out to be made. Given the identification, perdurance follows, since
spacetime perdures.[37]

'A region of spacetime bounded out the door and barked at the mail-
man'—it sure sounds strange to say! Indeed, it sounds like a 'category

---

[36] Quine (1976b) makes this identification, but then goes further and gives a construc-
tion of the regions in terms of pure sets. It is hard to go all the way with Quine here; even
the most devout reductionist has a strong sense of the difference in ontological category
between pure sets and blooming buzzing physical things. And even setting this aside, there
are reasons I give in Sider (1996b, esp. n. 22) for resisting this 'hyper-Pythagoreanism' of
Quine's.

[37] What of a non-standard view of enduring spacetime? This would face the objections
to the combination of relationalism and endurance discussed below.

mistake'. But this is not a good reason to resist the identification, any more than the strangeness of saying that pain is located in the brain is a good reason to reject the identity theory of mental states. As Paul Churchland (1988: 29–31) points out, Copernicus's claim that the earth moves may well have seemed like a category mistake at the time. Our language may well have a prohibition against saying that regions of spacetime bark. Perhaps this is due to ignorance of the metaphysical nature of dogs: our progenitors simply did not know that dogs are regions of spacetime. Perhaps if we became convinced of the identification of things with regions of spacetime we would reform our language. Or perhaps not. We might accept the identification and yet choose to treat thing-language and spacetime-language differently. We might regard the predicate 'barks' as inappropriate to apply to an object when the object is thought of as a region of spacetime, even if we acknowledge that the object is indeed a region of spacetime. Appropriateness of a predicate would be determined not only by its object but also by how that object is conceptualized. This sort of restriction on the appropriateness of predicate application emerges in unrelated cases: those who regard persons as identical with aggregates of subatomic particles can acknowledge the strangeness of saying 'I was just kissed by a swarm of quarks and electrons'.

It may be objected that the very fact that spacetime perdures is reason to resist the identification: spatiotemporal objects do not perdure and thus cannot be identified with anything that does. But what is the evidence for this claim? It is perhaps not part of ordinary belief that spatiotemporal objects perdure, but that should not stand in the way of a theoretical identification, any more than the fact that it is not part of the everyday concept of heat that heat is molecular motion. Philosophical arguments against perdurance will be taken up and rejected in Chapter 6; those do not stand in the way of the identification. Any remaining resistance should be weighed against the ontological extravagance of a redundant ontological category.

Some will claim that regions of spacetime differ from the occupants of spacetime by having their spatiotemporal size and location essentially. But given an appropriately flexible understanding of *de re* modality, the worry vanishes. On the counterpart-theoretic account I favor, the claim that *a* is essentially *F* means that all of *a*'s counterparts are *F*. The counterpart relation is a similarity relation: *a*'s counterparts are objects in other possible worlds that are similar to *a* in certain respects. But in different conversational contexts, different respects of similarity, and thus different counterpart relations, are relevant to the evaluation of the claim. In the case of modal claims about regions of spacetime there are two different counterpart relations one could utilize. One counterpart relation stresses spatiotemporal similarity; the other stresses similarity of a sort relevant to ordinary objects. The thought that spatiotemporal facts are essential to regions of spacetime is a result of thinking in terms of the former counterpart relation, whereas ordinary modal judgments are based on the latter counterpart relation. Thus, the fact that we make apparently different modal judgments about spatiotemporal objects and regions of spacetime does not preclude their identification: the judgments are judgments about the same objects under different counterpart relations.[38]

As with other cases of 'counterpart theory to the rescue' in this book, there will be doubters. But it strikes me as being fundamentally wrong-headed to allow conservatism about *de re* modality to dictate one's ontology in the way envisioned by the doubters. We have available to us a compelling reduction. It would be terrible methodology to forgo this reduction because of worries about *de re* modality. Moreover, most of the reasons people have for rejecting counterpart theory are fallacious, as I will argue in Chapter 5, Section 8.

It is worth stressing a point made by Harold Noonan (1991: 190; see also Lewis 1986*a*, sect. 4.5) that counterpart theory is not strictly needed to rebut modal arguments of the sort considered here. The modal argument against identifying things with regions of spacetime can be rejected by appeal to any account of *de re* modality according to which the content of a *de re* modal judgment depends on how its subject is conceptualized. (In Noonan's phrase, we need the claim that modal predicates are 'Abelardian'.) Counterpart theory is one way, but not the only way, of making good on this idea. And even if the *truth* of *de re* modal judgments is not held to depend on how their subjects are conceptualized, an analogous view about *modal intuitions* may yet be correct. A four-dimensionalist could grant that spatiotemporal objects have their spatiotemporal size and location essentially but go on to give an error-theory of ordinary modal intuitions. Intuitions about the modal properties of an

---

[38] See Lewis (1968, 1971).

object, on this view, depend on whether we think of it as an ordinary object or as a region of spacetime.[39] I think counterpart theory is the best of this lot, but these alternate views would also defuse the modal objection to the reduction.

Inflexible accounts of *de re* modality lead to trouble anyway, for example in the modal versions of familiar paradoxes of identity over time. A modal version of the statue/lump example, put forward by Alan Gibbard (1975), runs as follows. A lump of clay, which we may name Lump1, is created already in statue form. It composes a certain statue, which we may name Goliath; we then later destroy Lump1 and Goliath simultaneously by annihilating the clay completely while it is still in statue form. Surely Lump1 and Goliath are identical, for they coincide at all times. And yet modal differences appear to stand in the way of this identification: Lump1 appears to have, while Goliath appears to lack, the properties *possibly having survived flattening, possibly failing to be a statue*, and so on. Surely, this apparent difference should be resisted; surely it is due in some way to a shift in our conceptualization of a single object, rather than a difference between two objects; surely, adopting a flexible account of *de re* modal predication, or a flexible error-theory, is a more sensible alternative than multiplying entities corresponding to the apparent modal differences.[40] The counterpart-theoretic version of this is familiar. To say that Lump1 might have survived flattening is to say that Lump1 has *lump* counterparts that survive flattening; to say that Goliath could not have survived flattening is to say that Goliath has no *statue* counterparts that survive flattening. Nevertheless, Lump1 *is* Goliath.

So far the argument has been that substantivalists should identify spatiotemporal objects with regions of spacetime and must therefore admit that spatiotemporal objects perdure. Let us now turn to the other horn of the dilemma. Can relationalism be made to work without accepting perdurance? As mentioned in Section 4 above, recent published versions of relationalism have utilized perduring entities; but is this inevitable? Though I have no knockdown objection, I will argue that the combination

[39] Cf. e.g. the defenses of modal mereological essentialism in Heller (1990), Jubien (1993), as well as the more distantly analogous Della Rocca (1996); see also Ch. 5, Sect. 7.

[40] Cf. Lewis (1986a, sect. 4.5). There are, of course, other responses to the argument, for example rejecting the existence of the entities involved. I discuss (the temporal analogs of) various positions in Ch. 5.

of spacetime relationalism and endurance has unattractive consequences. My discussion will ignore relativity; I presume this begs no important questions.

Let us first examine what a perdurance-based relationalism looks like. The relationalist wants to capture temporal facts using temporal relations between objects existing in time. Given perdurance, the objects standing in these relations may be taken to be instantaneous stages, and the temporal relations will include the binary relations of *simultaneity, being temporally before, being one minute before, being two minutes before*, and so on. What object stages exist and how they stand in these relations determines the totality of temporal facts. Moreover, facts about intrinsic change involve the instantiation of monadic properties by these object stages. For example, when one of my object stages has the property *sitting*, and another has the property *standing*, and the second stage is *after* the first, then I have changed from sitting to standing.

This simple picture is made possible by the assumption of perdurance. Once that assumption is dropped, the statement of temporal relationalism gets much more complicated.

For one thing, the temporal relations from which all temporal facts are supposed to flow can no longer be the same binary relations used by the perdurantist. If two objects to be temporally compared are both instantaneous, then either they are simultaneous, or one is some definite temporal distance before the other (I continue to ignore special relativity). But now the objects to be compared exist throughout stretches of time; moreover, these stretches of time may overlap. Suppose I create a statue and then destroy it; the statue therefore starts existing after I do and stops existing before I do. What kinds of temporal relations relate me and the statue? Nothing quite so simple as the binary relations of the perdurantist.

Another feature of the relationalist picture complicated by enduring objects is the account of change. Change is no longer the instantiation of different monadic properties by different temporal parts. It is common for defenders of endurance to account for change by indexing property instantiation to time in some way (Sect. 6), but indexing makes best sense on a substantival picture of time. Otherwise what are properties indexed to?

The defender of the endurance-based relationalist theory of time should, it seems to me, pursue something like the following strategy.

The strategy overcomes both obstacles at once: it allows the defender of relationalism to make temporal comparisons between enduring things, and simultaneously yields an account of change that does not require indexing to substantival times. The endurantist relationalist should say that all facts about persisting objects are captured by statements of the form: $\ulcorner x$ is F n units of time after y is $G\urcorner$, which is officially primitive but explained informally as meaning that at *some* pair of times n units apart, x is F at the earlier time and y is G at the later.[41] Figure 4.3 gives the idea, indulging in the fiction of substantivalism for clarity of presentation. We have two objects: x, which exists between times t_0 and t_3 and is F throughout, and y, which exists between times t_1 and t_2 and is G throughout. In this situation the following facts hold: x *is* F *one unit after* x *is* F (informally, this holds in virtue of t_0 and t_1, for example, as well as t_1 and t_2, and t_2 and t_3); x *is* F *two units after* x *is* F (in virtue of t_0 and t_2, or t_1 and t_3); x *is* F *three units after* x *is* F; y *is* G *one unit after* y *is* G; y *is* G *one unit after* x *is* F (in virtue of e.g. x at t0 and y at t1); y *is* G *two units after* x *is* F; x *is* F *one unit after* y *is* G (in virtue of e.g. x at t2 and y at t1); and so on; *it is not the case that* x *is* F *four units after* x *is* F; and so on.

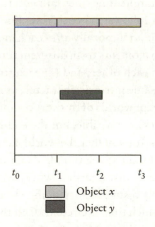

   Object x

   Object y

Fig. 4.3. Relational predication

---

[41] Similarly for cross-time relations: $\ulcorner x$ bears R to y n units of time hence/before$\urcorner$ means (unofficially) that at some pair of times n units apart, x as it is at the earlier/later time bears R to y as it is at the later/earlier time.

On this conception of property instantiation, change is easily described. An object x's being F for one unit of time followed by its being G for one unit of time, for example, would be (partially) characterized by the following facts: x *is* F *(0.1, 0.2, . . . 1) units of time after* x *is* F; x *is* G *(0.1, 0.2, . . . 1) units of time after* x *is* G; x *is* G *(0.1, 0.2, . . . 2) units of time after* x *is* F.

Moreover, temporal relations between objects are given by the totality of relative property ascriptions involving those objects. On some views, a property can be had by an object only at times at which it located; the totality of relative property ascriptions thus specifies the relative temporal locations of continuants. But even if some properties can be instantiated at times at which an object does not exist (perhaps the property *being famous*), others are existence-entailing (for example, the property of *having 50g mass*). Facts about the relative instantiation of these existence-entailing properties would then fix the temporal locations of objects.

This is an apparently consistent view. However, it seems to me to have two unattractive consequences. First, it collapses certain possibilities that seem, pre-analytically, to be distinct. Imagine, for example, worlds consisting of multiple time lines laid end to end, which may be intuitively described as follows: (1) each time line is infinite; (2) each moment of each time line is temporally *after* each moment of all the earlier time lines; (3) no two moments from different time lines are any finite temporal distance from each other; and (4) each time line contains the same objects, with the same intrinsic character, as the rest. One would have thought that different worlds of this sort containing different numbers of distinct time lines are possible, but the endurantist-relationalist view does not allow this, for whether the world has one, two, or twenty such time lines, the endurantist-relationalist's description is the same. Similarly, the view cannot distinguish a world with an infinite linear time line containing only a single unchanging electron from an otherwise similar world in which time is circular. Call the electron e, and let C be the property *having unit negative charge*. Presumably, in the circular world, for any n, e is C n units after e is C, since one can begin at any point and traverse the circle repeatedly until n units have elapsed. Since it is also true in the infinite linear world that e is C n units after e is C, for all n, the endurantist-relationalist cannot distinguish these possibilities. The endurantist might deny that in the circular world, for any n, e is C n

units after e is C, and hold instead that e is C n units after e is C only if n is less than or equal to the temporal circumference of the circle. But then the circular world cannot be distinguished from an otherwise similar world with a finite time line of temporal distance n. All of these possibilities can be distinguished if one gives up either endurance or relationalism, by appealing to the differing pattern of temporal relations among temporal parts or spacetime points.[42]

The possibilities envisioned in the preceding objection are admittedly distant from common opinion; the second objection must therefore bear a good deal of weight. It is this: the endurantist-relationalist view makes all predication objectionably relational. Recall Lewis's objection to turning temporary intrinsic properties into relations to times. As noted, one could perhaps stomach indexing if the indices were *times*, but now objects have shapes relative to other *objects*. What is more, my having a given shape is relativized to every other object in the universe. Very little remains of the intuition that an object can be just plain straight.

This last objection could be avoided by altering the fundamental predicational form from $\ulcorner x$ is F n units after y is $G\urcorner$ to $\ulcorner x$ is F n units after x is $G\urcorner$. This fundamental form only relates an object's properties at a time to its own properties at later times. The proposal amounts to turning every *pair* of ordinary property attributions to a single thing into an attribution of a single property. These properties are examples of what Josh Parsons (2000) calls 'distributional' properties. Examples include *being hot ten minutes after one is cold, being straight one second after one is bent*, and so on. The advantage of this approach is that predication is no longer relative to other objects. One still cannot say that anything is just plain straight, so a hard-line defender of the problem of temporary intrinsics (Sect. 6) may remain unsatisfied. But at least being straight is no longer a relation to other objects or times.

Just as there are temporary intrinsic properties, there are also temporary intrinsic relations. The present theory must account for these as well. Presumably it will do so using sentences of the form: $\ulcorner x$ bears R_1 to y n units of time after x bears R_2 to $y\urcorner$. Such predications bring in nothing other than x and y, and so appear to preserve the intrinsicality of R_1 and R_2.

---

[42] John Hawthorne and I hope to discuss these and related objections in more detail in a future paper.

However valuable this progress on the temporary intrinsics front may be, the proposed account is unacceptable as a version of relationalism. (Not that Parsons thinks otherwise. He only introduces distributional properties to respond to the problem of temporary intrinsics, not in an attempt to develop a version of spacetime relationalism.) Suppose x is at some time hot and y is also at some time hot. Given only sentences like 'x is hot n units after x is hot' and 'y is hot m units after y is hot', one cannot specify which of x or y is hot first, or whether they are hot at the same time. The whole point in moving to the new view was to remove the objectionably relational aspect of the original theory, which made all predication to objects relative to predications to *other* objects. But by ruling out relational predication the new theory loses the ability to capture certain temporal facts.

The defender of the new theory might try a divide-and-conquer strategy. First, account for intrinsic change using the proposed locution for property instantiation ($\ulcorner x$ is F n units after x is G$\urcorner$). Secondly, 'temporally line up' objects by introducing a new predicate 'x begins to exist n units after y begins to exist'. The hope is that once we specify the temporal interval between the beginnings of x's and y's existences, and further specify all the distributional properties of x and y, then the temporal intervals between x's and y's instantiating various properties will thereby be fixed. But this works only in the special case where x and y have temporal beginnings. Suppose two things have always existed (and, for good measure, always will exist). If each is hot at some point in time, the current theory still cannot say which is hot first, or whether they are hot simultaneously. The divide-and-conquer strategy fails.

My argument has been against relationalists that make use only of enduring objects. It does not apply to a relationalist who accepts enduring *and* perduring entities. The three-dimensionalist dualist mentioned in Section 7, for example, might utilize perduring events in her relationalism while holding that ordinary continuants endure. But dualism faces problems of its own. As noted in Section 7, the dualist has trouble explaining the relationship between the properties of things and the properties of events. Moreover, the dualist is subject to the first horn of the dilemma of the present section. An ontology that contains a (*sui generis*) history for each enduring continuant seems to contain a redundant ontological category: why not reduce the enduring continuants to the events?

Before concluding this section a loose end must be tied. The 'arguments from exotica' from the previous section assumed that, given certain philosophies of time, change must be accounted for either by postulating temporal parts or by indexing property instantiation to times. The relationalist theory of endurance discussed in this section now provides a third way of accounting for change. Objections have been given to this theory, but set them aside. How do the arguments from exotica fare against the combination of endurance and spacetime relationalism?

The argument from timeless worlds carries over with a slight modification. I can no longer characterize a 'timeless world' as one in which no times exist, since the relationalist says there are no such entities as times even in a temporal world like ours. A timeless world must be understood instead as one in which no temporal relations are instantiated. Since the actual relations that capture property instantiation, namely those of the form x *is* F n *units of time after* y *is* G, are temporal relations, no object in the timeless world could be straight in the same way that actual straight objects are straight. It may be replied that whether an object, *x*, is actual or timeless, it could be true that x *is straight* zero *units of time after* x *is straight*. But this locution is still temporal, and hence inappropriate to a genuinely timeless world. Compare the claim that an object *x* is straight zero units after another object, *y*, is straight. This requires that *x*'s straightness be *simultaneous* with *y*'s straightness—a temporal comparison.

The argument from time travel carries over as well. The argument was that anyone who indexes properties to times cannot distinguish what appear to be two distinct possibilities, one in which I am standing and my former self is sitting, the other in which our roles are reversed. Neither can the relationalist-endurantist distinguish these worlds, since each is a world in which *I am sitting zero units of time after I am standing*. One response considered and rejected was indexing property instantiation to space as well as time. The analogous (and equally unpalatable) response for the relationalist-endurantist would be to regard all property instantiation as having the form x *is* F n *units of time* and m units of space *from where* y *is* G.

9.   THE ARGUMENT FROM VAGUENESS[43]

The final argument of this chapter is, I think, one of the most power-ful. In outline, it runs as follows. Under what conditions do objects come into and go out of existence? As a believer in temporal parts and unrestricted composition, I say this *always* occurs. Any filled region of spacetime is the total career of some object. Others say that objects come into and go out of existence only under certain conditions. When bits of matter are arranged in certain ways, an object—say, a person—comes into existence; and that thing goes out of existence when the bits cease to be arranged in the appropriate way. But what sorts of arrange-ments are suitable? If one arrangement is suitable, then a *very* slightly different arrangement would seem to be as well. Iterate this procedure, and we have the conclusion that objects *always* come into and go out of existence, no matter how bits of matter are arranged. But this, it will be seen, is tantamount to admitting that four-dimensionalism is true. The obvious problem with 'slippery slope' arguments of this sort is that they neglect vagueness. But there cannot be vagueness of the sort needed to block the argument. The argument will at this point make some assumptions, most notably that vagueness never results from 'logic' (i.e. from boolean connectives, quantification, or identity). These assumptions could be coherently denied, but they are very plausible. I also suspect that they are widely held, even among those hostile to temporal parts. There is, therefore, considerable interest in showing that anyone who accepts the assumptions must accept four-dimensionalism.

Those familiar with David Lewis's *On the Plurality of Worlds* (1986*a*) will recognize a parallel here with his argument for the principle of unre-stricted mereological composition. In the next subsection I develop Lewis's argument for unrestricted composition in my own way, and then in the following two subsections show how it can be modified to yield an argument for temporal parts.

---

[43] An earlier version of this argument was given in Sider (1997). Compare Quine (1981: 10) and Heller (1990, ch. 2, sect. 9).

9.1. Unrestricted mereological composition

Here is Lewis's argument (1986*a*: 212–13):

We are happy enough with mereological sums of things that contrast with their surroundings more than they do with one another; and that are adjacent, stick together, and act jointly. We are more reluctant to affirm the existence of mereological sums of things that are disparate and scattered and go their separate ways...

The trouble with restricted composition is as follows... To restrict composition in accordance with our intuitions would require a vague restriction. But if composition obeys a vague restriction, then it must sometimes be a vague matter whether composition takes place or not. And that is impossible.

The only intelligible account of vagueness locates it in our thought and language. The reason it's vague where the outback begins is not that there's this thing, the outback, with imprecise borders; rather there are many things, with different borders, and nobody has been fool enough to try to enforce a choice of one of them as the official referent of the word 'outback'. Vagueness is semantic indecision. But not all of language is vague. The truth-functional connectives aren't, for instance. Nor are the words for identity and difference, and for the partial identity of overlap. Nor are the idioms of quantification, so long as they are unrestricted. How could any of these be vague? What would be the alternatives between which we haven't chosen?

The question whether composition takes place in a given case, whether a given class does or does not have a mereological sum, can be stated in a part of language where nothing is vague. Therefore it cannot have a vague answer. ... No restriction on composition can be vague. But unless it is vague, it cannot fit the intuitive *desiderata*. So no restriction on composition can serve the intuitions that motivate it. So restriction would be gratuitous. Composition is unrestricted...

It may be summarized as follows. (I follow Lewis in speaking of parthood atemporally; I consider temporally relativized parthood in the next subsection.) If not every class has a fusion then there must be a restriction on composition. Moreover, the only plausible restrictions on composition would be vague ones. But there can be no vague restrictions on composition, because that would mean that whether composition occurs is sometimes vague. Therefore, every class has a fusion.

There is a weakness in this argument. The first premise of my summary is that if not every class has a fusion then there must exist a 'restriction on composition'. On a natural reading, a 'restriction on composition' is a way of filling in the blank in the following schema:

A class, S, has a fusion if and only if—

such that what goes into the blank is not universally satisfied. That is, a restriction on composition would be an answer to Peter van Inwagen's 'special composition question'.[44] (For example, one answer might be that a class has a fusion iff its members are 'in contact'.) But perhaps the special composition question has no informative answer because whether composition takes place in a given case is a 'brute fact' incapable of informative analysis.[45]

There are two senses in which composition might be brute. Composition is brute in a strong sense if it does not even supervene on causal and qualitative factors. This is extremely implausible; one would need to admit a pair of cases exactly alike in terms of causal integration, qualitative homogeneity, and so on, but which differ over whether objects have a sum. But even if supervenience is admitted, composition might be brute in the weaker sense that there is no natural, finite, humanly statable restriction on composition. Since I do not wish to reject weak brute composition out of hand, I will reformulate Lewis's argument so as not to (directly, anyway) presuppose its falsity.

Let us understand a 'case of composition' ('case', for short) as a possible situation involving a class of objects having certain properties and standing in certain relations. We will ask with respect to various cases whether composition occurs; that is, whether the class in the case would have a fusion. In summary, my version of Lewis's argument runs as follows. If not every class has a fusion, then we can consider two possible cases, one in which composition occurs and another in which it does not, which are connected by a 'continuous series of cases' selected from different possible worlds, each extremely similar to the last. Since composition can never be vague, there must be a sharp cut-off in this series where composition abruptly stops occurring. But that is implausible. So composition always occurs.

More carefully. First, consider any case, C_1, in which composition occurs—the case of a certain class of subatomic particles that are part of

---

[44] Actually, the special composition question is slightly different, since it concerns when fusion takes place *at* a given time; see van Inwagen (1990*a*, ch. 2).

[45] Thanks to David Cowles and Ned Markosian here. See Markosian (1998).

my body, for example. Now consider a second case, C_2, which occurs after I die and am cremated, in which my molecules are scattered across the Milky Way. Some would say that in C_2, composition fails to take place: there is nothing that is made up of these scattered, causally unconnected particles. Next, let us further imagine a finite series of cases connecting C_1 and C_2, in which each case in the series is extremely similar to its immediately adjacent cases in all respects that might be relevant to whether composition occurs: qualitative homogeneity, spatial proximity, unity of action, comprehensiveness of causal relations, etc. I call such a series a 'continuous series connecting cases C_1 and C_2'.

My argument's first premise is:

P1: If not every class has a fusion, then there must be a pair of cases connected by a continuous series such that in one, composition occurs, but in the other, composition does not occur.

I can think of only two objections. Given 'nihilism', the view that composition *never* occurs (i.e. that there are no composite objects): since there are no cases of composition at all there cannot exist a continuous series connecting a case of composition to anything.[46] I argue against nihilism in Chapter 5, Section 6. The second objection is that not every pair of cases can be connected by a continuous series. No continuous series connects any case with finitely many objects to a case with infinitely many objects, for example.[47] However, P1 only requires that *some* pair of cases differing over composition be connected by a continuous series, if composition is restricted. No one will want to claim that the jump from finitude to infinity is the thing that makes the difference between composition and its absence. So even if no continuous series connects C_1 with C_2, one can choose another pair of cases C_1' and C_2', like C_1 and C_2 with respect to whether composition occurs, which are connected by a continuous series.

By a 'sharp cut-off' in a continuous series I mean a pair of *adjacent* cases in a continuous series such that in one, composition definitely occurs, but in the other, composition definitely does not occur. Surely there are no such things:

---

[46] On the usual terminology, a mereological atom is the fusion of its unit class; let us understand 'continuous series connecting cases C1 and C2' as excluding 'cases' involving only one atom.

[47] I thank Earl Conee for this observation.

P2: In no continuous series is there a sharp cut-off in whether composition occurs.

Adjacent members in a continuous series are extremely similar in certain respects. By including more and more members in a continuous
series, adjacent members can be made as similar as you like. Accepting a
sharp cut-off is thus nearly as difficult as rejecting the supervenience of
composition on the relevant factors. It would involve saying, for example, that although certain particles definitely compose a larger object, if
one of the particles had been 0.0000001 nanometers displaced, those
particles would have definitely failed to compose any object at all. Of
course, sharp cut-offs in the application of a predicate are not *always*
implausible—consider the predicate 'are separated by exactly 3
nanometers'. What I object to is a sharp cut-off in a continuous series of
cases of *composition*.

To postulate such a sharp cut-off would be to admit that the realm of
the macroscopic is in some sense 'autonomous' of the microscopic. By
'autonomous' I do not mean 'non-supervenient', since accepting a sharp
cut-off in a continuous series of cases of composition does not threaten
supervenience. Rather, I mean that there would seem to be something
'metaphysically arbitrary' about a sharp cut-off in a continuous series of
cases of composition. Why is the cut-off here, rather than there?
Granted, everyone must admit *some* metaphysically 'brute' facts, and it
is a hard question why one brute fact seems more or less plausible than
another. Nevertheless, *this* brute fact seems particularly hard to stomach.[48]

A possible objection to P2 would be based on precisely statable topological restrictions on the regions of space that can possibly be occupied by a composite object, perhaps regions in which any two points are
connectable by some continuous path confined to the region. But this
would rule out too many objects: galaxies, solar systems, and so on.
More importantly, under the classical physics conception of matter, all
macroscopic objects are discontinuous. This is less clear on a quantum-
mechanical picture, but a classical world should not turn out devoid of
macro-objects.[49]

---

[48] See, however, Markosian (1998).

[49] I thank John G. Bennett for helpful observations here. Another precise restriction of
fusions, to classes that are sets, seems unmotivated (and of little consequence even if
adopted).

The final premise of the argument is, I think, the most controversial:

P3: In any case of composition, either composition definitely occurs, or composition definitely does not occur.

P1, P2, and P3 imply the desired conclusion. P1 requires that if composition is not unrestricted, we have a case of composition connected by a continuous series to a case of non-composition. By P3, there must be a sharp cut-off in this series where composition abruptly ceases to occur; but this contradicts P2. It must be emphasized that this is not 'just another Sorites'. The correct solution to traditional Sorites paradoxes will surely involve a region in which the relevant predicate ('is a heap', 'is bald', and so on) neither definitely applies nor definitely fails to apply (note: the epistemic theory of vagueness is discussed below). But this is just what P3 prohibits.

I turn now to the defense of P3. Recall that a 'case' was defined as involving a *class* of objects, by which I mean a non-fuzzy class. Thus understood, classes have precisely defined membership, and so must be distinguished from class descriptions, which may well be imprecise. P3 pertains to classes themselves, not their descriptions. Thus, indeterminacy of truth value in the sentence 'The class of molecules in the immediate vicinity of my body has a fusion' would not be inconsistent with P3. In virtue of its vagueness, the subject term of this sentence may well fail to refer uniquely to any one class. Also note that P3 is not concerned with the nature of the resulting fusion, only its existence. It may well be indeterminate whether a given class of molecules has a fusion that counts as a *person*. This is not inconsistent with P3, for the class may definitely have a fusion which is a borderline case of a person.

Lewis's method for establishing P3 appeals to the 'linguistic theory of vagueness'.[50] This view's slogan is that 'vagueness is semantic indecision'. Whenever a sentence is indeterminate in truth value due to vagueness, this is because there is some term in the sentence that is *semantically* vague, in that there are multiple possible meanings for that term, often called 'precisifications', no one of which has been singled out as the term's unique meaning. There is no vagueness 'in the world'; all vagueness is due to semantic indecision. An oversimplified example: 'bald' is vague because no one has ever decided which of its precisifications it is to

[50] See e.g. Dummett (1978: 260) (although see Dummett 1981: 440); Fine (1975); Russell (1923).

mean, where the precisifications are properties of the form *having no more than* n *hairs on one's head*, for various integers *n* in a certain range. (Realistically, baldness depends on more than how many hairs one has on one's head. Distribution, length, and other factors also matter.)

In virtue of the definition of 'fusion' in terms of parthood, we can formulate the assertion that a given class, *C*, has a fusion as follows:

> (F) There is some object, *x*, such that (1) every member of *C* is part of *x*, and (2) every part of *x* shares a part in common with some member of *C*.

If (F) has no determinate truth value relative to some assignment to '*C*', this must be due to vagueness, for other potential sources of truth value gaps (such as ambiguity or failed presupposition) are not present. Given the linguistic theory of vagueness, one of the terms in (F) would need to have multiple precisifications. But it is difficult to see what the precisifications of logical terms, or the predicates 'is a member of' and 'part of', might be.

The weakest link here is the rejection of precisifications for 'is part of'. Notice that in ruling out 'part of' as a source of vagueness, Lewis is not ruling out all vagueness in *ascriptions* of parthood, for ascriptions of parthood may contain singular terms (e.g. 'the outback') with multiple precisifications. (F), however, apparently contains no vague singular terms. Vague ascriptions of parthood are therefore not a good reason *for* saying that 'part' lacks precisifications. But what is a good reason *against*? Lewis's reason is that it is difficult to see what the precisifications might be. But perhaps this is because they are not easily statable in natural language. *Some* non-logical terms, 'is bald' for example, have prima facie easily statable precisifications (namely, properties expressed by predicates of the form ⌜has a head with less than *n* hairs⌝, and even then stability is in doubt, given the vagueness of 'head' and 'hair'). But other vague predicates lack easily statable precisifications, for example 'person', 'table', and artifact terms generally. Someone might argue that 'part' has precisifications corresponding to precisifications of answers to van Inwagen's special composition question. I do not say that this response to Lewis can be made to work, but I cannot see how to show that it cannot be made to work.

Fortunately, P3 may be supported without making any assumptions about parthood, for if it were vague whether a certain class had a fusion then it would be vague how many concrete objects exist. Lewis's assumptions about vagueness can then be replaced by weaker assumptions that concern only logical vocabulary.

Let us stipulatively define *concrete* objects as those which do *not* fit into any of the kinds on the following list:

   sets and classes
   numbers
   properties and relations
   universals and tropes
   possible worlds and situations

If I have missed any 'abstract' entities you believe in, feel free to update the list. Suppose now for *reductio* that P3 is false—that is, that it can be vague whether a given class has a fusion. In such a case, imagine counting all the concrete objects in the world. One would need to include all the objects in the class in question, but it would be indeterminate whether to include another entity: the fusion of the class. Now surely if P3 can be violated, then it could be violated in a 'finite' world, a world with only finitely many concrete objects. That would mean that some *numerical sentence*—a sentence asserting that there are exactly n concrete objects, for some finite n—would be indeterminate. But numerical sentences need contain only logical terms and the predicate 'C' for concreteness (a numerical sentence for $n = 2$ is: $\exists x\, \exists y\, [Cx\, \&\, Cy\, \&\, x \neq y\, \&\, \forall z\, (Cz \rightarrow [x = z \vee y = z])\,]$). Mereological terms are *not* needed to express numerical sentences, and so need not be assumed to lack precisifications.

To support P3, then, I must argue that numerical sentences can never be indeterminate in truth value. First, note that numerical sentences clearly have no syntactic ambiguity. Secondly, note that the concreteness predicate, 'C', presumably has precise application conditions since it was defined by a list of predicates for fundamental ontological kinds that do not admit of borderline cases. And even if one of the members of the list is ill defined or vague in some way, the vagueness is presumably of a kind not relevant to my argument: any way of eliminating the vagueness would suffice for present purposes. So if any numerical sentence is to be indeterminate in truth value, it must be because one of the logical notions is vague.

Accordingly, the argument's crucial assumption about vagueness is that logical words are never a source of vagueness.[51] Any sentence containing only logical expressions, plus perhaps predicates with determinate application conditions (such as 'is concrete'), must be either definitely true or definitely false. This premise is extremely compelling. Logical concepts are paradigm cases of precision. At the very least, in no case is there evident indeterminacy as with 'bald' and 'heap'.

I am inclined to regard my assumption that logic does not generate vagueness as flowing from two further theses, first, the linguistic theory of vagueness outlined above, and secondly, the assumption that logical terms lack multiple precisifications. The first thesis I simply assume; the second I am about to argue for. But all the argument for four-dimensionalism requires is that the assumption holds, whether or not it is justified by these two theses.

It is overwhelmingly plausible that the boolean operators lack precisifications. That leaves the quantifiers and the identity sign.

Might an unrestricted quantifier have precisifications? It is important to be clear that there is no problem at all with *restricted* quantifiers having precisifications. The restricted quantifier 'all persons' will clearly have precisifications because the restricting predicate 'is a person' has precisifications. But this is irrelevant.

If predicates can have precisifications, why not unrestricted quantifiers? The asymmetry is due to the fact that predicates have subclasses of the universal domain of all things as their extensions, and the universal domain has many subclasses. But there seems to be only one 'everything' for the restricted quantifier to range over.

This can be turned into an argument against the possibility of multiple precisifications for the unrestricted quantifier. Imagine there were two expressions, $\forall_1$ and $\forall_2$, which allegedly expressed precisifications of the unrestricted quantifier. $\forall_1$ and $\forall_2$ will need to differ in extension if they are to make any difference to the kinds of sentences under consideration in this section; merely intensional difference will not do. Thus, there must be some thing, x, that is in the extension of one, but not the other, of $\forall_1$ and $\forall_2$. But in that case, whichever of $\forall_1$ and $\forall_2$ lacks x in its extension will fail to be an acceptable precisification of the

---

[51] Cf. also Fine (1975: 267, 274–5).

unrestricted quantifier. It quite clearly is a restricted quantifier since there is something—x—that fails to be in its extension.

This argument is directed only at those who share my assumption of the linguistic theory of vagueness. Those who believe that objecthood itself is somehow vague might resist the step where I concluded that some object is in the extension of one but not the other of $\forall_1$ and $\forall_2$ from the fact that $\forall_1$ and $\forall_2$ differ extensionally. Suppose, for example, that reality definitely contains objects a and b, but that it is indeterminate whether reality contains a third object, c. Somehow it is indeterminate whether c exists, where this is not due to semantic indeterminacy of any kind. The believer in vague objects might then claim that if $\forall_1$ ranges over a and b, and $\forall_2$ over a, b, and c, then even though $\forall_1$ and $\forall_2$ differ extensionally, it is at least not definitely the case that there is something in $\forall_2$ but not $\forall_1$, for it is not definitely the case that c exists. I mention this position only to set it aside; as I said above, I simply assume that this theory of vagueness is *not* correct.

Someone who shares the linguistic theory of vagueness might still attempt to resist this step of the argument. Its conclusion is that *there is* an object, x, in the extension of one of $\forall_1$ and $\forall_2$. But this 'there is', it might be claimed, must be one or another precisification of the unrestricted quantifier. In particular, it will need to be one that includes x. But then it might be argued that it is illegitimate to conclude that $\forall_2$ is not an acceptable precisification for the unrestricted quantifier just because under one of the *other* precisifications there is an object that is not in $\forall_2$'s extension. There is no Archimedean point from which to quantify, and say that $\forall_2$ is a restricted quantifier. All we have are many precisifications, each of which is complete by its own lights.

It is hard to understand what these precisifications are supposed to be. As mentioned above, precisifications for predicates are unproblematic, and should be acceptable to all since everyone admits the existence of the extensions of those precisifications. But what are these precisifications of 'everything'? It might be claimed that existence and objecthood are somehow relative to 'conceptual scheme', and that the precisifications for the quantifiers correspond to different conceptual schemes, or precisifications of conceptual schemes. This comes in tame and wild variants. The tame claim that different conceptual schemes involve different restrictions on quantifiers, is surely correct, but is irrelevant, concerning as it does merely restricted quantification. The wild claim is that all quantification, no matter how unrestricted, is relative to conceptual scheme. A claim so wild that I will not consider it is that the world is the way it is because we talk in a certain way. A still wild but nevertheless worthy-of-discussion claim is that the world is in a certain way independent of us, but there is no once-and-for-all correct description of it in terms of quantifiers and variables. Any description using such a 'thing-language' presupposes some division of reality into things, but this division may be done in various ways depending on one's conceptual scheme or linguistic framework. Various ways of doing this division count as precisifications of the concept of an object, and hence correspond to precisifications of the quantifiers. I reject this conception of existence for the reasons explained in the introduction. This book presupposes that existence of things is univocal, not relative to conceptual schemes or linguistic frameworks.

So I reject the idea that unrestricted quantifiers have precisifications. Might the identity predicate have precisifications? On the face of it, the answer is no: the nature of identity seems conceptually simple and clear. Identity *sentences* can clearly have vague truth conditions when they have singular terms that are indeterminate in reference: 'Michael Jordan is identical to the greatest basketball player of all time', for example. But the only singular terms in numerical sentences are variables relative to assignments, which are not indeterminate in reference. There are those who say that even without indeterminate singular terms, and even without precisifications for the identity predicate, identity ascriptions can be vague in truth value, despite the Evans (1978)/Salmon (1981) argument to the contrary.[52] I find this doctrine obscure but have nothing to add to the extensive literature on this topic; here I must presuppose it false.

In summary, then, the argument for P3 has been as follows. If it could be vague whether composition occurs, this could happen in a finite world; some numerical sentence would then be indeterminate in truth value. But aside from the predicate 'concrete', which is non-vague, numerical sentences contain only logical vocabulary, and logical vocabulary, I say, can never be a source of vagueness.

A loose end must be tied before proceeding to the parallel argument for temporal parts. Defenders of *epistemicism* claim that vagueness

---

[52] See Lewis (1988*b*); Parsons (1987); Pelletier (1989); Thomason (1982); van Inwagen (1990*a*, ch. 18).

never results in indeterminacy of truth value. Imagine removing the hairs from a man, one at a time. According to the epistemicist there will be a single hair whose removal results in the man becoming bald. Even though no one could ever know where it lies, this sharp cut-off for the predicate 'bald' exists.[53] Since epistemicists are already accustomed to accepting sharp cut-offs for predicates like 'heap' and 'bald', one might think they would also be happy with a sharp cut-off in a continuous series of cases of composition, thus rejecting P2. The epistemic theory seems to me incredible despite its current popularity, but set this aside. I will argue that even an epistemicist should accept P2.

As explained in the introduction, I assume a 'best-candidate' theory of reference and meaning, according to which meaning is determined jointly by 'use and intrinsic eligibility'. Recall the precisifications for the predicate 'bald': *having no more than* n *hairs on one's head*, for various positive integers *n*. Most of us think there is no fact of the matter as to which of these candidate properties is meant by 'bald'. The reason, I think, is twofold. First, the candidates appear equally intrinsically eligible. Secondly, it also appears that use does not distinguish between the candidates. Despite this, the epistemicist says that 'bald' means exactly one of them. If the epistemicist accepts the best-candidate theory of meaning (and I think he should), he must therefore say either (1) one candidate is more intrinsically eligible, carves nature at the joints better than the rest, thus granting it *metaphysical* privilege, or (2) one candidate fits use better than the rest, thus granting it *semantic* privilege.

The epistemicist should surely prefer option (2).[54] Somehow, something about our meaning-determining behavior singles out one of the many candidate properties to be the meaning of 'bald'. The epistemicist is therefore committed to the existence of bridge laws from use to meaning that are more fine-grained than one might have expected, but at least he avoids the highly implausible metaphysics of option (1). Epistemicism *per se* should not lead us to revisionary metaphysics.

So the epistemicist's sharp cut-offs would not be 'metaphysical'. Instead of corresponding to unexpected joints in reality, they would represent unanticipated powers of humans to draw metaphysically arbitrary lines. They cannot, therefore, be used to give a plausible objection to premise P2 in my argument. Premise P2 says that there are no sharp

---

[53] See e.g. Sorensen (1988: 217–52), and Williamson (1994).

[54] Williamson (1994, sect. 7.5) prefers option (2).

cut-offs in a continuous series of cases of composition. A sharp cut-off in whether composition occurs would (in a finite world) result in a sharp cut-off in the number of objects, and thus in the truth value of a sentence stated solely in terms of logical terms and the predicate for concreteness. But, as I have argued, there are no multiple candidates to be meant by these terms. So the epistemicist's explanation of sharp cut-offs due to vagueness—as being the result of use selecting among equally eligible candidate meanings—is unavailable in this case.

If, despite this, the epistemicist were to persist in believing in a sharp cut-off, he would need to revert to the metaphysical explanation. The sharp cut-off would represent a 'logical joint' in reality: on the one and only candidate set of meanings for the logical terms (and 'concrete'), at some point on a continuous series of cases of composition there is an abrupt shift in the truth value of a numerical sentence. This sharp cut-off would be starkly metaphysical. As I have claimed, it is very hard to believe in this sort of cut-off—it feels 'metaphysically arbitrary'. Moreover, at this point epistemicism is no longer playing a role in the objection to P2, for even a non-epistemicist will admit that *if* the *metaphysical* cut-off exists, then there is a sharp shift in the truth value of a numerical sentence. The objection to P2, therefore, is not aided by epistemicism, but rather rests on its own metaphysical credentials, which are unimpressive.

The argument for restricted composition, we have seen, leans most heavily on P3, which in turn rests on the view that logic, and in particular unrestricted quantification and identity, are non-vague. This view is attractive, and I have said some things in its defense, but I doubt I have said enough to convince a determined opponent. My argument for unrestricted composition, therefore, should be taken as showing that anyone who accepts that logic is non-vague must also accept unrestricted composition. In the next two subsections I show that everyone who shares this assumption about vagueness must also accept four-dimensionalism.

9.2. *Composition questions and temporally indexed parthood*

The argument of the previous section concerned the question of when a given class has a fusion, where 'fusion' was understood atemporally. To avoid begging any questions against my opponents, the argument for temporal parts will be stated using temporally qualified mereological terms (see Ch. 3, Sect. 3). When the relation *being a fusion of* is indexed to times, various questions of composition must then be distinguished.[55]

The simplest question is that of when a given class has a fusion at a given time. But we are also interested in 'diachronic', or 'cross-time' fusions: things that are fusions of different classes at different times. These are objects that gain and lose parts. One concept of cross-time summation may be introduced as follows. Call an 'assignment' any (possibly partial) function that takes one or more times as arguments and assigns non-empty classes of objects that exist at those times as values; and let us say that an object x is a *diachronic fusion* ('D-fusion', for short) of an assignment f iff for every t in f's domain, x is a fusion-at-t of $f(t)$. For example, consider two times at which I exist, and let f be a function with just those two times in its domain that assigns to each the class of subatomic particles that are part of me then. I am a D-fusion of f, since at each of the two times I am a fusion of the corresponding class of subatomic particles.

A second question of composition, then, is the question of when a given assignment has a D-fusion: given various times and various objects corresponding to each, under what conditions will there be some object that at the various times is composed by the corresponding objects? A third question would be that of the conditions under which there would be such an object that existed *only* at the specified times. This is the question of when a given assignment has a *minimal* D-fusion—a D-fusion of the assignment that exists only at times in the assignment's domain. I am not a minimal D-fusion of the assignment f mentioned above because I exist at times other than the two times in the domain of f. To get an assignment of which I am a minimal D-fusion, extend f to assign to any other time at which I exist the class of subatomic particles that are part of me then.

In an intuitive sense, a minimal D-fusion of some objects at various times consists of those objects at those times and nothing more. Though it required some machinery to state, the question of which assignments have minimal D-fusions is far from being remote and technical. Indeed, we can restate this question in the following woolly yet satisfying

---

[55] See Simons (1987: 183 ff.) and Thomson (1983: 216–17).

fashion: *under what conditions do objects begin and cease to exist?*
Suppose we make a model of a park bench from three toy blocks, b_1, b_2,
and b_3, by placing one on top of two of the others at time t_1; a few minutes later at t_2 we separate the blocks. Is there something that we
brought into existence at the first time and destroyed at the second? This
is the question of whether a certain assignment has a minimal D-
fusion—namely, the assignment that assigns the class $\{b_1,b_2,b_3\}$ to
every time between t_1 and t_2.

9.3.   *The argument from vagueness for four-dimensionalism*

Under what conditions does a given assignment have a minimal D-
fusion? I say that all assignments have minimal D-fusions; my argument
is parallel to the argument for unrestricted composition. Restricting
when minimal D-fusions exist would require a cut-off in some continuous series of pairwise similar cases. Just as composition can never be
vague, neither can minimal D-fusion. So the cut-off would need to be
abrupt, which is implausible:

P1′:   If not every assignment has a minimal D-fusion, then there must
be a pair of cases connected by a 'continuous series' such that in
one, minimal D-fusion occurs, but in the other, minimal D-
fusion does not occur.

P2′:   In no continuous series is there a sharp cut-off in whether minimal D-fusion occurs.

P3′:   In any case of minimal D-fusion, either minimal D-fusion definitely occurs, or minimal D-fusion definitely does not occur.

The notion of a 'case' must be adjusted in the obvious way. A 'continuous series of cases' will now vary in all respects thought to be relevant
to whether a given assignment has a minimal D-fusion, including spatial
adjacency, qualitative similarity, and causal relations at the various
times in the assignment, as well as the beginning and cessation of these
factors at various times of the assignment.

The justification of premise P1′ is like that for P1. Like P1, P1′ can be
resisted by a nihilist, who rejects the existence of all composites. For the
nihilist, only mereological simples exist; there are no composite objects.
The only cases of minimal D-fusion concern the entire lifetime of a single particle; such cases cannot be connected continuously with cases in

which minimal D-fusion does not take place.[56] Arguments against nihilism must wait until Chapter 5, Section 6. As for P2′, an abrupt cut-off in a continuous series of cases of minimal D-fusion—a pair of cases *extremely* similar in spatial adjacency, causal relations, and so on, but definitely differing in whether minimal D-fusion occurs—seems initially implausible. There is, however, a three-dimensionalist ontology that would secure such a cut-off: a version of mereological essentialism according to which, intuitively, nothing exists but mereological sums, which have their parts permanently, and exist as long as those parts exist. Minimal D-fusions could be restricted non-vaguely: an assignment has a minimal D-fusion, roughly, when and only when it is the temporally longest assignment for a given fixed class of objects. The idea is that mereological fusions of objects 'automatically' come into existence when their parts do, automatically retain those same parts, and automatically go out of existence when any of those parts go out of existence. (Less roughly: where S_1 and S_2 are sets of objects that exist at times t_1 and t_2, respectively, say that pairs $<t_1, S_1>$ and $<t_2, S_2>$ are *equivalent* iff every part-at-t_1 of any member of S_1 overlaps-at-t_2 some member of S_2, and every part-at-t_2 of any member of S_2 overlaps-at-t_1 some member of S_1. The idea is that S_1 and S_2 contain, if not exactly the same members, at least the same stuff, just divided up differently. The non-vague restriction is that an assignment f has a minimal D-fusion iff f is a maximal equivalence-interrelated assignment; that is (construing f as a class of pairs), iff (1) every two pairs in f are equivalent, and (2) if a pair $<t, S>$ is equivalent to some member of f, then some pair $<t, S'>$ (i.e. some pair with the same time) to which it is equivalent is a member of f.) My argument can therefore be resisted by this sort of mereologist.[57] Other arguments can be given against mereological essentialism; see Chapter 5, Section 7.

---

[56] More carefully, for the nihilist, an assignment A has a minimal D-fusion iff for some simple, x, A's domain is the set of times at which x exists and A assigns to any such time $\{x\}$.

[57] A variant of mereological essentialism would also secure precise cut-offs. According to both mereological essentialism and this variant, if x is ever part of y then whenever x and y both exist, x must be part of y. The mereological essentialist adds that x must exist and be part of y whenever y exists, whereas the variant adds instead that y must exist and contain x as a part whenever x exists. The variant allows a thing to survive the destruction of one of its parts. The criticisms of mereological essentialism in Ch. 5, Sect. 7 apply to this variant as well.

Just as topological restrictions on regions of space can provide precise restrictions on composition (although I find them unmotivated), topological restrictions on regions of time can provide precise restrictions on minimal D-fusion. Some may favor a restriction to continuous intervals (although cf. Hirsch's 1982: 22 ff. example of a watch that is taken apart for repairs), or to sums of continuous intervals. I regard each as unmotivated, but we need not quarrel. Given either restriction, the argument would still establish a restricted version of four-dimensionalism according to which there exist continuous temporal segments of arbitrarily small duration. For most four-dimensionalists that would be four-dimensionalism enough.

My argument for P3 was that if it is indeterminate whether composition occurs then it will be indeterminate how many objects there are, which is impossible. I use a similar argument to establish P3'. Indeterminacy in minimal D-fusion might be claimed in several situations. But in each case, I will argue, at some possible world there would result 'count indeterminacy'—an indeterminacy in the finite number of concrete objects. This was argued above to be impossible, assuming that logic is not a possible source of vagueness. (Recall the distinction between existence-at and quantification. Count indeterminacy is indeterminacy in how many objects *there are*, not merely in how many objects *exist at* some specified time. It is the former that my assumption about logic prohibits, and hence the former that I must argue would result from indeterminacy in minimal D-fusion.)

I distinguish four situations in which indeterminacy in minimal D-fusion might be claimed:

(1) Indeterminacy in whether objects have a fusion at a given time, because (say) they are moderately scattered at that time. This would result in count indeterminacy. For consider a possible world containing some finite number of quarks that are greatly scattered at all times except for a single time, *t*, at which they are moderately scattered. The quarks would then determinately lack a fusion except at time *t*, when it would be indeterminate whether they have a fusion. The result is indeterminacy in how many objects exist: there is one more object depending on whether the quarks have a fusion at *t*. (Similar remarks would apply if 'scattered' in this paragraph were replaced by various other predicates

deemed relevant to the question of whether a class has a fusion at a given time.)

(2) Indeterminacy in whether a fusion at t of certain particles is identical to a fusion at some other time, t', of some other particles. This, too, would result in count indeterminacy. Suppose I undergo amnesia in such a way that we feel indeterminacy in whether 'Young Man Ted is identical to Old Man Sider' is true. Presumably we will want to say the same thing about this case if it occurs in a world with only finitely many concrete things. But in this world, if it is really indeterminate whether a certain assignment has a minimal D-fusion (say, one that assigns to times before and after amnesia all my parts at those times), then there will result indeterminacy in the count of the concrete objects there, for if the identity holds there will be one less object than if the identity does not hold.

(3) Indeterminacy in when an object begins to exist. Again, this would result in count indeterminacy. Suppose that in some case, C, it is indeterminate when a certain statue comes into existence. Consider next a case much like C, but in which (i) only finitely many concrete things exist, and (ii) the molecules that would make up the statue are all annihilated after the time at which the statue is alleged to indeterminately exist. Then it will be indeterminate whether the statue exists at all, and hence indeterminate how many things there are in the world in question.

(4) Indeterminacy in when an object ceases existing. This case is similar to the previous case.

If, then, minimal D-fusion could be indeterminate, it could be indeterminate what the (finite) number of concrete things is. But then there could be a numerical sentence that is neither definitely true nor definitely false. Assuming that no indeterminacy can issue from logic, this is impossible. So P3′ is true: a given assignment must either definitely have or definitely lack a minimal D-fusion. This is not to say that the phenomena adduced in (1) to (4) are not genuine; they simply must be understood in some way not implying indeterminacy in minimal D-fusion: (1) The indeterminacy is due to indeterminate restrictions on everyday quantification. Typically, we do not quantify over all the objects that there are, only over fusions of objects that are not too scattered. If objects are borderline scattered they still definitely have a fusion, but we have a borderline resistance to admitting that fusion into an everyday domain of quantification. (2) This is a case involving three objects. Object 1 begins around the time of my birth and ends at the amnesia, Object 2 begins at amnesia and lasts until my death, and Object 3 lasts throughout this time interval. The name 'Young Man Ted' is indeterminate in reference between Objects 1 and 3; the name 'Old Man Sider' is indeterminate between Objects 2 and 3; hence the identity sentence is indeterminate in truth value. (3) There are many objects involved differing in when they begin to exist; the term 'the statue' is indeterminate in reference among them; hence the sentence 'The statue begins to exist at t' will be indeterminate in truth value for certain values of 't'. Case (4) is similar to (3).

P1$'$, P2$'$, and P3$'$ jointly imply:

(U) every assignment has a minimal D-fusion.

But (U) is a powerful claim, for it entails four-dimensionalism! The central four-dimensionalist claim, recall from Chapter 3, Section 2, is that every object, x, has a temporal part at every moment, t, at which it exists. Let A be the assignment with only t in its domain that assigns $\{x\}$ to t. (U) guarantees the existence of an object, z, that is a minimal D-fusion of A. It may now be shown that z is a temporal part of x at t. I do so by showing that z satisfies clauses (1) to (3) of the Chapter 3, Section 2 definition of a temporal part (see p. 58 for principles and definitions of temporal mereology):

(1) z is a fusion of $\{x\}$ at t. It follows from the definition of 'fusion at t' that every part of z at t overlaps x at t; by (PO) (p. 58), z *is part of* x *at* t.

(2) Since z is a *minimal* D-fusion of this assignment, z *exists at but only at* t.

(3) Let y be any part of x at t. Since z is a fusion of $\{x\}$ at t, x is part of z at t; thus, y is part of z at t; thus, z overlaps y at t. So: z *overlaps at* t *every part of* x *at* t.

A few people have objected in conversation that the conclusion of the argument, (U), does not entail four-dimensionalism. A thing-event dualist (Section 7), for example, might say that the objects guaranteed by (U) are temporal parts of events, not of continuants. These events would spatially coincide with continuants, but the continuants would nevertheless endure. This objection is a mistake. Line (1) of the argument shows that z is a *part* of x at t, not merely spatially coincident with x. So x could not be an enduring thing, given (U)—at any moment it (and every other object as well) would have an instantaneous part that overlaps all its parts.

An interesting feature of the argument from vagueness is that it forces one into taking an extreme position in the philosophy of persistence. Take on board the claim that minimal D-fusion can never be vague, and reject as well the existence of a sharp cut-off in a continuous series of cases of composition. What is out at this point are moderate views, such as those of David Wiggins (Ch. 5, Sect. 3) and Michael Burke (Ch. 5, Sect. 4), who admit minimal D-fusion in cases that match up with ordinary intuition, and even Peter van Inwagen (Ch. 5, Sect. 6), who admits minimal D-fusion only in the case of living things. The only views left open seem to be nihilism, mereological essentialism, and four-dimensionalism. Each gives a non-vague answer to the question of when minimal D-fusions exist and is thereby unaffected by the argument. I discuss each in the next chapter and argue that four-dimensionalism is the most attractive of the three.

CHAPTER 5

In Favor of Four-dimensionalism, Part 2: The Best Unified Theory of the Paradoxes of Coincidence

The final argument for postulating temporal parts is both powerful and popular: only with their help can we solve various puzzles in which distinct objects apparently share exactly the same parts and spatial location.

Four-dimensionalists usually argue that the best account of the puzzles is based on the *worm view*, on which the objects of our everyday ontology are sums of temporal parts—'space-time worms'. While I agree that the worm view gives a *good* account of the puzzles, I think that the *best* account is that of the *stage view*, according to which ordinary objects are momentary stages.

A point of methodology should be kept in mind. There are several competing resolutions of the puzzles, each with advantages and drawbacks. We should prefer the one that has, on balance, the most important advantages and the least serious drawbacks. I myself think that the balance favors the stage view, but lacking any systematic theory of how to balance these considerations, my role is restricted to their inventory. Since what ultimately matters is the overall balance of considerations, at no point do I claim that a counterintuitive consequence of one of the accounts is a decisive reason to reject it. Each account, including my own, has counterintuitive consequences. (Otherwise, the puzzles would not be so interesting.) This is not to say that counterintuitive consequences are irrelevant to evaluating theories, only that no one such consequence is decisive.

I.   THE THREAT OF COINCIDENCE

The heart and soul of the debate over coinciding entities is a cluster of examples in which distinct things appear to be located in the same place at the same time. Co-location is commonly considered puzzling: how could two things *fit* into a single spatial region? But notice that spatial co-location is not *impossible*. In a possible world with laws of nature under which objects made of certain types of matter do not causally interact at all, objects would simply pass right through each other; two such objects of exactly the same shape could share spatial location at a time. Moreover, as John Hawthorne pointed out to me, on some metaphysical views certain cases of co-location are ubiquitous, for example co-location of regions of space and their occupants, or immanent universals (or tropes) that share location with each other or with 'thin' particulars that instantiate them.[1]

What is really objectionable in the puzzle cases is twofold. First, the objects in the examples will be actual material objects that we ordinarily take *not* to be capable of co-location. The actual laws of nature presumably prohibit interpenetration of distinct material objects. And entities that allegedly can share location with material objects, for example regions of space or immanent universals, would be of a quite different ontological kind from the objects in the puzzle cases. Secondly, in the puzzle cases to be considered, the objects in question will share all the same microscopic parts. Inert entities that happen to spatially coincide, or material objects and numerically distinct immanent universals or regions of spacetime, would not share any parts in common. If we are given two material objects with the same microscopic parts, the pressure is on to identify them. Many philosophers have ridiculed distinguishing such entities, saying that this 'reeks of double-counting' and would 'manifest a bad case of double vision'.[2] The justification of this attitude will be discussed below.

Let us say that objects *coincide* at a time iff (1) they share the same spatial location at the time, and (2) there is some class of parts of which

---

[1] See Armstrong (1978*a*, 1978*b*), and Lewis (1986*a*: 64–9) on immanent universals and tropes; see Cover and O'Leary Hawthorne (1998) on the bundle theory.
[2] Lewis (1986*a*: 252), Noonan (1988: 222).

each is composed.[3] (It is plausible that the first clause is redundant, given the second clause.) Prima facie, distinct objects never coincide. But consider the following puzzle cases.

Artifacts and Natural Objects, and their Constituting Quantities of Matter

A case of this type was discussed in Chapter 1. When an artist forms a lump of clay into a statue, it seems that (1) a pre-existing lump of clay continues to exist, but (2) a statue is *created*. If so then the statue and the lump would be numerically distinct, since they would have different histories—only one existed before the artist's work. Moreover, they would have different modal properties: the lump, but not the statue, is such that it possibly survives being squashed. Despite their numerical distinctness, they would coincide since they would be made of the same microscopic parts and would share the same spatial location. Wiggins develops a similar case in which a tree coincides with an aggregate of cellulose molecules. Supposing that a branch of the tree is cut off and then burned so that the cellulose molecules are destroyed, the original aggregate of cellulose molecules goes out of existence—a tree but not an aggregate of cellulose molecules is capable of surviving the destruction of some of its cellulose parts. Thus, before the branch was cut off, the tree and the aggregate were numerically distinct, since their futures were different.

Undetached Parts

This powerful puzzle was known to the Stoics, but was introduced into the current scene by Wiggins, who attributed it to Peter Geach.[4] We begin with a cat, Tibbles, and a certain proper part of Tibbles, Tib, which consists of all of Tibbles except for the tail (see Fig. 5.1.). Tibbles and Tib are obviously numerically distinct. But suppose now that Tibbles loses her tail; it seems that both Tibbles and Tib survive: Tib because nothing has happened to it beyond having something external to it detached, and Tibbles because cats, like trees, can survive the loss of certain parts. As noted above, Tibbles and Tib are distinct; but they coincide after detachment.

---

[3] Cf. Simons (1987: 210–11).
[4] On the history of this puzzle see Rea (1997, p. xviii).

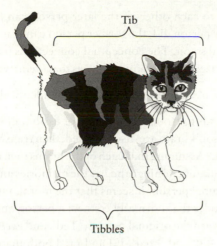

FIG. 5.1. Tibbles and Tib

Parfit's Cases: Fission, Fusion, and Longevity

Derek Parfit's paper 'Personal Identity' (1975) raised an important problem for the theory of personal identity: the fact that identity is a one–one relation conflicts with certain seemingly undoubtable propositions about the relationship between personal identity and certain moral, rational, and psychological relations. Some such principles were mentioned in Chapter 1:

- I can be punished for my past crimes, but no one can be justly punished for anyone *else's* crimes.
- I have a certain sort of fear or dread of my future pains, but no one can fear—in the appropriate way—the future pains of others.
- While others can wish that I had not done certain things in the past, only I can *regret* my past actions.

These connections have traditionally been used as tests for personal identity. To see whether our concept of personal identity applies in a certain thought-experiment to persons *A* and *B*, Bernard Williams asks whether *A* would fear the prospect of *B* being tortured, and Locke uses accountability as a measure of personal identity in his case of the prince and the cobbler.[5] Let us lump all these connections into one. Say that

---

[5] Williams (1975); Locke (1975) (who regards accountability as *constitutive* of personal identity). For an extensive discussion of the exact nature of some of these connections see Unger (1990: 27–34, 92–7, and ch. 7).

persons *matter* to each other iff the later person can be punished for what the former person did, the former person can fear the pains of the later person, and so on. The conceptual connections just adduced may then be summarized in the following thesis that *identity is what matters*:

(=WM) Person x matters to person y iff x is identical to y

This thesis leads to trouble in the case of fission, in which the hemispheres of a person's brain are disconnected, then transplanted into two brainless bodies.[6] Assuming that each of the brains then resumes normal (or nearly normal) functioning, and has the memories and psychological traits of the original person, it seems that the moral, rational, and psychological attitudes that normally connect a person and his future self are present between the original person, 'Ted', and *each* of the two successor persons, 'Ed' and 'Fred'. Ed and Fred both matter to Ted. Ted should rationally fear the future pains of both Ed and Fred, both Ed and Fred should regret Ted's misdeeds, and so on. This conclusion may be bolstered as follows. In a case of the preservation of a *single* hemisphere, the resulting person clearly matters to the original. If my entire body and one hemisphere of my brain had cancer, but my remaining healthy hemisphere could be saved and put into a clone with minimal loss of function and memory, I would regard this as full survival; I would care about the resulting person as much as I would if I had no operation at all. But the case of fission is just like this one-branch case, except that an extra branch has been *added*. Whether the resultant person of an operation matters to the original person surely is not affected by the addition of a second resultant person. How could whether Ed also exists affect whether *Fred* should regret Ted's misdeeds? Whether Ted matters to Fred should be a function only of the intrinsic connection between Ted and Fred (except in so far as causal relations between Ted and Fred are extrinsic, in virtue of involving the laws of nature or in virtue of their analysis in terms of global states of affairs); whether Ted matters to Fred cannot be affected by how things fare with Ed. Likewise, whether Ted matters to Ed cannot depend on facts about Fred. Thus, since the mattering relation holds in the *single*-hemisphere case, in the double-hemisphere (fission) case, both Ed and Fred matter to Ted. But then, by

---

[6] See Parfit (1975: 200 ff.) for a representative example of the division case, and his n. 2 on p. 200 for further references.

(=WM) Ed and Fred would each be identical to Ted; it would then follow, since identity is one–one, that Fred and Ed are identical to each other—an absurd conclusion.

This argument crucially relies on the assumption that what matters cannot be determined by extrinsic factors, and thus that whether Ed exists cannot affect whether Fred and Ted stand in the mattering relation. Principles like this are sometimes called 'only x and y principles', and have been discussed by Harold Noonan (1989, ch. 7) and David Wiggins (1980: 96). Note, however, that these and other authors formulate the principle as ruling out extrinsic determination of *persistence*, whereas I think the principle is much more compelling when formulated as a principle about what matters. The effect of the principle about persistence can then be recovered using (=WM).

We can distinguish between symmetric fission, where each of the resultant entities has an equal claim to be the original entity, and asymmetric fission, where one has a stronger claim. The case just discussed was symmetric. The standard Ship of Theseus case (see Ch. 1) can be thought of as asymmetric fission. We have two candidates: the discarded planks reassembled, and the continuously rebuilt ship. Though the intuitions of many seem to say that the latter is a stronger candidate, it seems intuitively clear, of *each* candidate, that were it not for the existence of the other, it would be the original ship. Each ship bears certain relations of importance to the original ship; a principle like (=WM) for these relations then generates our difficulty.

The problem raised by fission is that (=WM) requires the formal properties of the mattering relation to match the formal properties of identity; but in the case of fission, mattering is one–many. The case of fusion reveals a similar difference in formal properties: mattering, unlike identity, can be many–one. Suppose that two persons fuse to form another person. Let the fusion be psychological as well as physical. This is most easily imagined if the two persons to be fused are quite similar psychologically. Where their psychological traits differ, the fused person can be imagined to have a sort of 'average' of the differing traits. The fused person can also be stipulated to have apparent memories of everything that either of the two original persons could remember. In such cases, surely what matters to the original two people is preserved; surely each can say truly that the person after fusion matters to him or her.

In each case, then, the principle (=WM) can apparently be used to derive a contradiction. How should this contradiction be avoided?

Parfit recommends giving up the view that identity is what matters. Note that this would not *completely* sever the connection between mattering and identity with which we began this discussion. Our concept of a person is that of a being that can rationally fear its future pain, is responsible for its past misdeeds, and so on—a being that satisfies (=WM). If Parfit is right, then nothing *perfectly* fits the concept of a person; but there may yet be entities that satisfy the related principle that in non-branching cases, mattering coincides with personal identity. Such beings would be imperfect but good-enough satisfiers of the person concept. Nevertheless, given the depth of the conceptual connection between mattering and personal identity, there is significant pressure to respect that connection, if possible.

David Lewis (1983*a*) argues that the connection between identity and mattering can indeed be preserved if one admits coincident entities. For Lewis the coincident entities are spacetime worms, but a similar resolution of Parfit's puzzle goes through if they are enduring 'wholly present things'.[7] Consider the case of fission. Each branch person matters to someone beforehand.[8] (=WM) then requires that each branch person be identical to someone beforehand. This is consistent with the distinctness of the branch persons provided there were already two persons *before* fission. These are initially coinciding persons that part ways when fission occurs. Similarly, since it seems intuitive that one should not fear fusion as death, for each of the two fused persons there exists someone afterwards that matters to that person; by (=WM), each of those persons survives fusion; fusion therefore results in two coinciding objects.

Intransitivity of mattering 'in a straight line' also can be argued to result in coincidence. Consider Parfit's (1975: 217–19) everlasting bodies, which undergo perpetual psychological change but remain physically indestructible. It is plausible that there is a limit to how long mattering will extend in this case, for after a sufficiently long period of time the body will have almost nothing in common, psychologically,

---

[7] See Robinson (1985) and Noonan (1989, chs. 7–11).

[8] Why 'someone'; why not 'each branch person matters to *each* person beforehand'? I argue in Sect. 8 below that this stronger premise is indeed warranted, and that this undermines Lewis's solution.

with 'its earlier self'. Pretend with Lewis (1983a: 66–7) that mattering extends over spans of exactly 137 years or fewer—that one of Parfit's persons at t_1 matters to another at t_2 iff t_1 and t_2 are 137 or fewer years apart. Given (=WM), it follows that:

- for every span of 100 years, some person survives that span;
- no person survives a span of 200 years.

But now consider one of these bodies that is present from 1700 to 1900: by the first principle, some person, x, survives from 1700–1800, and some person, y, survives from 1800–1900; but by the second principle, no person survives from 1700–1900. Thus, x and y are numerically distinct, but both are coincident with the body and hence with each other in 1800. We therefore have another example of coincident entities. Indeed, we must admit that there are infinitely many coincident persons present then, for 1800 is part of infinitely many 137-year spans, and a similar argument to the one above establishes that each one contains a distinct person. This is coincidence in the extreme!

Essentially the same difficulty arises in any case where small changes are survivable but a big change composed of a sequence of small changes is not. Such cases are temporal versions of 'Chisholm's paradox'.[9] Begin with a person, and imagine a gradual series of changes that turns the person into something utterly different—a walrus, for example. Since the changes are gradual, we want to say that (*): for each change, something survives the change. Suppose for *reductio* that distinct entities never coincide. It then follows from (*) that (**): for each change, the one and only object present before is identical to the one and only object present after. But from (**) and the transitivity of identity, the person is identical to the walrus. This is absurd (if you disagree, let the person be transformed into a tree, or an automobile); hence the *reductio* assumption, that distinct entities never coincide, appears to be refuted. This is not just a problem about vagueness. While it may seem indeterminate after a while that the original person has survived, the argument only needs the very plausible assumption that it is definitely true of each gradual change that *something* survives it.

Statues and lumps, Tibbles and Tib, fusion, fission, and longevity are among the cases threatening coincidence that are frequently discussed. But some other cases are also worth mentioning.

---

[9] Chisholm (1968); for discussion see Forbes (1984) and Salmon (1986).

Vague Identity; Conventional Identity[10]

In my discussion of vagueness I will follow Robert Stalnaker's (1988) lead. There are clearly vague statements of identity over time. Here is Stalnaker's example:

In Philadelphia there are two prominent seafood restaurants named 'Bookbinder's' that carry on a rather unseemly rivalry. One calls itself 'Bookbinder's Seafood House,' . . .; I will call it 'B_1'. The other describes itself as 'The old original Bookbinder's' . . .; I will call this one B_2. Each lays claim to a tradition going back to 1865 when a single restaurant named 'Bookbinder's' was founded. I will call this original restaurant 'B_0'.

Both B_1 and B_2 claim to be identical to the original Bookbinder's. Let us assume with Stalnaker that each has an equally strong claim. Which is correct? Which of the following two sentences is true?

$B_1 = B_0$
$B_2 = B_0$

Surely the natural answer is that it is simply indeterminate which restaurant is the original Bookbinder's. Each of the two sentences is a vague identity statement, indeterminate in truth value. If we agree, there are then two roads leading to coincidence.

The first appeals to the linguistic theory of vagueness (see Ch. 4, Sect. 9). On that view, an identity sentence can be vague only if either '=' has precisifications, or one (or both) of the flanking singular terms have precisifications. But '=' does not seem to have precisifications—what could have a clearer meaning? The semantic indeterminacy must therefore be located in one of the terms flanking the identity sign—most naturally the term 'B_0', which had its reference fixed by the description 'the original restaurant'. Indeterminacy in reference between *two* entities, one of which is B_1, the other of which is B_2, would explain the indeterminacy in the identity sentences. But these two candidates must have been coincident in 1865, parting ways thereafter.

It might be objected that there are multiple candidates for '=' after all. Since in this case, the identity sign is expressing *identity over time*, perhaps there are multiple candidates corresponding to different criteria of

---

[10] Cf. Noonan (1989, ch. 6), and Shoemaker (1988: 208–9).

identity over time. On one such criterion, B_1 would be the correct successor; on the other, B_2. While I agree that B_1 and B_2 are the correct successors under different criteria of identity over time, the objection is confused. 'Identity over time' is nothing but identity itself. Criteria of identity over time are misnamed; the name gives the impression that there is a special relation other than identity whose analysis is provided by such criteria. In fact, to say that an object persists means nothing more than that an object that exists at one time is identical—identical *simpliciter*—with an object that will exist at some later time. Criteria of identity are better thought of as providing analyses of concepts like *being a person*, *being a restaurant*, or the temporal counterpart relation discussed in Section 8 below, or the temporal concept of existing at multiple times. The concept of identity itself is conceptually simple and not plausibly analyzed in terms of such criteria.[11]

The second route from vague identity statements to coincidence appeals to the argument by Gareth Evans (1978) and Nathan Salmon (1981: 243) against identity holding vaguely between things. Here is Salmon's version:

> Suppose there is a pair of entities x and y ... such that it is vague ... whether they are one and the same thing. Then the pair $<x, y>$ is quite definitely not the same pair as $<x, x>$, since it is determinately true that x is one and the same thing as itself. It follows that x and y must be distinct. But then it is not vague whether they are identical or distinct.

We have a dilemma: the Evans–Salmon argument appears to succeed in establishing that it can never be vague whether one object is identical to another, and yet it is clear that there can be vague identity *sentences*. Stalnaker's resolution of this dilemma is as follows. The Evans–Salmon argument shows that there can be no vague identity sentences 'A = B' in cases where the terms 'A' and 'B' are not vague in what they refer to. But if there is vagueness in what the flanking terms refer to, then vagueness in identity statements can be admitted, for in that case Salmon's argument cannot even get started: that 'A = B' is indeterminate in truth value does not imply that there is a pair of entities, x and y, such that it is vague whether $x = y$. 'A = B' could be indeterminate because 'A' is indeterminate in reference between two entities, one definitely identical to the referent of

---

[11] Cf. Lewis (1986*a*: 192–3); the introd. to Perry (1975); Stalnaker (1988: 357); and Sider (1999*c*, sect. II).

'B', another definitely distinct from it. If we accept this view of the Evans–Salmon argument we have a second route to the conclusion that vagueness in identity statements requires that the flanking terms be indeterminate in reference among multiple candidates. And applied to the case of Bookbinder's, we again get an argument for coincident entities.

I think that a proper view of *conventional* identities yields the same conclusion. In certain cases, it seems to be in some sense a *convention* that a certain object at one time is identical with an object at another. Conventional persistence would contrast with the presumably 'objective' persistence of, say, electrons (I neglect the issue of whether, because of quantum mechanics, facts about electrons are mind-dependent or indeterminate). Despite our best investigations, the truth about the persistence of electrons might well remain hidden from us. But for other objects this seems implausible. Parfit suggests this when he says we might 'give answers' to certain 'empty questions' about personal identity (1984: 260). He also discusses the case of a social club (1984: 213–14). It is hard to believe in hidden facts about the persistence of clubs; one is tempted to say: '*we* decide the persistence conditions of clubs'.

This is tempting to say, but what exactly does it amount to? On one hand it threatens to amount to nothing more than the banal point that if we had meant something different by 'club', different sentences would have been true. All facts, even facts about electrons, are conventional in this sense, for *any* bit of language could have meant something different. On the other hand, it threatens to imply that if you and I were to talk differently then clubs would vanish. But surely we have no such mystical powers.

The sensible idea behind the vague slogan is something in-between these two extremes: sentences about some domain are partly conventional if (and to the extent that) there were equally good alternate semantic choices for words contained in the sentences that would have resulted in different truth values for the sentences. An equally good alternate semantic choice for a word (or group of words) is one that (1) would have equally well suited our purposes for that word (or words), and (2) is just as intrinsically eligible to serve as a semantic value (recall the discussion in the Introduction to this book of intrinsic eligibility and the best-candidate theory of content). We make a conventional decision to use 'club' in a certain way. It is a banal fact about language that we could have used the word to mean something very different. It is also a fact, but not a banal one, that there were alternate ways of carving nature at its joints that would have suited our purposes for talking about clubs equally well. Suppose that, as we actually use the term 'club', we identify clubs with different membership, so long as the club rules have been preserved. Thus, a certain candidate meaning, C_1, on which clubs remain intact through changes in membership fits our use of the term 'club' better than another candidate meaning, C_2, on which a drastic change in membership results in a numerically distinct club. Nevertheless, with only slight alterations in how we talk about clubs we could have used the term 'club' for C_2 rather than C_1. Moreover, C_1 and C_2 are equally intrinsically eligible; neither carves nature at its joints better than the other. The case of electrons is very different: there is presumably a joint in nature separating the electrons from the non-electrons, and any language that divided up the world differently would be missing out on something. It is the lack of a joint in reality of this sort in the case of clubs that makes talk of hidden facts about their persistence seem implausible.

Here is a case, distant from those currently under discussion, where I think this model of conventionality is apt: constants in physics that involve particular units of measure. There is an element of convention, we say, in choosing the universal constant of gravitation to be 6.67 nm^2/kg^2, since our units of measure are conventional. The word 'conventional' is appropriate because there were equally good choices available to us for choosing units of measure, no one of which carves nature at the joints better than the others. Or consider conventionalism about morality. A conventionalist should *not* claim that infanticide (say) would have been morally permissible if we had adopted different conventions about morality. Rather, we in fact have certain standards governing morality that are constitutive of the meaning of 'morally wrong', but we would not have missed the joints of nature by meaning something very different by that term; and in some sense such an alternative meaning would have equally suited our purposes.

Suppose, then, that persistence is conventional in that there are multiple equally good conceptualizations of persistence among which we *could* have chosen. In fact we have chosen one (or perhaps several indeterminately, given the possibility of vagueness); but this choice was not mandated. What might these alternate candidates involve? The most natural answer is: coincident entities. Wherever a club is located, there are actually several coinciding entities differing only in their histories. Under our conventionally chosen conception of a club, only one of these entities is correctly called a club; the others we ignore. But none is any more real or intrinsically eligible to be meant than the others; we would not have carved nature any less by the joints had we singled out one of the other club-candidates for attention.

We have seen numerous cases in which there is pressure to admit coincident entities. There are various ways of coming to grips with these cases. The best way, I think, invokes the stage view. But as a sort of benchmark, I first examine how the cases of coincidence are handled by the more standard worm theory. I then consider and reject the worm theory's competitors, and finally give my own account.

2.   THE WORM THEORY AND COINCIDENCE

The worm theory's appealing account of coincidence is one of its most attractive features. Instead of providing a way to resist coincidence, the worm theorist gives an explanation of how coincidence is possible, and indeed, unobjectionable. Whenever distinct material objects coincide, they are never at that time wholly present, but rather overlap in a shared temporal slice or segment. Coincident objects are therefore no more mysterious or objectionable than overlapping roads. The diagram of overlapping roads from Chapter 1 can be expanded to display the relevant analogies for all of the putative cases of coincidence (Fig. 5.2). The statue and the lump are like a road and one of its subsegments; Tibbles and Tib like a road in which one lane merges into the main road; Fred and Ed like a road that forks. The picture for vague identity is like that for division except that the branches B_1 and B_2 are precisifications between which use of the name 'B_0' is indeterminate. The picture for the conventional identity of one club with another is also similar, except that one of the many candidate branches has actually been singled out as the referent of 'Club 1'; the others represent equally acceptable conceptual choices we could have made.

  Coincidence, as I have defined it, requires sharing of parts at the time of coincidence. As explained in Chapter 3, the fundamental mereological

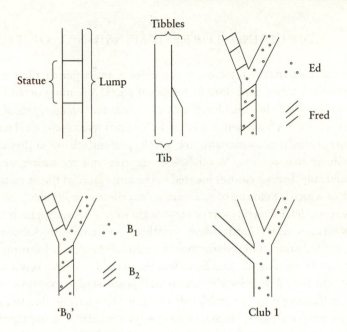

FIG. 5.2. Coinciding spacetime worms

locution for the four-dimensionalist is the atemporal relation of parthood whereas ordinary mereological predications are relativized to times, and thus must be understood as follows:

(P@T) x is part of y at t iff x and y each exists at t, and x's temporal part at t is part of y's temporal part at t.

According to the worm theorist, coinciding objects have the same temporal part at the time of coincidence; it then follows immediately, given (P@T), that coinciding objects share all the same parts at the time of coincidence.

The worm theorist, therefore, can accept the arguments in favor of coincidence but go on to explain why coincidence is not objectionable—its occurrence is as mundane as roads that overlap. This is an acceptable account of the puzzles; can anyone else match it? Can one account for coincidence without postulating temporal parts?

3.   COINCIDING THREE-DIMENSIONAL OBJECTS

A popular alternative is to accept coincidence and argue that it is unremarkable without appealing to temporal parts. A leading defender is David Wiggins, who considers the case of a tree and the aggregate of cellulose molecules from which it is made. Wiggins rejects temporal parts, saying instead that continuants are 'wholly present' whenever they exist (whatever that means). Nevertheless, the tree and the aggregate are numerically distinct entities located in the same place at the same time, each of which is made up of a certain set of cellulose molecules.[12]

Anyone defending this sort of view ought to give some explanation of how this can be. It is hard to deny that there is *something* odd about the claim that distinct things share the same parts and the same location. To just say 'things coincide' and leave it at that would be deeply unsatisfactory. The four-dimensionalist seems well-positioned to explain coincidence, likening it to unremarkable cases of part-sharing. But Wiggins rejects temporal parts. He must therefore give an alternate explanation of coincidence, of how it can be that the tree and the aggregate share the same parts and spatial location. We ordinarily think of distinct material objects (in the actual world, anyway) as being unable to fit into a single region of space. So how do aggregates and trees manage to do it?

Wiggins's *main* explanation, that the tree is *constituted by*, or *made up of*, the aggregate, will be discussed in a moment. I first want to consider something else Wiggins says: that coincidence is possible only between objects of different *kinds*. Trees and cats coincide with aggregates of matter, but never trees with trees or cats with cats. In fact, I think differences in kinds cannot play a serious role in explaining away the oddness of constitution. First, why should a difference in the kinds of the objects mitigate any implausibility in their coincidence? What is needed is a coherent metaphysical picture of the relationship between coinciding objects. Secondly, note that it is plausible that the tree and the aggregate have the same *momentary* properties, given their part-sharing. If so, then the difference in kind amounts merely to a difference

---

[12] See Wiggins (1968, and also 1980, ch. 1). Other defenders include Baker (2000, 1997), Doepke (1982), Johnston (1992), Lowe (1983*b*), Shoemaker (1999), Simons (1987), and Thomson (1983, 1998). See also Yablo (1987), though he defends coincidence for modal rather than temporal reasons.

in histories and modal properties. But how can the fact that objects have different histories and modal properties shed metaphysical light on how they can coincide *now, actually*? Finally (and most importantly), the difference-in-kinds explanation is unavailable in cases of coincidence where the entities involved do not differ in kind, for example the cases of fission and fusion, longevity, vague identity, and conventional identity.

The Wiggins-style explanation of coincidence must, then, rest on the notion of constitution. That notion is under-explained by Wiggins, but a suggestion of Judith Jarvis Thomson (1983: 218) is helpful: take the relation between the tree and the aggregate to be that of *mutual temporary parthood*: at the time of coincidence, the tree is part of the aggregate and the aggregate is part of the tree. This of course requires rejecting the analog for parthood-at-*t* of the Calculus of Individuals (Leonard and Goodman 1940) 'identity principle' that mutual parthood implies identity. As I see it, the defender of coincidence must indeed accept mutual parthood since the following principle seems correct (see p. 58):

(PO) If *x* and *y* each exists at *t*, but *x* is not part of *y* at *t*, then *x* has some part at *t* that does not overlap *y* at *t*.

Surely any part of the tree shares subatomic particles with the aggregate at the time of coincidence, and any part of the aggregate shares subatomic particles with the tree; by (PO), mutual parthood follows.

Mutual parthood seems inadequate as a definition of constitution since Wiggins and company want to say that constitution is asymmetric: although the tree is constituted by the aggregate, the aggregate is not constituted by the tree.[13] Nevertheless mutual parthood can play the role of explaining coincidence, to which the asymmetry between constituted and constituter is irrelevant. Mutual parthood allows the three-dimensionalist to take over part of the four-dimensionalist's explanation of coincidence. That explanation was that coincidence is

---

[13] Thomson (1998) extends her (1983) claim of mutual parthood into a definition of constitution, on which constitution is an asymmetrical relation. The definition (1998: 157) says, very roughly, that *x* constitutes *y* at *t* iff *x* and *y* have the same parts at *t*, and *y* is more tightly tied to its parts than is *x*. The second clause is to ensure asymmetry, but seems to do no better than did mere mutual parthood in *explaining* how coincidence is possible, for it concerns only modal facts about *x* and *y*, not facts about their actual, categorical relationship. Moreover, it is not clear that the definition will even apply to all cases of coincidence, for in the cases of fission and fusion, longevity, and vague and conventional identity, the coinciding objects are equally strongly tied to their parts, since they are of the same kind.

the overlapping of spacetime worms, and thus is no more objectionable than overlapping roads. But given mutual parthood, the enduring tree and aggregate also overlap. Indeed, given mutual parthood, the overlap is total.

It might be argued, then, that we have an appealing account of why aggregates and trees do not 'crowd each other out' that appeals to our ordinary conception of when material objects do not compete for space. It might even be argued that this explanation of coincidence is just as good as that offered by the worm theorist. However, the superiority of the temporal parts explanation emerges when we consider a further feature of the analogy between roads and spacetime worms. In addition to overlapping, the roads share a segment that exists *only* in the region of overlap. The four-dimensionalist can say an analogous thing: the tree and aggregate share a temporal segment that exists only during the times of coincidence. The tree and aggregate do not 'crowd each other out' because there is just one object wholly contained in the spatiotemporal region of coincidence. A *three*-dimensionalist, on the other hand, cannot say this, for she rejects the existence of temporal segments. The worm theorist's explanation of the oddness of coincidence is thus superior to the Wiggins–Thomson explanation.

The second reason to reject the Wiggins–Thomson view is that it is one of the views most directly undermined by the argument from vagueness in favor of temporal parts given in Chapter 4, Section 9, for Wiggins and Thomson take a moderate position on when minimal D-fusion takes place, whereas the argument from vagueness forces us into one of the extreme positions: four-dimensionalism, nihilism, or mereological essentialism.

A third reason for dissatisfaction is a worry about arbitrariness.[14] It is part of Wiggins's (1980, chs. 1–3) picture that every entity is associated with some sortal term that answers the question 'what kind of thing is this?', and determines its persistence conditions. Followers of Wiggins must then answer the question what kinds of entity there are. On one version of the view, the entities that exist correspond exactly with the categories for continuants in *our* conceptual scheme: trees, aggregates, statues, lumps, persons, bodies, and so on. How convenient! It would be nothing short of a miracle if reality just happened to match our conceptual

---

[14] Compare van Inwagen (1990a: 124–7) and Sosa (1993, sect. III).

scheme in this way. Or is it rather that the world contains the objects it does *because* of the activities of humans? This is an equally unappealing hypothesis. Everyone agrees humans have the power to select for attention a subset of the totality of objects that exist regardless of our activity. A worm theorist, for example, thinks that our sortal terms select ordinary continuants from a multitude of spacetime worms that exist regardless of our activity. What is incredible is the claim that *what there is*, rather than what we select for attention, depends on human activity. (Recall the rejection of Carnapian ontological relativity in the Introduction to this book.)

One might try to avoid the embarrassment by allowing the existence of entities corresponding to sortal concepts for which there are no sortal terms in our language. One might admit, for example, Eli Hirsch's incars and outcars (1982: 32), for example, or *wakers*—objects a worm theorist would describe as sums of all the awake stages of a person. Humans then select some of these entities to name, quantify over, and so on. This avoids the charge of granting special ontological significance to our conceptual scheme only if it holds that there exist continuants corresponding to the sortal terms of *any* possible conceptual scheme. But this maximally liberal position essentially amounts to four-dimensionalism, whereas Wiggins's goal was to maintain a three-dimensionalist solution to the paradoxes of coincidence. To admit the existence of continuants corresponding to any possible conceptual scheme would be to admit that there exists a minimal D-fusion for every assignment (in the sense of Ch. 4, Sect. 9); but that implies four-dimensionalism.

Followers of Wiggins, then, face a dilemma. The maximally liberal position on what there is implies four-dimensionalism, but the claim that what there is exactly matches our conceptual scheme seems arbitrary. Some remarks by Wiggins himself suggest an intermediate course. Though Wiggins allows continuants for natural kind terms, unlike many of his followers he is ambivalent about artifactual kinds (1980, ch. 3). I confess that I am not exactly sure just what Wiggins's position is here, but one way of avoiding the dilemma would be to claim that only 'natural objects'—things falling under natural kinds—exist. While this seems to be the version of Wiggins's view that fares best with the present objection, it has the disadvantage of failing to accommodate our intuitions about the persistence of artifacts. Artists do not bring statues into existence, factories do not create bicycles, tables and chairs do not exist (or at least, do not have the persistence conditions we think they have), and so on.

Two other reasons for rejecting Wiggins's view may be drawn from the recent literature. Each has some force, but (unfortunately) neither seems very decisive.

The first is the supervenience argument.[15] Persistence over time for macroscopic things must somehow supervene on (or be 'based on' or 'grounded in') certain other 'base facts', for example facts about spatio-temporal and qualitative continuity, and facts about the persistence of matter.[16] But this supervenience requirement seems inconsistent with Wiggins's view. Consider the case of the statue and the lump of clay. Before the statue is squashed, it is coincident with the lump, and hence does not differ at all from the lump with respect to the base facts. So if persistence supervenes on those facts, the statue should persist through the squashing iff the lump does. But this is precisely what followers of Wiggins deny.

I agree that persistence of statues and lumps supervenes, somehow; but the supervenience argument neglects a distinction between two ways persistence could supervene. Let the base facts include: (1) facts about *where* and *when* momentary qualitative properties are instantiated, and (2) facts about the persistence of matter; call the properties and relations involved in base facts 'base properties and relations'. Elsewhere (1999c) I have distinguished two versions of global supervenience, weak and strong. In the present case we have:

Weak global supervenience of persistence: any two possible worlds that have exactly the same base facts must have exactly the same facts about persistence.

Strong global supervenience of persistence: for any two possible objects, x and y, in the same or different possible worlds, and for any two times, t_1 and t_2, *if*: (1) x at t_1 has the same base properties as does y at t_2, (2) x at t_1 bears the same base relations to its worldmates as does y at t_2, and (3) x's worldmates have at all times the same base

---

[15] See Burke (1992), Heller (1990: 30–2), Oderberg (1996: 158), Simons (1987: 225–6), Sosa (1987, sect. G), and Zimmerman (1995: 87–8) for the supervenience argument; see Sider (1999c) for a more detailed presentation of my response.

[16] The latter is included to satisfy those who think that the problem of motion in homogeneous substances (Ch. 6, Sect. 5) shows that persistence of matter is ultimate or brute.

properties and stand in the same base relations as do the worldmates of y, *then*: x persists until some time after t_1 iff y persists until some time after t_2.

The statue and lump violate the strong global supervenience of persistence, since the lump persists whereas the statue does not despite the fact that they (1) share the same base properties, (2) stand in the same base relations to other things, and (3) inhabit the same possible world and hence have worldmates with the same base properties and relations. However, they do not violate the weak global supervenience of persistence. Weak global supervenience requires that any possible world like our world with respect to base facts must also be like ours in containing a statue and a lump with histories like those of the actual statue and lump. It can in fact be shown that it follows from this that a proposition that specifies the distribution of base properties and relations throughout all of the objects in the actual world must entail the *existential* proposition that there exists a statue and a numerically distinct lump with differing histories. But none of this is inconsistent with coincidence. Thus, Wiggins could ground statue and lump persistence by upholding merely weak global supervenience of persistence on base facts. Some will argue that strong global supervenience should hold as well as weak, and thus continue to maintain the supervenience argument against Wiggins, but the strength of the argument is compromised since Wiggins can at least uphold *some* supervenience claim.

The second argument against Wiggins is based on the doctrine of 'composition as identity'. On this view, when a thing, x, is composed of some other objects, the ys, then this is a kind of identity between x and the ys. Object x just is the ys. The relation of composition and the relation of identity are one and the same relation. We say that x is composed of the ys when we think of the ys as many, whereas we say that x is identical to the sum of the ys when we think of the ys as one, but each description is of the same state of affairs. Given composition as identity, no ys can compose two distinct things, since that would mean that the ys were identical to two things, which is impossible since identity is transitive and symmetric.

To my mind, the main attraction of composition as identity is that it allows us to explain the necessity of composition as being a species of logical necessity. As a believer in unrestricted mereological composition

(Ch. 4, Sect. 9), I believe it is a necessary truth that whenever the ys exist, so must another object, x, the mereological sum of the ys. But what is the explanation of this necessity? Why should every possible world containing certain objects also contain another one? The answer cannot be that it is part of the meaning of 'fusion' that the fusion of the ys exists whenever the ys do, because the definition of 'fusion' only specifies conditions under which some object x will count as a fusion of the ys, and cannot ensure that those conditions will necessarily be satisfied whenever the ys exist.[17] But given composition as identity, the necessity of the existence of fusions follows from the necessity of the laws of logic. The reflexivity of identity, in plural form, assures us that it is necessary that for any ys, there exist some xs that are identical to the ys. Composition as identity allows us to redescribe those xs that are identical to the ys as a single thing, x, that is composed of the ys. Thus, we have that it is necessary that for any ys, there is some x that is composed of the ys.

Composition as identity comes in full industrial strength as well as a watered-down analogical version. The industrial-strength version has been advocated by Donald Baxter (1988a, 1988b), the analogical version by David Lewis (1991, sect. 3.6). That presented above was Baxter's version, on which composition and identity are literally one and the same relation. It is difficult to argue against it,[18] but it is also difficult to believe it. How can many things really be identical to one thing? As Lewis puts it, 'What's true of the many is not exactly what's true of the one. After all they are many while it is one' (1991: 87).

Lewis's claim is that composition is analogous to identity in various ways, for example:

- If you believe in x then commitment to y is no additional ontological commitment if $x = y$; if you believe in the ys then commitment to x is no additional ontological commitment if x is composed of the ys.
- If x exists then something identical to x automatically exists; if the ys exist then something composed of the ys automatically exists.
- If $x = y$ then y is automatically located wherever x is; if x is composed of the ys then x is automatically located wherever the ys are.
- Nothing is identical to two things; no ys ever compose two things.

[17] Cf. van Inwagen (1990a: 6–12).
[18] Although see van Inwagen (1994) and Yi (1999).

The final feature of the analogy might then be enlisted in an argument against Wiggins, for Wiggins claims that the subatomic particles in the vicinity of the tree compose two distinct things, an aggregate of cellulose molecules and a tree.

The problem is that it is unclear how dialectically appropriate this argument is as an argument against Wiggins, for the final feature of the analogy between composition and identity is precisely the claim at issue. Wiggins will claim that at that point, the analogy fails. (He will, in fact, go on to point out further disanalogies, for example that identity is an atemporal relation whereas composition, like parthood, holds only relative to times.) The only argument against him here is weak, namely, that since some features of the analogy hold, others ought to hold as well.

This weakness in analogical composition as identity surfaces as well in explaining the necessity of the existence of fusions. Only the defender of the industrial-strength version can fully endorse the argument above, which depended on identifying the composition and identity relations. The defender of the analogical version must attempt to explain the necessity by the second feature of the analogy, that composition is like identity in fusions automatically existing, just as identical objects automatically exist. But this is not much of an explanation. *Why* is composition like identity in this respect?

I find myself, therefore, in a bit of an uncomfortable position. Composition as identity in its industrial-strength form is difficult to believe, but it is that form that has the advantage of explaining the necessity of unrestricted composition and it is that form that can be used against Wiggins's coinciding objects. Even without resolving this issue, however, the other considerations adduced against Wiggins motivate us to look elsewhere for a better resolution of the puzzles of coincidence.

4. BURKE'S DOMINANCE ACCOUNT

An interesting recent account that avoids distinguishing coinciding entities has been given by Michael Burke. Many of our puzzle cases involve two 'sortal terms' (e.g. 'statue' and 'lump'), with two associated persistence conditions, which then generate two coinciding objects. Burke avoids coincidence by disqualifying one of the competitors. In the statue/lump case, there is only a single object. That object satisfies both 'lump' and 'statue', but only the latter determines that object's persistence conditions, and therefore is that object's *dominant sortal* (1994*a*).

The argument for coincidence was this: when a statue is formed from a pre-existing lump, subsequently the lump and statue have different historical properties and hence are distinct. Burke agrees that a statue is created, but denies that the original lump survives. After the process, there does exist a lump of clay. But that entity, call it *X*, is also a statue, and in fact has 'statue' as its dominant sortal. The persistence conditions for statues rule out existence as an unformed lump of clay, and hence rule out the identity between *X* and the pre-existing lump. Thus, the artist's work results in the original lump of clay being replaced by a numerically distinct lump of clay.

The case of Tibbles is similar. Let us invent the sortal term 'torso' for all-of-a-cat-except-perhaps-a-tail. We thus initially have a torso, Tib, which is a large proper part of a cat Tibbles. After detachment, according to Burke, we have a single object that is both a torso and a cat. 'Cat', however, is that object's dominant sortal, and so determines its persistence conditions, which identify it with the original cat (Tibbles) rather than with the original torso (Tib). What has happened to Tib? Burke rejects coincidence; hence there is just one object present after detachment. Since that object has already been identified with Tibbles, there is no other object for Tib to be. Thus, when the tail is detached, Tibbles survives and Tib goes out of existence (1994*b*).

We can agree, I think, that it is odd to claim that Tib is destroyed by the removal of the tail, and that a lump of clay can be destroyed by forming it into a statue. But Burke argues that these claims can be supported by a plausible essentialist principle: for a number of different *sorts*, *S*, if something is *ever* an *S*, then it is *always* an *S*. Provided *being a cat* is one of the sorts in question, since Tib would become a cat if it survived, but is not a cat initially, Tib cannot survive detachment. Similarly, the initial lump would become a statue if it survived the artist's work, which is impossible if *being a statue* is one of the sorts in question. Burke is in a good dialectical position when he utilizes the essentialist principle, for in many cases the argument *for* coincidence appeals to that principle. Why is it claimed, for example, that the artist's action *created* a statue? The answer is, presumably, that the object created is essentially a statue, and thus cannot be identified with the unformed lump of clay with which the artist began.

Note, however, that Burke assumes that Tib would become a cat if it survived. The reason given is that Tib would, after detachment, have all of what it takes, at the time, to be a cat. But followers of Wiggins are accustomed to denying that kind-membership is intrinsic to a time; that is, they deny that two things that are intrinsic duplicates at a certain time must be of the same kind at that time. The statue and the lump, for example, are intrinsically alike at times when they coincide, yet differ in kind in virtue of their differing historical properties. They will, therefore, resist concluding that Tib would become a cat if it survived. After detachment, Tib comes to have all of what it takes at the time to be a cat but still is not a cat since it has the wrong historical (and modal) properties. Worm theorists will say similar things. Distinct overlapping space-time worms of different kinds stage-share when they overlap, and will therefore be intrinsic duplicates at those times. Thus, the essentialist argument will not persuade unbelievers; it can only be regarded as 'part of the package', as generating an explanation from within Burke's theory of why lumps and torsos can be so easily destroyed.

Burke's proposal does have the merit of doing away with coincidence, but it faces problems. The first is good old-fashioned implausibility. We are asked to believe that an artist can destroy a lump of clay by shaping it into a statue, and that a torso can be destroyed by detaching something external to it! Burke has his essentialist arguments for these conclusions, but as just noted those arguments fail if kind-membership is not intrinsic to a time. Other theories (such as the worm theory, and Wiggins's theory) do not have this unintuitive consequence. The undecided shopper for a good theory of coincidence should take this as a reason (defeasible, as always) to choose some other package deal.

Burke responds to this charge in several ways. The most important thing he says about the lump of clay is that while it is clear that the *same clay* is present both before and after the artist's work, this does not imply that *the lump of clay* survives. 'The clay' denotes plurally; it could be replaced with 'those clay molecules'. There is therefore no one object that is asserted to survive when we say the clay survives; what has been asserted is that the various clay molecules still exist afterwards (1994a: 597, 616–17). But I think that it still remains implausible to deny the persistence of the lump. If there are such things as lumps of clay, surely they can survive being shaped into statues. Moreover, the maneuver is less straightforward in the case of Tib. Torsos can survive the loss of small parts just as cats can; 'Tib', therefore, does not plurally denote cat molecules.

Burke's answer to the charge of implausibility in the Tibbles case is that it is not so implausible to claim that Tib goes out of existence, given the great changes that occur to Tib upon detachment of the tail from Tibbles. For one, Tib would become a cat if it survived detachment. For another, Tib would for the first time begin to eat, sleep, dream, and do many other things that cats do. Burke's reason for thinking that Tib does not eat, sleep, or dream *before* detachment is that those are activities that are done only by cats (and other living things), not their proper parts (1994*b*: 138–9). But suppose we grant Burke that a mere part of a cat cannot literally sleep, eat, or dream. Still, mere parts of cats do things very much like sleeping, eating, and dreaming. Before the detachment of the tail, Tib had four paws, a working mouth, whiskers, and a brain and spinal cord as parts, and its brain and spinal cord were connected in the way that cats' brains and spinal cords are usually connected. Tib moved in the way that a cat typically does when it sleeps, eats, and dreams; Tib's neurons fired in the way that a cat's do. We can say that Tib was 'pseudo-eating', 'pseudo-sleeping', and 'pseudo-dreaming'. The change that occurs in Tib upon detachment is simply that a former pseudo-dreamer, -sleeper, and -eater begins to do the real things by having an external part removed. This does not seem to be such a radical change. Surely, Tib ought to be able to survive it. Moreover, the radical change would *add* capacities to Tib, not remove them. We are familiar with destroying objects by robbing them of interesting capacities—dismembering a car and melting down the components—but not with destroying an object by, so to speak, making it more interesting!

There are other reasons to be dissatisfied with Burke's account. First, it requires an account of which one of the many sortal terms that apply to a given object is its dominant sortal. For Burke, the dominant sortal is the one 'whose satisfaction entails possession of the widest range of properties' (1994*a*, sect. V.) For example, both 'statue' and 'lump of clay' entail the possession of physical properties, but 'statue' in addition entails the possession of aesthetic properties, and hence is dominant. Of course, there are *particular* properties entailed only by the latter, but the criteria concerns only the 'range' (1994*a*: 611). The idea seems to be that there is a fixed set of *categories* of properties: physical, chemical, aesthetic, psychological, and so on; and dominance is determined by measuring the number of categories such that the sortal entails that some member of the category is instantiated. But as Michael Rea points out (2000, sect. 5.1), this criterion fails to pick out a unique dominant sortal in many cases. Consider a statue that is also a pillar, an axe that is a hammer, and a human that is a chess piece. Perhaps extensive Chisholming will solve the problem, but note that competing theories do not require this mess. Alternatively, one could give up on the analysis of dominance and follow Rea in taking the notion of dominance (or rather, the notion of an essential property) as unexplained. Here again is baggage that competing theories do not have. And on either way of dealing with the problem, there is an air of arbitrariness: why should the world contain just the continuants that answer to the dominant sortal terms of English? Here the problem for Burke is just like the problem of arbitrariness for Wiggins's account.

Other problems are even more serious. Like Wiggins, Burke has a 'moderate' position on when minimal D-fusion takes place, and is therefore ill-equipped to answer the argument from vagueness in favor of four-dimensionalism. Secondly, Burke's account is insufficiently general, for it cannot be applied to cases of coincidence between objects of the same kind, such as the cases of fission, fusion, longevity, and vague and conventional identity. I turn next to more general, and more radical, strategies.

5.   TEMPORARY IDENTITY

I am mostly ignoring accounts of coincidence based on 'logically deviant' theses about the identity relation, for example relative identity (Geach 1980; Griffin 1977; Noonan 1980) and the denial of the transitivity of identity. I do, however, want to consider the thesis of *temporary* identity, in light of its interesting recent defense by André Gallois (1998). Like Burke, Gallois is a three-dimensionalist who wants to avoid postulating distinct coinciding objects. To do so, he claims that identity can hold between two objects at one time and fail to do so at another.

Gallois primarily applies his approach to the case of fission. Suppose Ted splits into Fred and Ed. Gallois grants that Fred and Ed are distinct persons after fission, and that each existed before fission, but he denies that Fred and Ed were distinct before fission. Fred and Ed are at first identical, and then later distinct. It is never the case, according to Gallois, that x and y coincide at a time unless x is identical with y at that time. Distinct coinciding objects are in this way avoided.

One could give a similar account of the other puzzle cases. If lump L constitutes statue S at t, L and S are identical at t, despite the fact that they are not identical at times after L is squashed. Tibbles is identical to Tib after its tail is detached, but not before. In the cases of vague and conventional identity, one could claim that the names involved are ambiguous over multiple candidate referents that are identical at certain times but not others. For example, one could hold that the name 'Bookbinder's' is vague as between restaurants B_1 and B_2, which are not currently identical but were in 1865.

There is something very right about this idea. When confronted with the case of the statue and the lump, one *does* want to join the defender of temporary identity in asking: 'why should we distinguish the statue and lump *today* because of what will happen to them *tomorrow*?' But I think the thesis of temporary identity is not, in the end, defensible. What is right about the ideas can be preserved in a better way, as will be explained in Section 8.

The central problem involves Leibniz's Law. Let t_1 be some time before Ted has divided into Fred and Ed, and let t_2 be some time after division, a time at which Fred is being tortured and Ed is lying on a beach in Hawaii. The defender of temporary identities wants to claim that Fred and Ed are identical at t_1. But Leibniz's Law appears to dictate otherwise. Even at t_1, it seems true to say of Fred that he has the property *being in pain at* t_2, whereas Ed does not seem to have this property. By Leibniz's Law it seems then to follow that Fred and Ed are not identical at t_1 after all.

What is the defender of temporary identities to say about this argument? George Myro's response (1986) is to restrict Leibniz's Law. First of all, the usual formulation of the law as the claim that $x = y$ only if x and y have exactly the same properties has a hostile presupposition that identity is atemporal, for it includes the temporally unqualified '$x = y$'. At the very least, the law must be reformulated in terms of temporary identity: $x = y$ *at* t only if x and y have exactly the same properties *at* t. The problem, then, is that if *being in pain at* t_2 is a property had by Fred but not Ed at t_1, it would follow that Fred is not identical to Ed at t_1. Consequently, Myro's modification is to restrict Leibniz's Law so as not to apply to 'time-bound' properties like *being in pain at* t_2.

This weakening of Leibniz's Law is deeply unsatisfying. The defender of temporary identity intends his phrase '$x = y$ at t' to express genuine *identity*. (If the phrase just expresses an intimate relation between numerically distinct things, the position collapses into something like Wiggins's.) But if it is admitted that it is true of Fred but not Ed at t_1 that he will be in pain at t_2, it is hard to see how they could be genuinely identical at t_1. Restricting Leibniz's Law forfeits one's claim to be discussing identity. The demands of the notion of identity are high: identical things must share *all* their properties. If x and y are identical at t, then there really is only one thing there at t, and how can a thing differ from itself, even in a time-bound respect?[19]

Myro's restriction on Leibniz's Law is unacceptable. But Gallois claims that the defender of temporary identity need not make this restriction. According to Gallois, if $x = y$ at t, then x and y must share *all* of their properties at t, even time-bound ones like *being in pain at* t_2. Since Gallois thinks that Fred and Ed are identical at t_1, and that Fred has, at the time, *being in pain at* t_2, he concludes that Ed has this property at t_1 as well. That is, Gallois accepts:

G1:   at t_1: at t_2: Ed is in pain

But since Ed is on a beach at t_2, not being tortured, Gallois does *not* accept the following:

G2:   at t_2: Ed is in pain

Nor does he accept the following, which he claims to be equivalent to G2:

G3:   at t_2: at t_2: Ed is in pain

He therefore rejects what one might call the *transfer principle*:

Transfer principle: for any t, t', [at t: φ] iff [at t': at t: φ]

On its face, rejection of the transfer principle is extremely puzzling. In so far as one can make any sense at all of sentences like G1 with two temporal qualifiers, it would seem that the first temporal qualifier is redundant. G1, G2, and G3 would then all be equivalent, and the transfer principle would be vindicated. So for Gallois, the first of a pair of

---

[19]   Compare Gallois (1998: 182–4).

temporal qualifiers is *not* redundant. How, then, do temporal qualifiers work?

The temporal qualifier 'at t' is typically the tool of a defender of endurance who favors a B-theoretic account of time. An enduring poker changes from being hot to being cold by being hot *at* one time and cold *at* another. Thus, irreducibly tensed facts are not required to account for change; change can be described using tenseless attributions of properties to things at times. This is in contrast to the presentist's account of change, who does not relativize property instantiation to times but instead makes use of irreducible tense operators and says that the poker *is* hot, but WILL be cold.

Gallois's rejection of the transfer principle is an unsavory blend of these two approaches to change. On the one hand, Gallois qualifies his property instantiations to times. This suggests a B-theoretic elimination of irreducible tense. But the defining characteristic of a B-theoretic, tenseless property attribution like 'x is F at t', as opposed to the tensed 'x is F *now*', is usually taken to be that it does not change in truth value. Tenseless property attributions *constitute* change, but do not themselves change, on the usual picture. Gallois denies precisely this, for he claims that 'at t_2: Ed is in pain' is true at t_1 but not at t_2.

My central objection to Gallois is that his theory is incompatible with a B-theory of time—the philosophy of time I supported in Chapter 2. This can be seen in a few ways. First, let us inquire into the exact meaning of the temporal qualifier 'at t'. On one view, temporal qualification indicates a relation to a time. The sentence 'Fred is in pain at t' says that Fred bears a certain relation to time t, the *being in pain at* relation. This view appears to leave no room for a non-redundant second temporal qualifier. Sentence G1 is a statement about the times t_1, t_2, Ed, and the relation *being in pain at*. It would seem, then, that G1 could mean one of two things: either that Ed is in pain at t_1, or that Ed is in pain at t_2. The first reading is clearly not right: as uttered at t_1, the sentence is intended to concern what Ed is like in the future, not what Ed is like then. That leaves the second reading, which makes the outermost qualifier, 'at t_1' redundant, and which vindicates the transfer principle.

Other B-theoretic accounts of temporal qualification are of no more help to Gallois. For example, Gallois (1998: 38) expresses a preference for the view that 'x is F at t' says that a three-place instantiation relation holds between x, the property of being F, and the time t. But again, there seems to be no room for an extra temporal qualifier. In the case of G1 we have a single object, Ed, the property *being in pain*, and two times, t_1 and t_2. But the instantiation relation only has room for Ed, *being in pain*, and one of the times. Clearly we do not want to say that G1 attributes *being in pain* to Ed at t_1, and so we seem left with the conclusion that G1 attributes *being in pain* to Ed at t_2, which again renders the outermost temporal qualifier redundant.

Gallois suggests that double temporal qualification obeys the following rule (p. 84):

(E) (at t: at t': φx) $\leftrightarrow \exists y$ ($y = x$ at t & at t': φy)

This account relates double temporal qualification to single temporal qualification without rendering the outermost qualifier redundant. Given (E), G1 is true because Ed is identical at t_1 with someone—namely, Fred—who is, at t_2, in pain; it does not follow that G2 is true.

However, Gallois should not regard (E) as an account of what double temporal qualification *means*, or metaphysically consists in. For suppose he did. When 'at t' attaches to 'x is F', the truth condition is just that x instantiates F at t; but when it attaches to 'x is F at t', a quite different (and more complicated) truth condition would then apply. One would have expected that the temporal qualifier 'at t' has a single, uniform function. The introduction of (E) seems ad hoc, introduced only for the purposes of defending temporary identities. Moreover, (E) seems implausible, taken as an *analysis* of double temporal qualification. G1 is a statement about Ed, and Ed alone, whereas (E), taken as an analysis, would bring Fred into the account of its truth conditions. A counterpart theorist like myself would be happy with this, but Gallois is offering an alternative to counterpart theory. It is particularly hard to see why (E)'s indirect truth conditions for sentences like G1 should be thought correct given that Gallois admits the existence of facts linking Ed directly to time t_2. Ed fails to stand in the three-place relation of instantiation to *being in pain* and t_2; instead, he instantiates *being on a beach* at t_2.

So (E) is not an account of what double temporal qualification means. Gallois might leave double temporal qualification unexplained and simply claim that (E) is true. We would then be left wondering what double temporal qualification means, whether it makes sense at all, and why we should believe Gallois's claim that (E) is true.

Moreover, there is something dialectically inappropriate with claiming that (E) is true in order to answer the challenge from Leibniz's Law, for in a sense (E) has the truth of Leibniz's Law (in the case of time-bound properties) built into its account of the instantiation of time-bound properties. The dialectical inappropriateness may be brought out by the following sketch of the debate over Leibniz's Law. Gallois introduces a temporary relation, call it R, that he *says* is identity. We are skeptical, and bring up the challenge from Leibniz's Law: we claim that objects that stand in R at t need not be indiscernible with respect to time-indexed properties, for example the property *being in pain at* t_2. Gallois then claims that there is no conflict with Leibniz's Law because the instantiation of time-indexed properties obeys (E): x has *being* F *at* t' at t iff something that bears R to x at t is F at t'. But notice that this 'vindication' of Leibniz's Law in the case of time-indexed properties did not depend on any features of R itself. For example, let R be Wiggins's constitution relation (more carefully: constitution disjoined with its converse; let this be understood). (E) would then amount to the claim that x has, at t, *being* F *at* t', iff something that constitutes x at t is F at t'. It would then follow that if x constitutes y then x and y have all the same properties. For if one thing constitutes another they will share the same non-time-bound properties, and (E) thus understood guarantees that they will share the same time-bound properties as well. (Suppose x constitutes y at t, and has at t the property *being* F *at* t'. It then follows from (E), understood in terms of constitution, that y has this property at t as well, for there is something that constitutes y at t—namely, x—that is F at t'.) This is an unimpressive defense of the idea that constitution is identity, for no skeptic would accept (E). Granted, *if* constitution really is identity then (E) will be true, for (E) would then follow from Leibniz's Law. But whether constitution is identity is what is at issue. Likewise, *if* Gallois is right that his relation R is identity, then (E) is indeed true, for if R is identity then (E) follows from Leibniz's Law. But if we are skeptical that R is identity because we worry that R-related things need not be indiscernible with respect to time-bound properties, we will not be moved by a defense that appeals to (E), for (E) assumes the very indiscernibility we think does not hold.

There is a second way to bring out the conflict between temporary identity and the B-theory of time. The B-theorist says that reality can be given a complete tenseless description; reality is a 'block universe' on which an atemporal perspective is fundamental. So consider the block universe from the atemporal perspective, not from the perspective of any time in particular. Gallois admits that Fred is in pain at t_2 whereas Ed is not. Considering Fred and Ed from the atemporal perspective, this seems to be a sort of atemporal difference between Fred and Ed. One is tempted to conclude that Fred and Ed are *atemporally* numerically distinct.

Gallois's core claim is that the identity relation holds with respect to times, whereas we have just seen that taking the atemporal perspective tempts one to speak of identity and distinctness *simpliciter*. Gallois must resist this temptation and claim that there is no such thing as the relation of identity *simpliciter*. For if there were, then it would presumably fail to hold between Fred and Ed, given the differences between them viewed from the atemporal perspective. But if there is such a relation as identity *simpliciter*, and if Fred and Ed do not stand in that relation, that would take the wind out of Gallois's sails. Gallois's so-called relation of 'temporary identity' would seem not really to be identity, for it would sometimes hold between atemporally distinct things.

So Gallois must reject the notion of identity *simpliciter*. But there is considerable pressure on anyone who accepts the B-theory to admit this notion. We have already seen one instance of this. Viewed from the atemporal perspective, Fred and Ed seem different and so seem to stand in a relation of non-identity *simpliciter*. The notion of identity *simpliciter* is staring us in the face: it is a relation requiring the absence of any differences whatsoever from the atemporal perspective.

Here is another sort of pressure towards admitting atemporal identity. In the world of the B-theorist, there exist, atemporally, dinosaurs and computers. True, the computer is located *here* (in time) and the dinosaur is located *there* (at an earlier time), but each can be the value of a bound variable from the atemporal perspective. But then, can we not ask whether they are identical? The Quinean dogma of 'no entity without identity' might be modified here to read: no atemporal quantification without atemporal identity. Otherwise it is hard to understand the nature of atemporal quantification: the variables would range atemporally over a class of things to which questions of identity cannot be atemporally applied. Gallois allows us to ask with respect to various times whether the objects are identical then; but we have the class before us *simpliciter*, and yet cannot ask whether this member is the same, *simpliciter*, as that. Once atemporal quantification and the atemporal perspective are granted, atemporal identity seems to come along in their wake.

I have argued that a B-theorist should not claim that identity is temporary. I think, though, that certain A-theories can be coherently combined with the temporary identity thesis. Here is a sketch of the theory of an imaginary character called 'Presentist-Gallois'. Recall the real Gallois's description of fission:

(1) Fred and Ed are identical at t_1

(2) at t_2: Fred is in pain

(3) it is not the case that at t_2: Ed is in pain

(4) Ed and Fred are not identical at t_2

Presentist-Gallois would describe the situation differently. Presentists do not account for change by indexing properties like *being in pain*, or relations like identity, to times. The need for indexing vanishes with the rejected atemporal perspective. The presentist acknowledges that no atemporal description of the case can be given; a vantage point must be chosen for any description. This is not to say that there is some atemporal perspective from which all the vantage points may be described; only one of the vantage points—the view from *now*—is real. Suppose that it is now time t_2; suppose that t_1 is one day before t_2; and let WAS_n and $WILL_n$ be tense operators for 'it was the case n days ago' and 'it will be the case n days hence', respectively. Presentist-Gallois would offer:

(1′) $WAS_1(Fred = Ed)$

(2′) Fred is in pain

(3′) Ed is not in pain

(4′) Fred $\neq$ Ed

Does claim (1′) contradict claims (2′) and (3′) by Leibniz's Law? No, because (1′) is not an assertion of identity; rather it asserts the existence of a certain tensed fact about Fred and Ed. Granted, Presentist-Gallois will probably want to maintain the following tensed version of Leibniz's Law:

(LL$_P$) ALWAYS(for all x, y, if $x = y$ then for all properties P, x has P $\leftrightarrow$ y has P)

It then follows uncontroversially from (1′) and (LLᴘ), assuming that tensed predicates express properties, that:

(*) WAS$_1$ [WILL$_1$(Fred is in pain) $\leftrightarrow$ WILL$_1$(Ed is in pain)]

Does (*) conflict with (2′) and (3′)? It does given these additional principles:

Presentist transfer: $\varphi \vdash$ WAS$_n$ WILL$_n$ φ
$\qquad\qquad\qquad\qquad$ $\varphi \vdash$ WILL$_n$ WAS$_n$ φ
Closure:$\qquad\qquad$ If $\{\varphi_1, \ldots, \varphi_k\} \vdash \psi$, then
$\qquad\qquad\qquad\qquad$ $\{$WAS$_n$ $\varphi_1, \ldots$ WAS$_n$ $\varphi_k\} \vdash$ WAS$_n$ ψ, and
$\qquad\qquad\qquad\qquad$ $\{$WILL$_n$ $\varphi_1, \ldots$ WILL$_n$ $\varphi_k\} \vdash$ WILL$_n \psi$

'$\varphi \vdash \psi$' means that formula ψ is a tense-logical consequence of formula φ; '$\Gamma \vdash \varphi$' means that φ is a tense-logical consequence of the formulas in set Γ. Here is a derivation of a contradiction from (*), (2′), (3′), presentist transfer, and closure. By presentist transfer, (2′) and (3′) imply:

WAS$_1$ WILL$_1$ (Fred is in pain)
WAS$_1$ WILL$_1$ ~ (Ed is in pain).

From these and (*), via closure we obtain:

(+) WAS$_1$: [WILL$_1$(Ed is in pain) & WILL$_1$ ~ (Ed is in pain)]

Now let '$\bot$' stand for a generic contradiction. Since {Ed is in pain, ~ (Ed is in pain)}$\vdash \bot$, closure assures us that {WILL$_1$(Ed is in pain), WILL$_1$ ~ (Ed is in pain)}$\vdash$ WILL$_1 \bot$, and so WILL$_1$(Ed is in pain)&WILL$_1$ ~ (Ed is in pain) $\vdash$WILL$_1\bot$. From this and (+), we get via closure that:

(−) WAS$_1$ WILL$_1$ $\bot$

But the negation of (−) is uncontroversially a tense-logical truth.

So Presentist-Gallois must reject either Presentist transfer or closure. Which? I would recommend rejecting closure. This can be motivated by considering how Presentist-Gallois might describe the situation when the time is t_1, before division. At this point we do not have the names 'Fred' and 'Ed'. Instead, there is just the name 'Ted', a name for the one and only person before us. (We cannot take the atemporal perspective and introduce 'Fred' and 'Ed' for, respectively, the person that is tortured at t_2 and the person that is on the beach at t_2, for the presentist rejects the atemporal perspective. We could try introducing the names by the descriptions 'person that will one day hence be tortured' and 'person that will one day hence be on a beach', but given what I am about to argue, each would just pick out Ted.) What is about to happen to Ted? One day hence, will he be tortured or will he be on a beach? Presentist-Gallois should, I think, say that he will be tortured *and* that he will be on a beach. Presentist-Gallois should deny, however, that he will be both tortured and on a beach, for in the example it is never the case that someone is both tortured and on a beach. These claims:

WILL$_1$ (Ted is tortured)

WILL$_1$ (Ted is on a beach)

not: WILL$_1$ (Ted is tortured & Ted is on a beach)

jointly contradict closure. It must be granted that making these claims would require adopting a somewhat surprising tense-logic, and further that too much divergence from common-sense tense-logic would render presentism implausible. But Presentist-Gallois might be willing to pay this price for an otherwise attractive account of fission.

Temporal counterpart theory, to be defended in Section 8 below, also violates closure. This emerges straightforwardly from the counterpart-theoretic analysis of the tense-operators. Presentist-Gallois would of course reject a counterpart-theoretic explanation of the failure of closure since he rejects temporal parts. My suggestion is that Presentist-Gallois advocate the tense-logic generated by temporal counterpart theory but reject the counterpart-theoretic analysis of tensed statements.

In making these claims, Presentist-Gallois would rule out the possibility of giving a standard Kripke-style semantics for tense-logic, for that semantics validates both closure and presentist-transfer.[20] So much the worse for Kripke semantics! For the presentist, the tense-operators are primitive, and so the Kripke semantics cannot be regarded as meaning-giving anyway. Presentist-Gallois needs to go further and

---

[20] See Hughes and Cresswell (1996). Pages 218–19 deal briefly with (propositional) tense-logic; part III deals with quantified modal logic. The basic idea is that Kripke-models for *modal* logic can with minor revisions be treated as models for tense-logic. The accessibility relation is thought of as a relation of temporal precedence, the 'worlds' of the model are interpreted as times, the objects in the domain are thought of as continuants, and so on. The truth condition for 'WILL$_1$ (x is F)' 's holding at t in such a model (outfitted with an appropriate metric for its earlier-than relation) is that the object assigned to 'x' is in the extension of 'F' at the time one day after t. It can easily be seen that closure and presentist-transfer are valid in these models.

claim that Kripke semantics does not even succeed in capturing the logic of tense.

Such, then, is Presentist-Gallois's response to the Leibniz Law argument.[21] If he is willing to pay the price of accepting a non-standard tense-logic he can give a coherent account of fission that does not require postulating coincident entities. Avoiding coincident entities in the other puzzle cases is less straightforward. Suppose a quantity of clay is created, already in statue form. We have before us a statue, S, and a lump, L. Suppose, further, that tomorrow the lump will be flattened but not destroyed. It would seem that two days hence, L but not S will exist. That is, the following two tensed claims seem true:

(L) $WILL_2$ (L exists)

(S) $\sim WILL_2$ (S exists)

But (LLp) then implies that $L \neq S$. Thus we have an argument for coincident entities that does not appeal to closure or any other controversial tense-logical principle.

With more radical revisions to presentism, Presentist-Gallois might avoid concluding that $L \neq S$. He might, for example, claim that *de re* tensed statements about a thing express propositions only relative to sortal properties. On this view, where x is the single object that is both a statue and a lump, x WILL in two days exist *qua* lumphood, but not *qua* statuehood. The names 'L' and 'S' each name this single object x, but 'L' is associated with lumphood whereas 'S' is associated with statuehood. A tensed statement involving one of these names must be understood relative to the name's associated property. As a consequence, the property attributed to x by (L)—*existing in two days*, qua *lumphood*—is not the same as that withheld from x by (S): *not existing in two days,* qua *statuehood*. (LLp) therefore does not imply that $L \neq S$. This is obviously a major departure from the usual presentist position. It would also require significant development. A systematic account of the sortal-relativity of primitive tense operators is needed, the account must be extended to sentences with multiple occurrences of names of continuants, and so on. I will not consider it further.

Presentist-Gallois's advantage over the real Gallois is that his claims about identity and time are in harmony. I claimed above that Gallois can

---

[21] Arthur Prior (1957*b*) once presented a very similar account of fission.

give no B-theoretic account of the meaning of double temporal qualification, and that a B-theorist ought to admit the existence of an atemporal
relation of identity *simpliciter*. The first problem does not confront
Presentist-Gallois, since presentists never qualify property instantiation
to times in the first place. Neither is the second a problem, for the presentist rejects the atemporal perspective on the world, which was what
generated pressure to admit the relation of identity *simpliciter*.
Unfortunately, the very thing that makes it possible for Presentist Gallois
to avoid these problems—presentism—was argued in Chapter 2 to be an
unacceptable theory. (Might the thesis of temporary identity be combined with some other A-theory? As I argued in Chapter 2, these other
theories are unattractive as well. Moreover, non-presentist A-theories
admit atemporal quantification, and so would not escape the argument
that atemporal quantification presupposes atemporal identity.) The
thesis of temporary identity should be rejected, for it can be defended
only by embracing an unacceptable philosophy of time.

6.   ELIMINATIVISM

The paradoxes of coincidence are generated by reflection on the persistence conditions of ordinary material objects. If those objects did not
exist, the paradoxes would not arise. A bury-one's-head-in-the-sand
solution is to deny that certain of the objects involved in the paradoxes
really exist. This is Peter van Inwagen's (1981) solution to the Tibbles
puzzle: Tib does not exist. Nor do statues and lumps of clay exist. What
objects, then, *do* exist? Other than *simples*—objects with no proper
parts—his answer is: only *living things*, such as persons, cats, and trees
(1990*a*).

A more radical form of eliminativism is what van Inwagen calls
'nihilism': *no* composite objects exist; the world consists only of mereological simples. This view is more theoretically satisfying than van
Inwagen's own view, since it is eliminativist about all composites. I am
unconvinced by van Inwagen's reasons for preferring his view to nihilism.
He argues that we are certain of the existence of our own first-person
thoughts, and also of the principle that 'thought requires a thinker';
he then argues that this thinker must be a composite entity. But the principle that thought requires a thinker—that is, that thinking cannot be a

'cooperative activity' (1990a: 118) of mereological simples, but rather requires a single entity having the thought—seems to me no more convincing than analogous principles that van Inwagen must reject, for example that what one would commonly describe as the striking of a baseball by a bat cannot arise simply from the multigrade relations between the involved simples, but rather requires a single bat striking a single baseball.

In his book *Material Beings* (1990a), van Inwagen's main route to his eliminativism is through consideration of the concept of composition. Van Inwagen asks his 'special composition question': under what conditions do a given plurality of objects compose some larger object? After considering and rejecting alternative answers, he concludes that the best answer is that a plurality composes something iff the resulting composite would be a living thing. Among the rejected alternative answers is my preferred answer that *every* plurality has a sum (i.e. the principle of unrestricted composition), as well as others (examples: objects have a sum iff they are in contact; objects have a sum iff they are fastened to each other; nihilism).

There are reasons to be dissatisfied with some of these arguments, particularly the argument against unrestricted composition (1990a: 75–9). That argument is based in part on the following premise:

(F) If Universalism [i.e. unrestricted composition] is true, then the xs cannot ever compose two objects. That is, the xs cannot compose two objects either simultaneously or successively. More formally, if Universalism is true, then for any xs, it is not possible that $\exists y \exists z \exists w \exists v$ (the xs compose y at the moment w, and the xs compose z at the moment v, and y is not identical with z)

In support, van Inwagen first says that since most universalists use the term 'the sum of the xs' without temporal qualification, they must be presupposing (F). Secondly, he argues that since universalists say that any xs 'automatically' have a sum at any time, regardless of how they are arranged, their arrangement should likewise be irrelevant to the identity of the composed object.

How would a four-dimensionalist react? (Stick to the worm theory, for simplicity.) When 'compose' is used in its temporally relative sense, as it is in (F), it is defined via (P@T). But then (F) is false because distinct spacetime worms can share stages.

How should Wiggins react? As follows: 'I use "aggregate" without temporal qualification because I do not use "aggregate of the cellulose molecules" in van Inwagen's sense of being composed at a time. Both the tree and the aggregate would count as being composed *at the time* by the molecules (cf. Thomson 1983: 217–18). "The aggregate" does not need temporal qualification because it denotes an object of a certain natural kind, which is *essentially* and *permanently* composed of the molecules in question. Any class "automatically" composes a member of the natural kind *aggregate*. But iff the members of the class are arranged in a certain way, there will exist *in addition* another object, a *tree* for example. It might be arbitrary to refuse to identify the object automatically associated with the class at one time with the object automatically associated with it at another; but it would *not* be arbitrary to refuse to identify an *additional* object composed by a class at some time, whose existence is contingent on the members of the class being appropriately arranged, with some object composed by the class at some other time.'

Thus, at least one of van Inwagen's objections to unrestricted composition can be resisted by at least two of his opponents. But never mind: one could always regard eliminativism as being motivated by the very paradoxes of coincidence under discussion. To the extent that one is unsatisfied with alternate accounts, rejecting the culprit entities becomes attractive.

An immediate objection is that the eliminativist's existence denials are so implausible that any alleged theoretical advantages would be outweighed. Surely, the existence of statues, cats, and persons is more certain than any competing philosophical claim! But van Inwagen has a powerful response. An ordinary assertion of 'there is a chair here' is consistent with the non-existence of composite inanimate objects. What is ordinarily expressed by this sentence might be more perspicuously expressed as follows: 'there are some subatomic particles here arranged chair-wise'. Statements apparently about macroscopic objects, which do not exist, may be paraphrased as being plural statements about mereological simples, which do.

Grant van Inwagen this method for reconciling eliminativism with common sense. There are other reasons to resist his solution to the paradoxes. First, generality is a worry. Once living things are accepted, the difficulties of fission, longevity, and vague and conventional identity remain. As it happens, van Inwagen would reject the arguments for coincident entities in these cases. His explicit acceptance (1990*a*, ch. 18) of the possibility of genuine vague identity without semantic indeterminacy undermines the argument from vague identity. He undermines the argument from fission by arguing that fission results in the annihilation of the original person.[22] It is in the spirit of *Material Beings* to flatly reject conventional identity for living things. It is less obvious how he would handle the case of longevity. But note that the more extreme position, nihilism, requires none of these *additional* (and, I think, implausible) moves. Nihilism on its own provides a completely general solution to the paradoxes.

(Or does it? Might there be cases of apparent coincidence involving simples—electrons for instance? The candidate cases are difficult to imagine. Vague or conventional identity seem to be out, since electron-identity seems determinate and 'objective'; the Tibbles puzzle is out since it essentially involves composites. For an analog of the statue and the lump case we would need an electron to take on some temporary property during some interval in such a way that we would be inclined to regard the interval as the entire career of some object. The only possible cases that come to mind seem stretched: imagine that having negative charge is not always a permanent property of electrons, and that someone creates a 'statue' entitled *Negative Charge* by causing an electron to have negative charge. As for fission, the argument for coincidence depended on denying that the original object survives as exactly one of the branches. This seems right for certain macroscopic objects, where one is inclined to resist 'hidden facts' about persistence. But such hidden facts are perhaps more plausible at a subatomic level; some might view them as the upshot of the rotating homogeneous disk (Ch. 6, Sect. 5).)

Set aside all other objections. The real problem with any sort of eliminativism is that van Inwagen's reconciliation of eliminativism with 'common sense' depends on a contingent feature of reality and hence does not work in all cases. Talk of macroscopic objects becomes plural talk of simples, but it is at best a contingent truth that there are any such things as simples. It is a metaphysical possibility, and even, I would say, an epistemic possibility, that every material object has smaller parts, *ad*

---

[22] 1990*a*: 188–212. The discussion is long and complex; I will only make the autobiographical remark that I find it unconvincing.

infinitum. But surely the truth[23] of ordinary beliefs about macroscopic objects is not tied to the empirical question of atomism; surely there might have been tables, chairs, and planets even if everything had been made of 'atomless gunk': matter such that each of its proper parts has further parts—'parts all the way down'. Some deny the possibility of gunk, others, the possibility of simples (e.g. McTaggart 1921, ch. 22). But surely the natural view is that both simples and gunk are possible.[24]

7. MEREOLOGICAL ESSENTIALISM

The final view I want to consider before presenting my own resolution of the paradoxes of coincidence is mereological essentialism, the doctrine that an object's parts are all essential to it.[25] I consider it last because, along with nihilism about composites, it is a three-dimensional view that is untouched by my argument from vagueness for four-dimensionalism, and thus is in my mind one of four-dimensionalism's strongest competitors.

One doctrine that goes by the name 'mereological essentialism' is of no help in the present case. Mark Heller (1990) and Michael Jubien (1993) uphold four-dimensionalism, and claim further that the *atemporal* notion of parthood always holds of necessity: if one spacetime worm is part of another then it is essentially part of it. This view presupposes temporal parts, and is therefore not the alternative to four-dimensionalism that we are after. The version of the doctrine we want presupposes three-dimensionalism and says that the relation *parthood-at*-t is permanent: (necessarily:) if x is ever part of y, then x is always part of y (provided y exists).[26]

---

[23] Van Inwagen could grant typical quantification over macroscopic objects some status other than truth (see van Inwagen 1990a: 102–3): perhaps assertibility, or truth-loosely-speaking, or even quasi-truth in the sense of Sider (1999b). My objection then is that ordinary quantification over macroscopic objects could have had this status even if atomism were false.

[24] For more details see Sider (1993). The term 'gunk' is from Lewis (1991: 20). For another objection to eliminativism, see Sider (1997).

[25] Defenders include Chisholm (1973, 1975, 1976, app. B), van Cleve (1986), and (in a sense) Zimmerman (1995).

[26] This leaves out the *de re* modal claim that x is *necessarily* part of y. The *de re* modal claim plays no role in defusing the temporal paradoxes of coincidence (though it does help defuse the modal paradoxes of coincidence).

In fact, we need more than this to solve the problem of coincidence. Ruling out mereologically inconstant objects does solve the Tibbles puzzle (since that puzzle assumes that Tibbles survives the loss of her tail), but not the puzzle of the statue and the lump, which need not involve loss of parts. A further mereological doctrine is needed. Mereological essentialism says that an object's parts are necessary for its existence; the further doctrine says that they are sufficient as well. Continuing to presuppose three-dimensionalism, the combination of these two doctrines may be called the 'Nothing-but-3D-sums' view:

'Nothing but 3D sums': if x is ever composed of the ys, then: at any time at which each of the ys exist, x exists and is composed of them; and at any time at which x exists, it is composed of the ys.

(For completeness we could add that it is never the case that there are ys that compose two distinct objects, provided we were not persuaded by modal versions of the paradoxes to admit permanently coincident entities. If desired, the doctrine could be restricted so as not to imply the existence of scattered objects.)

The name is intended to remind us of a picture: the world consists exclusively of three-dimensional objects that are individuated by, and whose persistence conditions are given by, their parts. Given this view, we can say that the statue and lump case involves a single thing. Forming this thing into a statue does not create any new thing, for if it did the new thing's parts would predate it, violating the nothing-but-3D-sums doctrine.

The doctrine solves most if not all of the paradoxes of coincidence. As noted, the Tibbles and statue/lump puzzles are immediately dissolved. It would be natural to regard the persistence of 3D sums as being objective; hence the puzzle of conventional identity would not arise. Neither would the puzzle of vague identity, if persistence of matter is definite. The puzzle of longevity arises only when we have an apparently intransitive relation providing necessary and sufficient conditions for persistence, which the defender of nothing-but-3D-sums can sensibly reject; the necessary and sufficient condition of persistence is the transitive relation *being composed of exactly the same parts*. Finally, the only possible fission case that could arise would be fission for a simple, and the argument for coincidence in that case was noted above to be weak. Prospects for generality, then, are good.

Like nihilism, mereological essentialism appears to be at odds with ordinary thought about persistence. This appearance may, however, be challenged. The challenge I will consider is inspired by analogous claims about modality made by Michael Della Rocca (1996) and Michael Jubien (1993, chs. 2, 3). Here I focus on Della Rocca's account.[27]

In Gibbard's case (Ch. 4, Sect. 8), a statue Goliath and its constituting lump Lump1 coincide at all times, but appear to differ in their modal properties. Some conclude that Lump1 and Goliath are two numerically distinct coinciding things. It would be nice to resist this argument. As I mentioned in Chapter 4, Section 8, I prefer a counterpart-theoretic response, but how else might the argument be resisted? A crucial step in the argument is the assumption that:

(1) Lump1 might have failed to be a statue.

According to Della Rocca, we can *redescribe* the modal intuition behind (1) as follows:

(2) It might have been the case that there exists *a* lump of clay (not necessarily Lump1 itself), created in a certain way, that failed to be a statue.

After all, we introduced the term 'Lump1' by the description 'the lump of clay we created in such and such a way'. Perhaps we substitute in thought this description for the name 'Lump1', and thus misreport the genuine modal intuition (2) as (1), failing to distinguish using a description to fix the reference of a name from using it to supply a synonym. (1) itself is false; we only think it is true because we confuse it with the true (2). (Note the analogy with Saul Kripke's (1972, lecture 3) defense of the identity between heat and molecular motion.)

Della Rocca challenges the argument's claim (1) about the modal properties of the lump, but one could similarly challenge the claim about the modal properties of the statue, or, to return to the current topic, challenge analogous claims about the temporal properties of statues in a defense of temporal mereological essentialism. Temporal mereological essentialism appears to differ with the common belief that persons (for example) can survive the loss of certain parts, but following Della Rocca one might claim that the common belief is regularly misdescribed. We

---

[27] I discuss Jubien's approach in more detail in Sider (1999a).

think we have an intuition that Descartes survives the loss of a finger. But this intuition could be redescribed as the intuition that, after the loss of the finger, there exists *a* person (not necessarily Descartes) with a certain property P. The confusion between this and the intuition that *Descartes* survives might be attributed to the fact that the description 'the person with property P' was used to fix the referent of 'Descartes'.

(A variant of this strategy could be employed in certain cases to avoid coincidence without assuming mereological essentialism. One could, for example, argue that in the statue and the lump case, the artist's work does not create a new thing, a statue, but rather causes a lump of clay to come to have the property *being a statue*. Intuitions to the contrary could be explained away in Della Rocca's way. The guiding picture here would be that alterations to the *shape* of a thing do not cause a new thing to come into existence. However, as Michael Burke (1994*a*: 592) points out, this move would not solve the Tibbles puzzle; mereological essentialism is required for a general solution.)

Della Rocca claims, in the modal case, that any attempt to argue that (1) rather than (2) is our modal intuition would be 'question-begging'—we would need to already have established the non-identity of the statue and the lump. But this seems incorrect. Apprised of the difference between fixing the referent and supplying a synonym, I remain convinced that (1) is true, in addition to (2). This need not beg any questions; intuition may be sophisticated enough to pertain directly to (1). Similarly for the temporal case: I do not think that my belief that the artist's work *creates* something is based on confusing names with reference-fixing descriptions. The intuition is robust; it persists after distinctions about descriptions have been made. In this way the case of the statue and the lump is unlike Kripke's cases. Once one makes the Kripkean distinctions, the original intuitions one had, for example, that heat might have been present without molecular motion, or that Hesperus might have been distinct from Phosphorus, no longer remain. I conclude that the attempt to reconcile mereological essentialism with ordinary beliefs about persistence fails.

One could attempt to reconcile mereological essentialism with ordinary belief in a different way, by using an appropriate strategy of paraphrase. Chisholm's (1976, ch. 3) method of *entia successiva* is an example. Although a ship cannot *strictly speaking* survive the loss of a part, we can in a 'loose and popular sense' speak of a distinct future ship as if it were the original ship, if it is sufficiently similar to the original ship, or if it is connected to the original ship by a series of ships that are pairwise sufficiently similar.

Still, according to Chisholm, it is never literally correct to say that a thing survives a change in parts. This is a point of massive departure from ordinary belief. Since four-dimensionalism has no such consequence, this has to be considered a major advantage for four-dimensionalism. But a more liberally minded mereological essentialist might argue that *entia successiva* persistence is, in fact, literal persistence. An analogy: it seems right to say that ordinary folks truly ascribe the predicate 'contact', despite the fact that (1) ordinary folks consider it definitional of 'contact' that objects in contact cannot be separated in space, but (2) given the atomic theory of matter, any two objects are always spatially separated. 'Contact' applies because there is an excellent candidate for our predicate 'contact', a certain causal relation that holds between objects when they are very close together, are not visibly separated, cannot be visibly forced closer together, and so on, and which holds in paradigm cases of contact. (Recall the best-candidate theory of meaning from the Introduction.) Compare David Lewis (1994: 489):

It's an old story. Maybe nothing could perfectly deserve the name 'sensation' unless it were infallibly introspective; or the name 'simultaneity' unless it were a frame-independent equivalence relation; or the name 'value' unless it couldn't possibly fail to attract anyone who was well acquainted with it. If so, then there are no perfect deservers of these names to be had. But it would be silly to lose our Moorings and deny that there existed any such things as sensations, simultaneity, and values. In each case, an imperfect candidate may deserve the name quite well enough.

Might it be plausible to hold that our talk of persisting ships is literally true after all, since the method of *entia successiva* provides good-enough candidates for ship-talk?

In fact I think not, for the mereological essentialist is forced to admit that *entia successiva* persistence is not *persistence in the fullest sense*. The persistence enjoyed by 3D sums is strict endurance over time, and is therefore very different from the loose and popular persistence of *entia successiva*. The persistence of 3D sums would be a much stronger candidate to be meant by persistence-talk; *entia successiva* persistence would be a second-class citizen. Our pre-analytic conception of the nature of persistence fits the persistence of 3D sums best; moreover, this persistence would be extremely intrinsically eligible. So it would be the strongest candidate to be meant by persistence-talk. Only the persistence of 3D sums would be *genuine* persistence.

What I am arguing is that given the best-candidate theory of meaning, talk of things persisting through change of parts would be false if mereological essentialism is true. The candidacy of *entia successiva* persistence to be meant by persistence-talk would be *trumped* by the genuine persistence of 3D sums. So, if respecting ordinary beliefs about persistence is a desideratum in our choice of theory, we should reject mereological essentialism. Ordinary belief is not the sole guide to belief in metaphysics. But there is, so far as I know, no strong *direct* reason in favor of mereological essentialism; the doctrine seems justified merely by its role in preserving as many of our most sensible convictions about identity over time as possible. My point, then, is that this sort of reasoning should lead us elsewhere.

It might be argued that even though genuine persistence is much more *eligible* than *entia-successiva* persistence, still *entia-successiva* persistence is the best candidate to be meant by ordinary talk since *entia-successiva* persistence fits *use* better, in particular our use of persistence-talk in 'paradigm cases'. After all, we do ordinarily speak of things surviving mereological change. However, even though *entia-successiva* persistence matches 'paradigm cases' better than does the persistence of 3D sums, it does not follow that it fits use better, since another facet of our use of persistence language is our intuition that animals, planets, bicycles, and other mereologically inconstant things persist in the same way as do hunks of matter. Moreover, another facet of use is the fact that the persistence of 3D sums best matches a kind of pre-analytic picture we have of the nature of persistence—a kind of 'ideal of persistence'. Compare the belief that objects are in contact only if there is no space whatsoever between the objects, or the belief that one has free will only if there are no external constraints whatsoever on one's actions. The ideal of contact and the ideal of free will are not decisive in the correct assignment of content to 'contact' and 'free will' because no actual cases live up to the ideals. But the mereological essentialist admits that there are cases that match the ideal of persistence. This favors the fit of the persistence of 3D sums with use. So I am inclined to think that use does not decisively favor *entia-successiva* persistence. At best, use is indeterminate between *entia- successiva* persistence and the persistence of 3D sums. Since the persistence of 3D sums is much more eligible than *entia-successiva* persistence, it is the winning candidate.

Still, it must be admitted that the trumping argument is weakened by vagueness in the slogan 'meaning is determined by use plus eligibility'. I have not specified just what use is, nor have I specified how exactly use and eligibility balance off against each other. It is, therefore, worth noting that even if the objection is conceded—even if ordinary talk of persistence through mereological change would turn out true, given mereological essentialism—we can still give sense to the idea that such persistence would not be 'full-blooded' persistence. We can still say that bicycles, animals, and planets do not persist in the fullest sense, if mereological essentialism is true. For the kind of persistence bicycles, animals, and plants enjoy is mere *entia-successiva* persistence, and is far less eligible than the persistence of 3D sums. The fact that ordinary talk of persistence through mereological change turns out *true* then starts to feel a little thin, since the kind of persistence in this case would be second-rate.

Dean Zimmerman's (1995) solution to the paradoxes of coincidence is similar to Chisholm's. According to Zimmerman, mereologically inconstant things (like bicycles and planets) are of a different ontological category from the concrete 3D sums for which mereological essentialism is true. He is neutral whether bicycles and planets are fictions, as Chisholm's *entia successiva* are, or abstract objects, perhaps functions from times to 3D sums, or processes, like water waves which are disturbances in quantities of water. But the genuine persistence enjoyed by 3D sums would trump the candidacy of fictions, functions, or processes.

The trumping argument also applies to the paraphrase strategy for defending nihilism (and, *mutatis mutandis*, van Inwagen's view). The nihilist gives sentences about persisting macroscopic objects 'devious' truth conditions that quantify plurally over simples, while sentences about persisting simples have far more straightforward truth conditions. This non-uniformity is implausible. Sentences about simples should concern the same sort of existence and persistence as do syntactically similar sentences about macroscopic objects. According to the nihilist, there is such a thing as genuine existence and persistence, which is enjoyed by simples alone. Genuine existence and persistence would trump the nihilist's devious candidates. So if nihilism is true, sentences about macroscopic things would not be true after all (though they might still have some other positive status—see n. 23).

Before concluding this section I would like to mention another view, which bears some similarities both to mereological essentialism and nihilism. Peter Unger once claimed that there are no persons, cats, statues, lumps of clay, and so on. Superficially this seems close to nihilism, whereas it is in fact closer to mereological essentialism. Unger's position was not that no composites exist, but rather that if any composites do exist, they do not satisfy ordinary sortal terms. If they did, he argued, they would fall prey to a 'sorites of decomposition' argument: if a *person* existed, then it would persist if a single atom were removed; but repeated application of this procedure yields the absurd conclusion that the person would remain even when only a single atom is left.[28] This argument, as Unger noted, does not generalize to objects with precise existence conditions, for example atoms, molecules, 'certain crystal structures', and 'physical objects'. Removal of a single simple from a physical object, for example, always results in another physical object, except when the physical object is just one simple, in which case the removal results in no object (1979*a*: 240–2). Unger does not himself commit to the existence of these 'precise' entities; he only points out that his arguments do not rule them out. Nevertheless, his remarks cohere with the nothing-but-3D-sums ontology, for those sums all have precise existence conditions.

Unlike nihilism and the nothing-but-3D-sums view, Unger's position must face its conflict with common sense full-on, unprotected by any paraphrase strategy that renders the conflict only apparent. Unger is therefore vulnerable to the Moorean criticism that any argument in its favor must appeal to premises less plausible than the denial of the view itself. The reason is that any paraphrase of a sentence, *S*, about ordinary objects would be just as vulnerable to Unger's sorites of decomposition as is *S*. Unger's argument that 'there is a table in the room' is false does not depend in any way on how this sentence is understood: the argument is simply that if it is true in one case, however understood, then it must also be true in a case in which just one simple has been removed, leading to the absurd conclusion that it is true in a case with no simples whatsoever.

---

[28] See Unger (1979*a*, 1979*b*, 1979*c*). A second route also concerns vagueness, but in the form of Unger's (1980) 'problem of the many' rather than the sorites of decomposition. Unger has since given up his rejection of ordinary objects (1990: 192).

The sorites of decomposition should not be taken lightly, but it is hard to follow Unger in his reaction to it. Vagueness is a notoriously puzzling phenomenon; surely the paradoxical conclusion can be blocked in some way by attending properly to its nature. Unger quickly dismisses an appeal to vagueness by reconstructing the argument in terms of definite survival rather than survival (1979*a*: 247–8). But this simply ignores higher-order vagueness. At present, the theory of vagueness is in flux, with none of the prominent theories being perfectly acceptable. If paradoxical conclusions emerge in the area, it is hard to justify attributing them to the postulation of ordinary objects, as Unger did, rather than to an inadequate understanding of vagueness. Similarly, the right moral to draw from Zeno's paradoxes is not that motion is impossible but rather that an adequate philosophical theory of motion is needed; the right moral to draw from the paradox of the liar is not that truth and falsity are incoherent categories, but rather that we need an adequate philosophical theory of truth.

The goal of this chapter is to find the best account, on balance, of the paradoxes of coincidence. So far I have provided arguments against various three-dimensional theories. While I have not considered every such theory, I hope I have considered the most plausible ones. The worm theory, on the other hand, seems to resolve the paradoxes: though the worm theorist must admit coincidence, she can explain its possibility. Of course, the worm theory has its detractors, but their arguments will be answered in Chapter 6. The worm theory is therefore the front-runner of the theories considered so far. But I will argue in the next section that there is a four-dimensionalist alternative to the worm theory that does even better, by avoiding coincidence altogether.

8.   THE STAGE VIEW[29]

'Coinciding objects are no more mysterious than overlapping roads.' In this way the worm theorist answers the *metaphysical* objection that coincidence is impossible. But a semantic objection lingers. Even if we

---

[29] See my Sider (1996*a*) for an earlier presentation of the stage view. Related views are discussed briefly in Forbes (1985: 188–9), Perry (1972), and van Inwagen (1990*b*).

knew that fission was about to occur, we would not *say* that there are two persons before us. It seems wrong to *say* that there are two statue-shaped objects before us, the statue and the lump; the more natural thing is to say that there is just one.

In response, David Lewis (1983*a*: 64) defends a revisionary theory of counting. If roads *A* and *B* coincide over a stretch that *S* must cross, when she asks how many roads she must cross to reach her destination it would be appropriate to say 'one'. In counting the roads we go through the roads and count off positive integers, as usual. But we do not use a new number for each road—rather, we use a new number only when the road to be counted fails to bear a certain relation to the roads we have already counted. In this case, the relation is that of *identity along S's path*, which is born by one road to another iff they both cross *S*'s path and share sections wherever they do. Say that persons are identical-at-*t* iff their stages at *t* are identical. Counting by the relation *identity-at*-t, there is only one person in the room.

I doubt this procedure of associating numbers with objects is really *counting*. Part of the meaning of 'counting' is that counting is by identity; 'how many objects' means 'how many numerically distinct objects'. Counting must be by identity when we count objects not in time (numbers, for example), and surely we count persons in the same sense in which we count numbers. Moreover, the intuition that just one person is present before fission arguably remains even if one *stipulates* that counting is to be identity.

The example of counting one road while giving directions, however, is designed to show that we *do* sometimes count by relations other than identity. I grant that we would indeed say that *S* needs to cross one road, but I would prefer to say that we have counted *road segments* by identity. What matters to *S* is how many road segments she must cross, and we have told her: one. Granted, the question was about roads. But it is plausible that the predicate 'road' sometimes applies to road segments rather than 'continuant' roads. Whether road segments or continuant roads are meant depends on the speaker's interests (and may sometimes be indeterminate).

I support this view with an additional example. Suppose *S* is walking to the farm. As far as we know, her path is as shown in Figure 5.3. If she asks: 'how many roads must I cross to get to the farm?', we will answer 'three'.

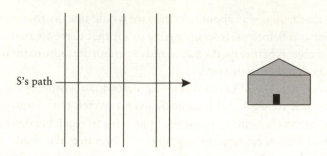

FIG. 5.3. Roads 1

But suppose that, unknown to us, because of their paths miles away the 'three' roads are connected, as in Figure 5.4. In a sense, she only crosses one road (albeit three times). If we count continuant roads, we count one road that she crosses, whether we count by identity or by identity-across-S's-path. But I think we gave the correct answer when we said 'three'. We told her what she wanted to know: the number of road segments she needed to cross. If someone later asked me for directions, my short answer would still be 'three'. I might add 'actually, you cross one road three times'. This might indicate that her question was ambiguous: does she want to know the number of roads or the number of road segments? But the first answer was satisfactory, for it is likely that she is more interested in road segments.

This way of understanding the case of directions is, I believe, more attractive than counting by relations other than identity. Lewis cites the roads case as evidence that we sometimes count by relations other than identity, but the evidence does not require Lewis's explanation. Counting is by identity.

I suggested that in the case of the winding road, 'road' meant road segment. The analogous view in the case of persistence would be that the predicate 'person' often—indeed, usually—applies to person stages, not spacetime worms. Then, we would never have 'over-counts', since in any possible case, no matter what episodes of fission or fusion the future or past holds, the current count of persons would be determined by the number of person stages present. The view should not be confined to persons. I have been using the term 'continuant' for the objects we typically discuss, name, quantify over, and discuss, whatever those objects turn out to

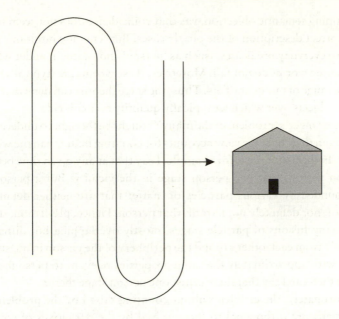

FIG. 5.4. Roads 2

be. The view I am suggesting is that all continuants are stages. I call this view the stage view. The opposing four-dimensionalist view is the 'worm view', according to which continuants are temporally extended space-time worms. So far, the point in the stage view's favor is that it provides the correct 'count' in the fission case. It also provides the correct counts in other cases of apparently coinciding objects (Tibbles and Tib, statues and lumps, and so on). All these cases involve distinct spacetime worms that share a single stage in common. Since on the stage view the names for the continuants involved name the shared stage rather than the distinct worms, the stage theorist does away with distinct coinciding continuants.

Given unrestricted mereological composition, I grant the existence of all the worm theorist's worms. My ontology is therefore the same as the worm theorist's: four-dimensionalism. I therefore admit the existence of coinciding entities, for given unrestricted composition, spacetime worms that share temporal parts automatically follow. But I deny that these or any other spacetime worms are *continuants*; they are not ordinarily named or quantified over. Coincidence between spacetime worms is *metaphysically* unobjectionable, as was argued in Section 2 above. The remaining semantic objection was that coincidence does not seem to be the correct description of the puzzle cases. But semantic intuitions pertain to everyday predicates, (such as 'person' and 'statue'), under which spacetime worms do not fall. Moreover, these worms are (typically) not in the range of our quantifiers. Thus, the stage theorist can deny that any of the objects over which we typically quantify ever coincide.

Peter Unger's 'problem of the many'[30] might be thought to undermine my claim that the stage view accounts for counting better than the worm view. In the fission case, for example, I say that at any given time before fission there is just one person stage in the vicinity. But a person is surrounded by various particles of matter that are neither definitely part of, nor definitely not part of, that person. Hence, pre-fission, there are many fusions of particle stages, mostly overlapping but differing slightly from each other around the periphery of the person in question, each with approximately the same properties relevant to personhood. How then can I say that there is just one person stage there?

Fortunately, the problems about counting raised by the problem of the many are orthogonal to those raised by the paradoxes of coincidence. Once the problem of the many is solved in some acceptable way, the coincidence-based problems remain, and can still motivate the stage view. Consider for example, the two solutions advanced by Lewis (1993), as applied to the case of a person alone in a room. According to the first approach, that of supervaluations, 'there is just one person in the room' is true since on any admissible precisification of the vague term 'person', exactly one of the candidate persons falls under its extension. According to the second, identity is the limiting case of mereological overlap; each of the many candidates is indeed a person; though these persons are numerically distinct from each other they extensively overlap, and so each is *almost* identical to the rest. Though it is not strictly true that there is just one person, it is almost true that there is just one person, and that is good enough. Each of these solutions seems promising. When applied to the case of a person stage, each generates the result that, at any time before fission, (it is at least almost true that) there is just one person stage. Thus, if persons are person stages, we have one person. But if persons are spacetime worms, there are two persons, given either of Lewis's solutions to the problem of the many. On any

---

[30] See Unger (1980), Lewis (1993), and Hudson (forthcoming, chs. 1, 2).

precisification of 'person', there are two worms that count as persons. (If some precisifications counted only one of the two overlapping worms as a person then a *post*-fission utterance of 'there are two persons in the room' would not turn out true—an unacceptable result.) Moreover, while the two worms overlap, the overlap is nowhere near total; hence the worms are not almost identical.

The stage view thus has the virtue of generating the proper counts in the cases of coincidence. But is it an acceptable view? The first and most obvious objection is that it denies persistence over time. How could continuants be stages? Stages don't *continue*. If persons are instantaneous stages, then no person lasts more than an instant. However, as I will develop it, the stage view includes a counterpart theory of *de re* temporal predication, according to which instantaneous stages may nevertheless have temporal properties such as *being* F *in ten minutes*.

According to my temporal counterpart theory, the truth condition of an utterance of 'Ted was once a boy' is this: there exists some person stage x prior to the time of utterance, such that x is a boy, and x bears the temporal counterpart relation to Ted.[31] Since there is such a stage, the claim is true. Despite being a stage, Ted *was* a boy; he has the historical property of *once being a boy*. Similar accounts of 'I was a boy twenty years ago' and 'I lived in Massachusetts in 1990' may be given, as having the truth conditions, respectively, that I have a temporal counterpart twenty years prior to the time of utterance that is a boy, and that I have a temporal counterpart in 1990 that lives in the 1990 counterpart of Massachusetts.[32]

---

[31] In Sider (1996, sect. VII) certain semantic complications are explored in more detail. A proper name denotes different objects relative to different times. There then arises a distinction between a *de re* and a *de dicto* reading for temporal predications. 'I was *F*' can be taken to be *de re* about my present stage; it is to these uses that the counterpart theoretic account is directed. But 'Socrates was *F*' cannot be, since Socrates has no present stage; the truth condition here is that at some time in the past, the referent of 'Socrates' with respect to that time—a stage—is *F*. Mixed cases are also possible. In fact, some of the sentences I discuss later in this chapter should be taken in this mixed way, for example the sentence 'Ted will be identical to Fred'. This should be interpreted as *de re* with respect to 'Ted', but *de dicto* with respect to 'Fred'; that is, it should be taken as having the following truth conditions: the current referent of 'Ted' has a future counterpart that is identical to the referent of 'Fred' with respect to that time.

[32] Note that the metalanguage locutions 'is a boy' and 'lives in' in these truth conditions are intended to express tenseless predication, not present-tense predication. The stage theory is an account of the truth conditions for a tensed language like English, but it is given in a tenseless language (though sometimes I will slide into a tensed metalanguage for ease of expression).

The temporal counterpart relation is the same relation used by the worm theorist to unite the stages of spacetime worms. Also known as the 'genidentity relation', the 'unity relation', the 'I-relation', and so on,[33] it may be analyzed in some way (in the case of persons perhaps in terms of memory or bodily continuity), or taken as primitive; the stage theorist has no particular commitment to any of these alternatives.

There is a close analogy here with modal counterpart theory. According to modal counterpart theory, an object, x, has the property *possibly being* F iff some counterpart of x in some possible world has F. The temporal operators 'was' and 'will be' are analogous to the modal operator 'possibly'. (The analogy is only partial, for there are no modal analogs of metrical tense operators like 'will be in 10 seconds' or 'was in January'.)

This analogy will be important in what follows. For example, it indicates the line of defense against the following objection: 'According to the stage view, statements that look like they are about what once happened to me are *really* about what once happened to someone else. And that's absurd.' John Perry gives something like this objection to a view something like my temporal counterpart theory:[34]

... [on (a view like) the stage view] the little boy stealing apples is *strictly speaking* not identical with the general before me. ... [The stage view] denies what is clearly true: that when I say of someone that he will do such and such, I mean that he will do it. The events in my future are events that will happen to me, and not merely events that will happen to someone else of the same name.

Compare Saul Kripke's (1972: 45) famous objection to Lewis's modal counterpart theory:

[According to modal counterpart theory,] ... if we say 'Humphrey might have won the election (if only he had done such-and-such)', we are not talking about something that might have happened to *Humphrey* but to someone else, a 'counterpart'. Probably, however, Humphrey could not care less whether someone *else*, no matter how much resembling him, would have been victorious in another possible world.

---

[33] See the introd. to Perry (1975) ('unity relation') and Lewis (1983a) ('I-relation'). Carnap (1967, sects. 128, 159) uses 'genidentity', attributing the term to Kurt Lewin (1923).

[34] Perry (1972: 479, 480). Nathan Salmon also appears to be giving an objection of this sort to a theory like the stage view in Salmon (1986: 97–9).

But according to Lewis, counterpart theory does *not* imply that we are talking about what might have happened to someone other than Humphrey. Granted, 'Counterpart theory does say . . . that someone else—the victorious counterpart—enters into the story of . . . how it is that Humphrey might have won.' But what is important is that Humphrey himself has the modal property:[35] 'Thanks to the victorious counterpart, Humphrey himself has the requisite modal property: we can truly say that *he* might have won.' The reply is the same in the temporal case. Perry is wrong to say that the stage view denies that 'You will do it' means that *you* will do it. 'Ted was once a boy' attributes a certain temporal property, the property of *once being a boy*, to me, not to anyone else. Of course, the stage view does analyze my having this property as involving the boyhood of another object, but *I* am the one with the temporal property, which is the important thing. The stage view is consistent with stages having temporal properties; it's just that temporal properties are given a counterpart-theoretic analysis.

It is a common complaint that modal counterpart theory does not *really* allow individuals to have modal properties.[36] Perhaps a residue of dissatisfaction remains in the temporal case, based on something like this sentiment. But I reject the complaint, both against modal and temporal counterpart theory. What is certain is that modal and temporal properties, however analyzed, apply to everyday objects. The *theory* about the proper analysis of such properties is another matter. If a theory can save the appearances—if it can account for the distribution of temporal and modal properties we take things to have; if it does not require an objectionable ontology or ideology; and if it meets these desiderata better than competing theories—then it is reasonable to adopt.[37] I do not say that intuitions about theoretical analyses carry no weight at all, only that they are not sacrosanct. Indeed, I partially based my rejection of the worm view on theoretical intuitions about counting. I grant that my analysis of tensed predication is unexpected, but this is not a *decisive* consideration, and is outweighed by the stage view's benefits.

The matter may profitably be viewed in light of the best-candidate theory of content, as presented in the Introduction to this book.

[35] See Lewis (1986a: 196). See also Hazen (1979).
[36] See e.g. Plantinga (1974, ch. 6), and Salmon (1981: 235 n. 16).
[37] See also Hazen (1979: 320–4) and Forbes (1987: 143).

Ordinary beliefs about persistence and modality lay down a persistence-role and a modal-role. Candidates for being meant by talk of persistence and modality satisfy these roles to greater or lesser degrees. I say that the counterpart-theoretic candidates satisfy the roles best. (In the temporal case this is in large part because of the attractive stage-theoretic solution to the paradoxes of co-location to which I will return shortly; this would need to be argued in the modal case.) Moreover, the counterpart-theoretic candidates are just as intrinsically eligible to be meant as their competitors. (In the temporal case, assuming four-dimensionalism is true, the competing candidate is worm-theoretic persistence, and it is clear that neither of these candidates carves nature at its joints more than the other. In the modal case this claim about eligibility would need to be argued.) The counterpart-theoretic candidates are thus the best candidates to be meant by talk of persistence and modality. And that is all it takes to be meant.

The difference between temporal counterpart theory, on one hand, and mereological essentialism and nihilism, on the other, may now be brought more clearly into focus. Recall the trumping argument against these views. *Entia-successiva* persistence would be a weaker candidate for being meant by persistence-talk than the *genuine* persistence of mereo-logically constant objects. For the nihilist, persistence of simples would be genuine persistence; statements about persisting macroscopic tables and chairs would turn out false. But assuming four-dimensionalism is true, counterpart-theoretic persistence is as good as it gets, and is thereby the best candidate, and is thereby true persistence. It might be argued that worm-theoretic persistence would trump stage-theoretic persistence, but it is precisely the arguments of the present section that show this is not the case. Stage-theoretic persistence best accounts for our intuitions about counting and other intuitions to be discussed below. At any rate, the stage theorist need admit no distinguished class of continuants whose persis-tence is more 'ideal' than that of others.

The stage theorist can therefore account for the possession of tem-poral properties by stages. I must concede, however, that tenseless state-ments of 'cross-time' identity are false, for example 'I am identical to a young child'. This strikes me as no bad thing, given that the tensed sen-tence 'I am identical to something that *was* a young child' *does* turn out true. More simply: I was a young child. That is the way we say it in English, and that is what is important to vindicate.

I therefore find the Kripke–Perry objection to temporal counterpart theory unpersuasive. There is, however, a different objection that I take very seriously, which ultimately seems to require a concession. Certain sentences involving 'timeless counting' are ill-handled by temporal counterpart theory, for example 'fewer than two trillion persons have set foot in North America throughout history'. The problem, of course, is that if 'person' refers to person stages, this sentence will turn out false, since more than two trillion (indeed, infinitely many if time is dense) person stages have set foot in North America throughout history.

As I say, a concession seems required. Some—perhaps most—talk of continuants receives a stage-theoretic analysis, but in some cases we need a worm-theoretic account after all. My considered view, therefore, is that a sort of indeterminacy or ambiguity should be postulated. Sentences involving counting of the non-timeless variety, for example 'there is one person in the room with me now', receive a stage-theoretic analysis, as do certain sentences to be discussed below, since this analysis makes the best sense of our intuitions about those sentences. But in cases like that of timeless counting, a worm-theoretic analysis seems required. The concession perhaps makes the stage view a little less attractive since, arguably, candidate semantics that postulate this sort of ambiguity or indeterminacy seem, other things being equal, weaker than candidates that do not.[38] Nevertheless, the stage view's advantages outweigh this defect.

A further objection to the identification of continuants with stages is that stages do not exist long enough to have many of the properties we attribute to continuants. The sentence 'Ted believes that four-dimensionalism is true' attributes, according to the stage theorist, a belief to my current stage. But how can an instantaneous stage believe anything? Beliefs take time.

Having a belief does indeed require *having had* certain features in the past. This is not inconsistent with the stage view, which interprets the past having of the relevant features as amounting to having temporal counterparts that have those features. In order to have a belief, a stage

---

[38] Jeremy Pierce pointed out in conversation that an ambiguity theory may have more attractive consequences than either the worm or stage view in the case of a time traveler talking to his former self. How many persons are involved in the conversation? The stage theorist says *two*, the worm theorist *one*. But perhaps our intuitions are indeterminate between one and two, just as the ambiguity theory predicts they should be.

must stand in an appropriate network of counterpart relations to other stages with appropriate features. Thus, the property *having a belief* is a highly relational property. It nevertheless can be instantiated by instantaneous stages. Notice that I do not claim to be able to *analyze* relational properties of this sort in terms of intrinsic features of stages and the counterpart relation. Such questions about analysis are no more my responsibility than anyone else's.

A final question one might have about the stage view is whether it can be reconciled with the special theory of relativity. What counts as a *temporal* stage of a spacetime worm varies with frame of reference. Clearly the stage theorist must in some way relativize his central claim, that continuants are temporal stages, to frames of reference.

Suppose a speaker refers to an object. Is the object to be identified with a temporal stage construed relative to the *object's* or the *speaker's* frame of reference? Not the former, I think. For suppose a speaker makes a tensed utterance about two objects at once, for example:[39]

> Next year it WILL be the case that Greg Maddux strikes out Mike Piazza.

'Greg Maddux' and 'Mike Piazza' refer to objects M and P that count as temporal slices, relative to a pair of frames of reference F_M and F_P, of the Maddux and Piazza worms at the time of the sentence's utterance. In addition, a frame of reference must be chosen to interpret the tense operator 'WILL'. The counterpart-theoretic truth condition for this sentence, as uttered at t, is that M and P have temporal counterparts at some time *future* to t, the first of which strikes out the second. But futurity (and the notion of 'time t') must be relative to some frame of reference, F_{WILL}. So there are three frames of reference floating about: F_M, F_P, and F_{WILL}. It would be very odd to choose either of the object-stages by a different frame of reference than that used to evaluate the WILL operator. Thus it should turn out that $F_M = F_{WILL}$ and $F_P = F_{WILL}$, and hence that $F_M = F_P$. Thus, the object stages M and P cannot be construed as temporal parts relative to the frames of reference of Maddux and Piazza, since Maddux and Piazza may well be moving in different frames of reference. The easiest way to ensure that $F_M = F_P = F_{WILL}$ is to set each identical to the frame of reference of the speaker.

---

[39] Maddux and Piazza are professional baseball players.

The central claim of the stage view is supposed to be that *a speaker refers to stages of worms sliced at the time of utterance*. If we could assume that every speaker follows a one-dimensional worldline through spacetime, and that each of her utterances occur at a single point along this worldline, then the stage view's central claim could be given a clear sense: when a speaker makes an utterance at a point p of spacetime, she refers to temporal stages of worms at the time that contains p, where 'time' and 'temporal stage' are relativized to her frame of reference when she passes through p. But each of the assumptions is an idealization. Utterances cannot in general be associated with single points in spacetime since they take time and cannot be spatially confined to a point. Moreover, speakers themselves follow four-, not one-, dimensional paths through spacetime. So just how is the central claim of the stage view to be understood?

The solution is to abstract away from utterances. A stage theorist should provide an account of a somewhat theoretical notion, that of *a sentence type's being true as uttered at a time* t, *understood relative to frame of reference F*. The stage theorist should claim, for example, that the sentence type 'Ted will be bald', as uttered at t, interpreted relative to F, is true iff the Ted-stage at t, relative to F, has a temporal counterpart in the future, relative to F, that is bald. How, then, is this theoretical notion to be *applied*? How can the stage theorist leave the ivory tower and make claims about truth values for real live utterances of sentences? The stage view can be applied provided we are willing to live with a lot of harmless indeterminacy. The principle of application is as follows. For any utterance u of a sentence type T, there will be a range of spacetime points where u could be regarded as occurring, and a range of frames of reference that could be regarded as the speaker's on the occasion of making utterance u. Call any pair $<F, p>$ of one of these frames of references, F, and points, p, an 'admissible pair'. For any admissible pair $<F, p>$, p counts as being at a certain time, t, relative to F. The stage view's account of the theoretical notion then supplies a truth value for T as uttered at t relative to F. Thus, for any admissible pair, the stage theory generates a truth value for u. For most utterances, the truth value will be constant for all admissible pairs, and in those cases we can harmlessly approximate the truth by saying that the utterance has this truth value *simpliciter*. When the truth value does not remain constant for all admissible pairs, it seems right to say that the utterance has no determinate truth value.

So much for answering objections. Let us now systematically examine the stage-theoretic account of the paradoxes of coincidence, beginning with the statue and the lump of clay. It is a great advantage of the stage view that it vindicates the natural reaction to such cases: the statue should not be distinguished from the lump today just because 'they' will differ tomorrow. The stage view thus preserves the core insight of the thesis of temporary identity (Sect. 5) while avoiding its pitfalls. Identifying lumps and statues with stages implies the desired claim that the statue is identical to the lump, at the time of coincidence.[40] But we also want to say that 'they' differ in their histories:

(L) The lump will exist tomorrow.

(S) The statue will not exist tomorrow.

How can (L) and (S) be true, if the statue *is* the lump?

The answer is that the expressions attributing temporal properties are ambiguous, so there is no one property that (L) predicates of the lump but (S) withholds from the statue. 'Existing tomorrow' expresses different properties in different contexts since the relevant temporal counterpart relation can vary from context to context.

A temporal counterpart relation specifies what sort of 'continuity' a thing must exhibit over time in order to continue to exist. But there are different kinds of continuity on which speakers focus. A certain kind of continuity is destroyed when a statue gets squashed, since the item has not retained a statue shape. Let us say that the *statue counterpart relation* does not hold between the statue stage before and the lump stage afterwards. But there is another kind of continuity that is not destroyed: the holding of a *lump-of-matter counterpart relation* underwrites our intuitive judgment that the same lump is present.

The lump counterpart relation is used in a typical interpretation of (L) because we denote the object in question using the term 'the lump'. (L)

---

[40] Ensuring that 'the statue = the lump' turns out true requires some subtlety if we solve the problem of the many using supervaluations. If the supertruth condition for this sentence begins simply with: 'for every admissible precisification of "statue" and every admissible precisification of "lump", . . .', the sentence will not be supertrue since some precisifications of 'lump' contain in their extensions a different one of the many stages in the region than do some precisifications of 'statue'. The supertruth conditions should reflect a kind of 'penumbral connection' (in the sense of Fine 1975) between 'the statue' and 'the lump': 'for every admissible precisification of "statue" and every *corresponding* admissible precisification of "lump" . . .'.

thus means that the lump (= the statue) has a lump counterpart tomorrow. When we denote that same object by the term 'the statue', this triggers the use of the statue counterpart relation. (S) means that the statue (= the lump) has no statue counterpart tomorrow. This is all consistent with the identity of the statue and the lump. Here I have again exploited the analogy between the stage view and modal counterpart theory: Lewis (1971) has accounted for contingent identity in a parallel way using multiple counterpart relations.[41]

The case of Tibbles and Tib is similar. The identification of Tibbles with Tib after detachment of the tail seems precluded by the apparent truth of the following claims:

Tibbles once had a tail.

Tib never had a tail.

The stage-theoretic solution is that the first sentence claims that Tibbles has *cat* counterparts with tails, whereas the second claims that Tib has no *torso* counterparts with tails.

The case of fission has a particularly nice resolution. The original puzzle was that both branch persons, Fred and Ed, seem to matter to the original person, Ted; the principle that identity is what matters then seems to imply that each will be identical to Ted. A resolution appealing to coincident spacetime worms was provided, but the stage theorist can do better. He can say that there is only one person before fission, namely Ted; that Ted will be identical to Ed; *and* that Ted will be identical to Fred! This seems like the right thing to say about the case: the person about to divide *will be* the one branch, and it is also true that he will be the other. This does not imply the paradoxical conclusion that the branch persons Fred and Ed are identical to each other. To say that Ted will be identical to Ed is to say that Ted has a future (person) counterpart that is identical to Ed. More simply, it is to say that Ed is Ted's counterpart. To say that Ted will be identical to Fred is to say that Fred is Ted's counterpart. But this does not imply that Ed is Fred, provided a person can have two distinct temporal counterparts at a single time in the future.

---

[41] I claim that I am identical to an *instantaneous* stage, and also that I will exist for more than an instant—how can I have it both ways? When I say that a 'stage' is instantaneous and so will not exist tomorrow, I am denying that it is *stage-counterpart* related to any stage in the future; the stage-counterpart relation is that of identity. When I say that 'I' will exist tomorrow, I mean that I have *person-counterparts* that exist tomorrow.

This resolution is particularly welcome given a difficulty in Lewis's resolution of the case, which was brought out originally by Parfit (1976), and which I reconstruct somewhat differently as follows. The Section 1 argument for coincidence based on fission (and the arguments from fusion and longevity as well) appealed to (=WM):

(=WM) Person x matters to person y iff x is identical to y.

I said that since *each branch preserves what matters to **someone***, (=WM) implies that there were two persons all along. But in fact, in addition to the italicized sentence, the following may be argued to be true:

(*) For any person beforehand, x, each of the post-fission persons, Fred and Ed, matters to x.

Between *any* initial pre-fission person and either Fred or Ed there hold the same intrinsic relations as in a non-branching case where only a single hemisphere of the original person survives. What matters is preserved in the non-branching case; since mattering is an intrinsic relation it must hold between any pre-fission person in the branching case and either Fred or Ed as well. (*) therefore is true. But (*) is inconsistent with Lewis's account of the fission case, given (=WM). According to Lewis, Ed exists beforehand; by (*), Fred afterwards matters to Ed; by (=WM) we have the conclusion that Fred = Ed, which Lewis must reject since Fred and Ed are, on his view, distinct spacetime worms.

In 'Survival and Identity' (1983*a*), Lewis claims to have reconciled the principle that identity is what matters with the idea that both branches preserve what matters by claiming that the I-relation (that is, the genidentity, or unity relation for persons) holds between pre-fission stages and stages on *both* branches.[42] If the mattering relation in question were a relation over *stages* this would perhaps be adequate, for in that case the thesis that identity is what matters and the principle that each branch preserves what matters would become, not (=WM) and (*), but rather the following theses:

- Stage x matters to stage y iff stages x and y stand in the I-relation.
- Stages of Fred matter to stages of Ted; and stages of Ed matter to stages of Ted.

[42] Lewis actually discusses the view that relation R is what matters, where R is a relation of psychological continuity and connectedness; but the issues are parallel for any view on which each branch preserves what matters.

Given that the I-relation need not be both transitive and symmetric, no contradiction would result. But Lewis's goal was to reconcile the *common-sense* platitude, as he puts it, that identity is what matters, with the idea that each of the branches preserves what matters. If the platitude is to be one of common sense, it must concern a mattering relation that applies to *persons*. For Lewis, persons are spacetime worms, not stages. In that case, the platitude and the claim that both branches matter must be cashed out as (=WM) and (*) above, and the solution collapses.

Lewis's response to Parfit in the postscript to his paper 'Survival and Identity', as I understand it, is that (=WM) is false. As he puts it (1983*a*: 74): '[A single person stage shared by Ed and Fred before division] does the thinking for both of the continuants to which it belongs. Any thought it has must be shared. It cannot desire one thing on behalf of [Ed] and another thing on behalf of [Fred].' I responded to this objection on behalf of Parfit in Sider (1996*a*); I would like now to take up the matter again. Lewis's claim seems to be that since Ed cannot desire anything uniquely on behalf of himself, we cannot say that Ed, but not Fred, matters to Ed; therefore, (=WM) is false. This is conceding defeat. The goal was to say that identity is what matters. But this requires that what happens to *another* person cannot matter to me. So if, as Lewis seems to be claiming, *both* what happens after fission to Ed and what happens then to Fred matter to Ed before fission (and also to Fred), then the goal of preserving the common-sense platitude that identity is what matters has not been reached. Lewis's argument seems to be that if we consider his description of the situation, we will see that (=WM) is false. But isn't that just to concede that his description of the situation violates the common-sense platitude?

Moreover, we can restate Parfit's argument so that it is invulnerable to Lewis's observations about Ed's desires. My earlier attempt (1996*a*: 436) was to argue that we have a concept of rational self-interested concern that is independent of what we are capable of desiring, and therefore that Ed's inability to *desire* anything uniquely on his own behalf is no impediment to Ed's being uniquely concerned, in the relevant sense, with Ed. But such a notion of concern, so divorced from desiring, may be regarded as too distant from ordinary belief to provide a basis for theory choice, so I will introduce a new example. Let us consider fusion, not fission, and let the relevant principles concern responsibility for a past crime, rather than concern. The common-sense platitude that no person can be held responsible for another's crime must be reconciled with the evident truth that the person who results from fusion seems responsible for crimes committed by either of the branches. And now the relevant attitude—responsibility—is not one that must be underwritten by anything like desire. There is, therefore, no room for a response like that in Lewis's postscript. Lewis can still, of course, say that once his description of fusion is appreciated, we will see that there is no impediment to punishing the resulting person for crimes of one of the original branches, despite the fact that this means punishing an innocent person (the innocent branch, who now shares stages with the guilty branch; of course, the guilty person is punished along with the innocent one). But this is simply giving up on, not preserving, the common-sense platitude that a person cannot be held responsible for crimes she did not commit. It would be better to preserve the platitudes.

As argued above, the stage theorist can indeed preserve the platitudes. She must simply hold in the fission case that a stage can have two temporal counterparts at a single future time, and in the fusion case that two distinct stages can share a common counterpart in the future. The principle that identity is what matters, and the principle that both branches preserve what matters, will be understood by the stage theorist as follows:

- Person x matters to an earlier person, y, iff x *was* identical to y.
- Ed matters to Ted; Fred matters to Ted.

In the fission case these claims imply that Ed was identical to Ted and that Fred was identical to Ted; it does not follow that Fred is identical to Ed.

The stage theorist can avoid admitting coincident persons in the longevity case by admitting intransitive counterpart relations. Return to Parfit's everlasting bodies, and consider persons P_{1700}, P_{1800}, and P_{1900}, which are, according to the stage theorist, three distinct stages, existing at times 1700, 1800, and 1900. The puzzle was driven by the assumption that mattering extends over intervals of up to, but not more than, 137 years. The following claims follow:

P_{1800} matters to P_{1700}

P_{1900} matters to P_{1800}

P_{1900} does not matter to P_{1700}

Then by the stage-theoretic version of the principle that identity is what matters, it follows that:

P_{1700} will be identical to P_{1800}

P_{1800} will be identical to P_{1900}

P_{1700} will not be identical to P_{1900}

But the latter three claims do not violate the transitivity of identity. They are, syntactically, the results of applying tense operators to identity statements; on analysis they become:

P_{1800} is a counterpart of P_{1700}

P_{1900} is a counterpart of P_{1800}

P_{1900} is not a counterpart of P_{1700}

The final triad is consistent, provided the counterpart relation can be intransitive.

Finally let us consider the cases of vague and conventional identity. We were driven to accept coincident entities to account for *multiple candidates*, candidates among which singular terms were indeterminate in reference, in the case of vagueness, and equally acceptable but unchosen candidates for reference, in the case of conventionality. The stage view allows us to provide the requisite candidates but still avoid coincidence: the candidates are different counterpart relations. We can attribute the vagueness in whether the original restaurant B_0 is identical to B_1 or B_2 to indeterminacy in which counterpart relation to use in evaluating claims like: 'Restaurant B_1 was restaurant B_0.' And we can attribute the element of conventionality in identifying one club with another to the existence of equally good alternative counterpart relations to the one chosen counterpart relation used in evaluating tensed claims about clubs.

The stage theorist can resist the arguments for coincident entities in all of the puzzle cases we have discussed. All competing theories, as argued above, fail to do away with coincidence in at least some cases, or deny deeply held beliefs about persistence. This, then, is a powerful argument in favor of the stage view, and hence of its presupposed ontology, four-dimensionalism.

A common complaint against the worm theory is that it provides a solution only to the temporal versions of the paradoxes of coincidence, whereas many of the puzzles have interesting modal versions. The worm theory on its own cannot explain the apparent modal differences between Gibbard's Lump1 and Goliath, since Lump1 and Goliath stage-share at every moment at which either exists and hence seem to be the very same spacetime worm. Either the argument in favor of coincidence must be resisted, or some alternate explanation of coincidence must be given. But admitting either of these alternatives would undermine the case for temporal parts, which is in part based on the rejection of alternative responses to the paradoxes of coincidence.[43]

Given the stage view, however, a single unified treatment of the paradoxes, both temporal and modal, is possible. That account is thoroughly counterpart-theoretic. We have already met the counterpart-theoretic solution to the modal statue and lump puzzle (Ch. 4, Sect. 8); the counterpart-theoretic solution to the modal paradox of undetached parts will be discussed in Chapter 6, Section 4. The other puzzles also have familiar modal analogs. All these modal puzzles can be resolved with modal counterpart theory just as the temporal puzzles have been resolved with temporal counterpart theory. Unlike a worm theorist, then, a stage theorist need not 'shift gears' when moving to the modal case. It is satisfying that the same medicine cures what appears to be the same disease. Some, of course, do not like counterpart theory, especially modal counterpart theory. Van Inwagen (1990*b*), as we will see in Chapter 6, Section 4, opposes four-dimensionalism by arguing that it implies (modal) counterpart theory! Many share this attitude towards modal counterpart theory; it is a philosophical bogeyman of the first magnitude, as bad as solipsism or logical positivism. But what is the problem? Counterpart theory does not require the modal realism defended by its most visible advocate, David Lewis (1986*a*); it is consistent with a number of views about the metaphysics of possible worlds and individuals (e.g. that defended in Sider 2000*b*).[44] Set aside this guilt by association; and set aside the Humphrey objection that has already been addressed. What is the big deal?

Perhaps the big deal is, paradoxically, counterpart theory's greatest strength. Dean Zimmerman has suggested to me that counterpart theory's flexibility in solving modal and temporal puzzles—the very feature that makes it attractive in the present context—is what lies behind pervasive

---

[43] See Burke (1994*a*: 593–4); Rea (1995).

[44] This point is made in Stalnaker (1986) (van Inwagen is fully aware of the point; see his 1990*b*: 254.)

queasiness about counterpart theory. 'So you have conflicting intuitions about *de re* modality or temporality? The conflict is only apparent, since the intuitions concern different counterpart relations. In fact, I can produce a counterpart relation corresponding to any intuition you might have!' Perhaps these words of the counterpart theorist make life too easy. Perhaps one of our deeply held beliefs about modality and temporality is that there is always a *single, univocal, non-conventional* answer to the questions 'What will happen to this thing tomorrow?' 'What might have happened to this thing?' The counterpart theorist must admit that pretty much any answer to these questions could, in principle, be correct, given an appropriate choice of a counterpart relation. Actual spoken languages may well have significant restrictions on what counterpart relations are chosen, and it need not be that an individual speaker has the freedom to choose whatever counterpart relation she likes. Nevertheless, it seems that a counterpart theorist cannot accept the existence of 'deep', 'non-conventional' facts about *de re* persistence and modality.

But the non-existence of such facts is precisely the moral of the puzzles of persistence and their modal analogs. Suppose I point to a lump of clay/statue and ask 'will *it* survive being squashed?' Must this question have a 'deep', univocal, non-conventional answer? Must this question: 'Did Bookbinder's survive as Bookbinder's Seafood House or The old original Bookbinder's'? Or consider Terence Parsons's (1987) pile of trash lying on the road for a day, undergoing partial but not total replacement of constituent refuse. Is the pile of trash at the end of the day the same as the pile of trash there at the beginning? When we consider these cases, our overwhelming feeling is surely that the answers to the questions depend on how we conceptualize the objects involved, that the world does not force single answers upon us. Any pre-reflective belief to the contrary is a casualty of philosophical reflection, disappearing once the puzzle cases are taken seriously.

If it is counterpart theory that really does the work in solving the paradoxes of coincidence, might four-dimensionalism be dispensed with? Might counterpart theory be combined with three-dimensionalism? We have already met one theory that pretty much amounts to a three-dimensionalist counterpart theory: Chisholm's theory of *entia successiva*. Its problem, as noted above, is that the *real* persistence enjoyed by mereological sums would trump the claim of counterpart-theoretic persistence to be referred to by ordinary talk of persistence.

A certain kind of presentist, on the other hand, could be a temporal counterpart theorist and avoid the trumping argument. Suppose the presentist accepts only primitive '*de dicto*' or 'qualitative' tenses—tense operators whose scope cannot contain proper names, demonstratives, indexicals, or quantified-in variables. Ersatz past and future individuals could then be constructed using purely qualitative formulas and the tenses, just as an actualist can construct ersatz possible individuals using qualitative formulas and the modal operators.[45] The open formula '*x* is a farmer & *x* lives on the moon & . . .' would represent a future possible individual iff the following tensed claim is true: 'WILL $\exists x$ (*x* is a farmer & *x* lives on the moon & . . .)'. A temporal counterpart relation could then be introduced over these ersatz past and future individuals, and sentences ascribing *de re* temporal predication, for example '$\exists x$ WAS (*x* is a boy)', could be analyzed using temporal counterpart theory.

Why the restriction to qualitative tenses? Because otherwise the primitive tenses on their own would suffice for the truth values of *de re* temporal predications, and counterpart theory would be superfluous. The primitive tenses would trump counterpart theory's claim to give the meaning of temporal predication, just as did the genuine persistence of 3D sums according to the mereological essentialist. (A similar trumping argument, it seems to me, shows that the primitive modal operators of an actualist counterpart theorist must be *de dicto*.) This sort of presentist would avoid the trumping argument against mereological essentialism, because given the abandonment of primitive *de re* temporal predication, counterpart-theoretic persistence would be 'as good as it gets'. No presentist I know of accepts this limitation of the tenses, but I see no obstacle to its imposition. Nor do I see any obstacle to this version of counterpart theory other than the underlying presentism. But that, as argued in Chapter 2, is obstacle enough.

---

[45] See Lewis (1986*a*: 148–50).

CHAPTER 6

Arguments against Four-Dimensionalism

In ontology, positions are supported by refuting the positions of others. There is nothing wrong with this. Rational belief requires assessing one's alternatives and selecting the most palatable, or least unpalatable. Chapter 5 was an unabashed argument by elimination, in which I gleefully shot down four-dimensionalism's competitors. But sooner or later one's own turn comes around; objections to one's own position must be faced. In the present chapter I will attempt to answer some of the most formidable, or at least most influential, objections to four-dimensionalism.

Complete vindication is not to be hoped for; every position has its drawbacks. But when all the arguments are in, in the end I think the balance favors four-dimensionalism. Of course, no objective measuring stick exists for these matters. For each argument my goal will be to assess the intellectual cost of maintaining four-dimensionalism. I leave to the reader the final reckoning.

1. LINGUISTIC AND EPISTEMIC OBJECTIONS[1]

As articulated in Chapter 3, four-dimensionalism is a *metaphysical* thesis about the nature of persisting objects. It is *not* a thesis about language, nor about the analysis of predicates of continuants, nor about the conceptual epistemic priority of predicates of stages and predicates of continuants. (The question within the four-dimensionalist camp of whether ordinary terms refer to spacetime worms or stages *is* a question

---

[1] See also Graham (1977).

about language. The objections discussed in this section do not concern that issue.) Several common objections to four-dimensionalism are therefore misguided, at least as applied to four-dimensionalism as I conceive it. P. T. Geach, for example, objects to four-dimensionalism by complaining about four-dimensionalists like Quine who analyze sentences of the form $\ulcorner x$ is F at $t\urcorner$ as involving a subject term for a stage, $\ulcorner x$ at $t\urcorner$, and a predicate F.[2] Whatever the merits of the objection, it does not apply to four-dimensionalism as such, for one's metaphysical account of the nature of persistence is separable from one's analysis of temporal language. A four-dimensionalist could follow Geach in construing $\ulcorner x$ is F at $t\urcorner$ as a predication of $\ulcorner$ is F at $t\urcorner$ to subject x, but then go on to give a metaphysical account of the truth of such a predication in terms of stages.

One also hears the complaint that predicates of stages cannot be defined without reference to continuants. This, too, need not embarrass the four-dimensionalist, who claims merely that temporal parts exist, not that one vocabulary is analytically prior to another. A worm theorist is under no obligation to translate person-predicates, for example 'believes that snow is white', into predicates of stages. Persons are composed of subatomic particles, but few think that language about persons can or should be translated into the language of physics. Facts about persons may well supervene on physical facts, and facts about continuants may well supervene on facts about stages, but the objection provides no reason to doubt supervenience. (The stage theorist has an even easier time with the objection, since for him, predicates of stages *are* predicates of continuants.)

Just as the four-dimensionalist is not committed to thinking that stage-vocabulary is analytically prior to continuant-vocabulary, the four-dimensionalist is also not committed to regarding stages as being epistemically prior to continuants. It is sometimes urged against four-dimensionalism that we cannot 'individuate' stages without making

---

[2] Geach (1972b: 308–11); Quine (1960: 173). The dialectic is actually a bit more complicated: Geach is arguing that the argument from change *for* four-dimensionalism is undermined by the implausibility of the Quinean analysis. Chisholm (1976, app. A) rebuts the argument from change in a somewhat similar fashion, by arguing that the temporal parts theorist cannot provide a definition of genidentity relations purely in terms of facts about stages, but must presuppose in that definition the concept of a continuing thing. But the temporal parts resolution of the problem of change (see Ch. 4, Sect. 6) does not depend on a reductive analysis of genidentity; it only requires the existence of temporal parts.

reference to continuants, by which it is meant, I suppose, that we could not pick out particular stages unless we had the ability to pick out particular continuants, whereas the converse does not hold.[3] But this argument is a *non sequitur*; its epistemic premise concerning our ability to pick out particular temporal parts lends no support whatsoever to its metaphysical conclusion that temporal parts do not exist. One might just as well argue that electrons do not exist because our ability to identify particular electrons asymmetrically depends on our ability to identify particular macroscopic objects.

Another point sometimes urged against four-dimensionalism is that natural language contains a distinction between things, on one hand, and processes or events on the other.[4] A process, for example a symphony, *occurs*. Processes have temporal parts—a symphony has first and second halves. But we do not say that a person is occurring or happening; we say rather that she *exists*. Nor do we say that a person has a first or second half. Things *change*; processes *are* changes, but do not themselves change. A thing *exists at* various times, whereas a process *lasts* from one time until another. A process *begins* and *ends*, whereas it makes no sense to speak of a thing as beginning or ending; things *come into*, and *go out of* existence. We pick up baseballs, but it sounds strange to say that we pick up events. Four-dimensionalism, it is argued, does not respect this deep difference between thing-talk and process-talk, because four-dimensionalists tend to place events and things in the same ontological category. As C. D. Broad (1923: 393) puts it, 'A thing . . . is simply a long event, throughout the course of which there is either qualitative similarity or continuous qualitative change, together with a characteristic spatio-temporal unity'. In the words of Nelson Goodman (1951: 357), 'a thing is a monotonous event; an event is an unstable thing'.

This difference between thing-talk and process-talk in no way undermines four-dimensionalism. It is consistent with things and events being in the same ontological category that natural language contains different ways of speaking of things and events. Natural language contains different vocabulary for speaking of persons and inanimate physical

---

[3] Compare Strawson's (1959, ch. 1) notion of a basic particular.

[4] See Mellor (1981, esp. 8–10); Wiggins (1980: 25 n. 12); Strawson (1959: 56–7). Broad (1933: 142–51) discusses the apparent difference between thing-talk and process-talk, though he does not accept a corresponding metaphysical distinction.

objects, but this is no argument against materialism. Nor is the oddness of saying that my thought is spatially located in my brain a compelling argument against the mind-brain identity theory. The objection might have bite if four-dimensionalism were a thesis of ordinary language philosophy, but it seems ineffective against the metaphysical thesis I uphold.

Let us turn to more metaphysical objections.

2. THE NO-CHANGE OBJECTION

In *Principles of Mathematics* (1903, sect. 442), Bertrand Russell says: 'Change is the difference, in respect of truth or falsehood, between a proposition concerning an entity and a time *T* and a proposition concerning the same entity and another time *T'*, provided that the two propositions differ only by the fact that *T* occurs in the one where *T'* occurs in the other.' Russell has in mind propositions like these:

The poker is hot on Monday.

The poker is hot on Tuesday.

If these propositions differ in truth value, then according to Russell the poker changes. The poker changes because it is hot *at* one time, but not hot at another.

For someone like Russell who accepts the B-theory of time (eternalism + the reducibility of tense), this is the natural account of change to give. Four-dimensionalists typically accept the B-theory and this account of change, and add an account of what it is for a poker to be hot at a particular time: it is for the poker's temporal part at the time to be hot *simpliciter*. The poker thus changes from hot to cold by first having a hot temporal part, then a cold one. Change is qualitative variation between the distinct temporal parts of an object.

In *The Nature of Existence*, as a part of a general attempt to prove that time is unreal J. M. E. McTaggart argued that a B-theory of time is inconsistent with the possibility of change. An important part of this argument is an attempted refutation of Russell's theory of change. His arguments are not particularly directed at the temporal parts version of the theory, but they do apply to it. The many arguments from change against temporal parts that have appeared in the literature since volume ii of *The Nature of Existence* appeared in 1927 have been, largely, echoes of McTaggart; his arguments thus form an important starting-point for our discussion.[5] Here McTaggart states the Russellian theory of change, then goes on to criticize it:

> If my poker, for example, is hot on a particular Monday, and never before or since, . . . the poker changes, because there is a time when this event is happening to it, and a time when it is not happening to it.
>
> But this makes no change in the qualities of the poker. It is always a quality of that poker that it is one which is hot on that particular Monday. And it is always a quality of that poker that it is one which is not hot at any other time. Both these qualities are true of it at any time—the time when it is hot and the time when it is cold. And therefore it seems to be erroneous to say that there is any change in the poker. The fact that it is hot at one point in a series and cold at other points cannot give change, if neither of these facts change . . .
>
> Let us consider the case of another sort of series. The meridian of Greenwich passes through a series of degrees of latitude. And we can find two points in this series, S and S', such that the proposition 'At S the meridian of Greenwich is within the United Kingdom' is true, while the proposition 'at S' the meridian of Greenwich is within the United Kingdom' is false. But no one would say that this gave us change. Why should we say so in the case of the other series? (1927, ch. XXXIII, sects. 315–16).

This passage contains two distinguishable arguments, which we might call the *argument from unchanging facts* and the *argument from spatial analogy*. Let us discuss them in turn.

The argument from unchanging facts is that things cannot change unless the facts change; but if the poker is hot *at* a particular time then it is always true that it is hot *at that time*; therefore, B-facts like that expressed by the sentence 'The poker is hot on Monday' do not change, and so neither does the poker. If the B-theory of time is true, the same is true for all facts about the poker, and so the poker would not change; nor would anything else. This is what people have in mind when they say that the four-dimensional universe is 'static':

> The [enduring] individual, Venus, moves in an ellipse about the sun. The [perduring] individual, Venus, does not move at all (rather, could not significantly be said either to move or not to move); it occupies a four-dimensional helix lying

---

[5] See Geach (1972*b*, sect. 10.2); Lombard (1986: 108–9); Mellor (1981: 110–11); Simons (1987: 126, 134–7).

about the world line of the sun. . . . In passing from a [perdurance]-language to an [endurance]-language we pass from a four-dimensional manifold of *change-less* individuals to a three-dimensional manifold of individuals enduring through time. (Wilson 1955: 590)

McTaggart's second argument is that the Russellian theory of change makes genuine change too much like spatial variation. No one says that the relative locations of the Greenwich meridian and the United Kingdom change, and no one says that a poker that is hot at one end but cold at another is thereby changing. But on the Russellian theory, change is the instantiation of different properties *at* different times, and is thus analogous to these cases of the instantiation of different properties *at* different places.

The analogy between spatial variation and genuine change becomes even closer if temporal parts are brought into the picture. A poker that is hot at one end and cold at another has a hot spatial part and a cold spatial part; the temporal parts theorist says that the poker changes by having a hot temporal part and a cold temporal part. The difference between merely spatial variation and four-dimensional change, according to the argument, is vanishingly small.

These McTaggartian arguments contain no subtle fallacy, no hidden technical mistake, and there is no reply making use of elaborate distinctions or theory. The objections may simply be met head-on. Change *is* analogous to spatial variation. Change *does* occur in virtue of unchanging facts about temporal parts. There are no good arguments to the contrary.

McTaggart says that the poker does not change unless the facts about it change. Let us use the term 'fact' so that he is right that the facts do not change. Thus, the fact that the poker is hot on Monday but not on Tuesday does not change. What is the barrier to saying that the poker itself changes? It always has been the case, and always will be the case, that the poker is hot on Monday; likewise, it always has been and always will be the case that the poker is cold on Tuesday. It seems natural to conclude that the poker thereby changes, since it is first hot and afterwards cold. We could add for good measure that this fact about the changing of the poker, like all other facts about the poker, does not change: it always has and always will be the case that the poker changes between Monday and Tuesday. Change *just is* variation in the (intrinsic) properties of a thing between one time and another.

(Incidentally, McTaggart's decision about how to use the term 'fact' seems to some degree arbitrary. Even the B-theorist admits that some *sentences* change in truth value, for example 'It is raining in Syracuse now'. Other sentences do not, for example the sentence 'It is raining in Syracuse at 12 a.m., on 30 October 2000'. Suppose we say that the latter sort of sentence expresses an *eternal proposition*, and, when true, an *eternal fact*. The former sort of sentence is associated with what I called in Chapter 2, Section 1 a temporal proposition: a function from times to eternal propositions, in this case the function that assigns to any time *t* the eternal proposition that it is raining in Syracuse at *t*. A temporal proposition is true at a time iff the value of that function, for that time, is true *simpliciter*. Call a true temporal proposition a *temporal fact*. Which are The Facts, the eternal facts or the temporal ones? I doubt there is a single correct answer.)

The objector might press a slightly different objection. Since it is the temporal part that is, in the first instance, hot, the poker itself is neither hot nor cold. This should be granted: a spacetime worm is neither hot *simpliciter* nor cold *simpliciter*, but is rather hot or cold *at times*. But, the objector might say, why should we apply the predicate 'hot' to the worm at all, when it is only a temporal part of the worm that is hot?

This version of the objection obviously fails when applied to the stage view of Chapter 5, Section 8; it is only the worm-theoretic version of four-dimensionalism that is potentially threatened. But even that theory has little to fear. Any philosophical theory of persistence, change, property instantiation, and related matters must save the appearances. What is certain is that things persist, somehow, that things change, somehow, and that things have properties at times, somehow. It is not part of reasonable common belief just how this occurs. The worm theory provides one picture of how this occurs, and it preserves the core of our ordinary beliefs in the neighborhood. It provides a conception of persistence (temporally extended spacetime worms), instantiation of 'properties at times' (instantiation of properties by slices), and persistence through change (worms with dissimilar segments). Ordinary belief contains a role for changing things, and the four-dimensional candidates satisfy that role in a way that involves little (if any) departure from our pre-analytic thoughts about changing things. Given the best-candidate conception of content (see the Introduction to this book), four-dimensionalism therefore provides an acceptable theory of change.

(Provided there are no better candidates, that is. If there were wholly present entities, the best candidate for change might involve them. In this section I am not trying to *establish* perdurance, only to reply to the objection that if objects did perdure then they would not change.)

Similar to the no-change objection is the no-persistence objection: if objects perdure then they do not *really* persist over time, 'real' persistence presumably requiring an object to be wholly present whenever it exists. The response is likewise similar: perdurance best fills the persistence-role in ordinary thought, which is all it takes to be genuine persistence.

Let us focus next on McTaggart's second argument, the complaint that four-dimensionalism collapses spatial variation and genuine change. The four-dimensionalist ought to grant that spatial variation *is* in many ways analogous to temporal change; it is unclear why this should be thought problematic. We *do* sometimes use the language of change for spatial variation, when we speak of a road becoming bumpier as one travels in a certain direction, for example. Perhaps talk of change is somewhat more natural in the temporal case, but the four-dimensionalist has a simple explanation: it is because the dimension of variation in that case is temporal rather than spatial. (Some then reply that this explanation is legitimate only if we have some independent method for distinguishing time and space, and that no such method is available to a B-theorist.[6] I do not accept this argument. The B-theorist can distinguish between time and space in other ways, for example by appealing to entropy or the structure of the laws of nature. The distinction might even be primitive. But a detailed discussion of these issues in the philosophy of time is not something I will take up here.)

3.   A CRAZY METAPHYSIC

Another objection comes from the following influential paragraph by Judith Jarvis Thomson (1983: 213), discussing the metaphysic of temporal parts:

. . . this seems to me a crazy metaphysic. It seems that its full craziness comes out only when we take the [analogy between spatial parts and temporal parts]

---

[6] See the first part of Mellor (1981, ch. 6) for a description of this sort of argument.

seriously. The metaphysic yields that if I have had exactly one bit of chalk in my hand for the last hour, then there is something in my hand which is white, roughly cylindrical in shape, and dusty, something which also has a weight, something which is chalk, which was not in my hand three minutes ago, and indeed, such that no part of it was in my hand three minutes ago. As I hold the bit of chalk in my hand, new stuff, new chalk keeps constantly coming into existence *ex nihilo*. That strikes me as obviously false.

The four-dimensionalist does indeed claim that the piece of chalk has a temporal part at every moment at which it exists, and that those temporal parts are white, cylindrical, and dusty. But in saying that temporal parts come into existence *ex nihilo*, Thomson makes it sound as if a *miracle* is constantly occurring. That isn't right. The sensible four-dimensionalist will claim that current temporal parts are caused to exist by previous temporal parts. The laws that govern this process are none other than the familiar laws of motion. A law of motion *just is* a law which guarantees the future existence of temporal parts given previous temporal parts (see Sect. 5 for a further discussion). Thus, if emergence *ex nihilo* is understood as uncaused or inexplicable emergence, Thomson is mistaken; and it is unclear what other sense these words may be given on which the argument is compelling.[7]

Thomson's argument, moreover, is subject to the following *tu quoque*. Why don't enduring particles just stop existing? Thomson ought to respond that the laws of motion ensure continued existence. But if this explanation is acceptable, so should be the response of the four-dimensionalist.

The temporal procession of temporal parts is analogous to the spatial procession of spatial parts one gets by running the mind's eye across any extended object, a branch of a tree, say. At the left end of the branch we begin with a certain spatial part, which 'ceases' to exist as we focus our

---

[7] Heller (1990) and Oderberg (1993: 86) make similar responses to Thomson. Heller (1984, 1990, ch. 1, sect. 8) and Paulo Dau (1986: 470–1) suggest a further response, that Thomson's objection is based on combining temporal parts with a 'three-dimensional' picture, on which objects 'exist at' instants rather than 'through' regions. I am not completely confident I understand these claims.

It is worth mentioning a question asked by C. Brock Sides: can the fact that temporal parts not only continually come into existence, but also subsequently *go out of existence*, be given a parallel nomic explanation? I suspect not. A possible alternate explanation is that temporal parts go out of existence 'automatically' since four-dimensionalism is a necessary truth.

attention on parts of the branch further to the right. Assuming the B-theory of time, our passage through time is analogous. 'The present' is simply a particular perspective in time, and other temporal parts of a present object are just as real as spatial parts of the branch other than the one of current focus. The succession of temporal parts we experience is simply a change in perspective, just like a change in perspective from left to right along the branch. (The analogy is only partial, however, since simultaneous spatially adjacent spatial parts of the branch are not causally related.)[8]

There are residual objections in the neighborhood. The succession of temporal parts has been shown to be law-governed, but one might regard the procession, implying as it does the existence of instantaneous objects, as being contrary to common sense, or as being unwarranted by the evidence. As for the former, it is quite clear that we do not typically speak of instantaneous objects, but nor do we speak of arbitrary spatial parts of ordinary objects, or of fusions of miscellaneous or scattered classes of objects. In each case, the strangeness of speaking of these things is adequately explained by their exclusion from ordinary domains of quantification. As for instantaneous objects being unwarranted by the evidence, *empirical* evidence seems neither to favor nor disfavor temporal parts (see the discussion of a Russellian argument for temporal parts in Ch. 4, Sect. 1, and the discussion of temporal parts and relativity in Sect. 4 of that chapter). As for philosophical evidence, that is the topic of this book. I think it favors four-dimensionalism. Perhaps ordinary thought contains disbelief in temporal parts. This might count as a defeasible reason against them. But no such belief seems very strong. Moreover, it is not clear that it always exists: in my experience, unprejudiced folks seem to find the idea of temporal parts a natural one.

4.   THE MODAL ARGUMENT

The next argument is that sums of temporal parts have the wrong modal properties to be identified with everyday continuants. It was argued in Chapter 5, Section 8 that the strongest version of four-dimensionalism identifies continuants with stages rather than spacetime worms, and it

---

[8] Cf. also Dau (1986: 470).

will become apparent that the modal argument has no force against the stage view. Nevertheless, I wish to rebut the argument anyway, for my defense of the stage view is more tentative than my defense of four-dimensionalism in general. Moreover, I was forced to admit that in certain contexts we do refer to spacetime worms.[9]

The main defense of the modal argument is in Peter van Inwagen's paper 'Four-Dimensional Objects' (1990*b*).[10] Following van Inwagen, call an object *modally inductile* iff it could not possibly have existed longer than it in fact did. Van Inwagen's first version of the modal argument is the following:

> The [worm-theorist] will want to say that it would make no sense to say of the temporal part of Descartes that occupied the year 1620 that it might have had an extent of a year and a half. . . . We may summarize this point by saying that the [worm-theorist] will want to maintain that temporal parts are 'modally inductile' . . .
>
> But then the argument against [the worm theory] is almost embarrassingly simple. If [the worm theory] is correct, then Descartes is composed of temporal parts, and all temporal parts are modally inductile. But Descartes himself is one of his temporal parts—the largest one, the sum of all of them. But then Descartes is himself modally inductile, which means he could not have had a temporal extent greater than fifty-four years. But this is obviously false, and [the worm theory] is therefore wrong. (1990*b*: 253)

Van Inwagen claims that this and the next version of the argument may be answered only if one presupposes a counterpart-theoretic account of *de re* modality. Many would read between the lines here an unstated further conclusion: that since *sensible* people reject counterpart theory, sensible people should reject four-dimensionalism. As argued in Chapter 5, Section 8, the common distrust of counterpart theory is ungrounded; and below, the counterpart-theoretic solution to the problem of modal inductility is considered (and endorsed). However, the argument merits more scrutiny before the need for counterpart theory is evident.

We must first ask why van Inwagen's argument should be thought to succeed, given that the following spatial analog fails: as everyone believes, I am made up of spatial parts; my spatial parts, for example any of the electrons that compose me, have their spatial size essentially, that

---

[9] Much of my discussion overlaps with Mark Heller's excellent 'Varieties of Four Dimensionalism' (1993).

[10] See also Shoemaker (1988: 203–4).

is, are spatially modally inductile; I am one of my spatial parts; therefore I am spatially modally inductile. The parallel argument fails by moving too quickly from the observation that *certain* of my spatial parts—my electrons—are spatially modally inductile, to the conclusion that *all* of my spatial parts have this feature. Some of my parts do not have this feature; most notably, *I* do not have this feature. Similarly, van Inwagen argues by reasonably plausible examples that certain temporal parts of Descartes are modally inductile, namely, the year-long ones; it does not follow that all of his temporal parts are modally inductile.

The analogy between the temporal and spatial arguments might be denied on the grounds that all of Descartes's *proper* temporal parts are modally inductile, whereas not all of my spatial parts are spatially modally inductile—my hands, for example, might have been larger than they in fact are. (Van Inwagen himself would not accept the existence of my hands, but the objection has a life of its own.) There are two problems with this response. First, it is not entirely clear that all of a person's proper temporal parts are modally inductile. It seems plausible that my adolescence, for example, might have lasted longer than it in fact did. Granted, this *could* be understood as not involving a *de re* modal predication about my adolescence; the intuition we have here might be claimed to pertain to the *de dicto* claim that I might have had an adolescence that was longer than the adolescence that I in fact had. But it is not clear that the intuition *must* be thus understood. Secondly, this disanalogy does not rescue the temporal version of the argument. Even if *all* of Descartes's proper temporal parts are modally inductile, it still does not follow that Descartes himself is modally inductile. Perhaps every proper temporal part of a person is (partially) modally individuated by its time span; still, Descartes might have had more temporal parts, and thus might have lived longer.

Van Inwagen's second argument is a modal version of the temporal paradox of undetached parts (Ch. 5, Sect. 1). Imagine a world much like ours, but in which Descartes is destroyed at age 40. It seems that D, the object that in fact is Descartes's temporal part for the first 40 years, would have in that case still existed, as would Descartes himself. On pain of admitting distinct permanently coinciding objects, Descartes and D would then have been identical. But this violates the principle of the necessity of distinctness, for Descartes and D are in fact distinct.

Let D be all of Descartes save his left foot; Descartes might have existed even if his left foot hadn't; surely D would then have existed as well; but again, on pain of admitting permanently coinciding objects, D and Descartes would then have been identical, despite being, in the actual world, distinct. The argument here—from van Inwagen (1981, sect. 3) himself!—is parallel, but does not involve temporal parts.

Since what seems to be the very same paradox can be generated without the assumption of temporal parts, temporal parts are not to be blamed. I will not leave the response at this, for reasons that will emerge below. But the very first thing to keep in mind about this argument is that the modal version of the paradox of undetached parts confronts everyone, not just a defender of temporal parts. A reasonable attitude about this sort of modal paradox might be a bit like one attitude towards the liar paradox: 'well *that's* a difficult problem, and must be solved somehow, but until I learn how to solve the problem I will carry on believing what seems to be right on other grounds'.

Of course, the only feasible solution to the paradox might threaten something I believe. This is particularly likely if the believed proposition is intimately connected to the generation of the paradox. As we have seen, temporal parts do not seem intimately connected with the generation of the modal paradox of undetached parts. But matters are different for certain propositions presupposed in certain arguments *for* temporal parts, as I will explain.

As I said, the modal paradox of undetached parts is parallel to the temporal paradox of undetached parts. Solutions to one are therefore often solutions to the other. Here are some potential solutions to the modal puzzle of Descartes and his proper temporal part D; in parentheses I mention theorists discussed in Chapter 5 with parallel temporal views: (1) numerically distinct objects sometimes permanently coincide; if Descartes had been destroyed halfway through his life there would have been two distinct objects standing in the relation of constitution but not identity (Wiggins). (2) The principle of unrestricted summation is false; objects do not in general have arbitrary undetached temporal parts; D does not exist (van Inwagen). (3) Like (2), except that there are *no* fusions of instantaneous temporal parts (nihilists). (4) D would not have existed if the second half of Descartes had been lopped off (Burke). (5) Descartes is modally inductile (Chisholm).[11] Now, there is nothing inconsistent in offering any of these solutions to the modal paradox and

---

[11] Response(s) to van Inwagen's argument is explicitly endorsed by Mark Heller (1990, ch. 1, sect. 14, and ch. 2.)

simultaneously accepting four-dimensionalism. However, certain *arguments* for temporal parts would be undermined by some of these solutions. Example one: none of these solutions can be offered by someone who defends temporal parts as the basis of the best solution to the paradoxes of coincidence, as I did in Chapter 5, for that argument is premised on the rejection of the temporal analogs of the responses just canvassed. Typically (though not inevitably), a reason to reject a solution to the temporal version of one of these paradoxes is itself a reason to reject the modal version of the solution. Example two: if the principle of unrestricted composition is false then my argument from vagueness in Chapter 4, Section 9 for temporal parts presumably fails since it is closely parallel to an argument for unrestricted composition. Thus, no one who defends the argument from vagueness can solve the present puzzle by rejecting unrestricted composition. On the other hand, someone who believed in temporal parts on the basis of the problem of temporary intrinsics, or the analogy between time and space, or contemporary physics, could make use of many of these solutions, for example Wiggins-style acceptance of permanently co-located objects.

Van Inwagen does not conclude from the case of Descartes and D that four-dimensionalism is false, only that the best defense open to its defenders invokes counterpart theory. As I have said, there are other solutions available, none of which is inconsistent with four-dimensionalism, and only some of which are inconsistent with only some arguments for four-dimensionalism. And there may be unforeseen solutions to the paradox consistent with four-dimensionalism, given that temporal parts play no essential role in generating the paradox. Nevertheless, the best solution seems to be the counterpart-theoretic one. As argued in Chapter 5, the *temporal* versions of this and other paradoxes are best solved by temporal counterpart theory. Modal counterpart theory is therefore part of a unified front. Secondly, the arguments of that chapter against the competitors of temporal counterpart theory carry over in many cases to the competitors of modal counterpart theory. Thirdly, we need counterpart theory (or something a lot like it) to solve Gibbard's Lump1 and Goliath puzzle (see Ch. 4, Sect. 8). Fourthly, counterpart theory has so much else going for it; it is an attractive unified account of a wide range of modal phenomena. And fifthly, as argued in Chapter 5, Section 8, the common suspicion of counterpart theory is unfounded; there is no good reason not to accept it.

Counterpart theory does indeed supply the means to escape van Inwagen's argument. That argument appeals to the necessity of distinctness, in particular the claim that if Descartes and D are actually distinct then they are necessarily distinct. A typical argument for this claim runs as follows:

(i)	D ≠ Descartes	(Assume)
(ii)	□ ◊ (D ≠ Descartes)	(i)
(iii)	□ (D lacks the property of *being necessarily identical to Descartes*)	(ii)
(iv)	□ (Descartes has the property of *being necessarily identical to Descartes*)	(premise)
(v)	□ (any objects with different properties are distinct)	(Leibniz's Law)
(vi)	so, □ (D ≠ Descartes)	(iii, iv, v)

(Note the use of the Brouwersche principle that whatever is actual is necessarily possible in moving from (i) to (ii).) According to the counterpart theorist, the argument equivocates, since there is no one property *being necessarily identical to Descartes*. Something is necessarily identical to Descartes iff all its counterparts are counterparts of Descartes (I simplify by ignoring the possibility of multiple counterparts under a single counterpart relation). But the counterpart theorist will invoke different counterpart relations in different contexts of utterance. A counterpart relation is a similarity relation. Since there are different dimensions of similarity, there are different counterpart relations. We can distinguish a *person* (P-) counterpart relation from a *temporal part* (TP-) counterpart relation. The P-counterparts of a thing must be persons (that are appropriately similar to that thing); the TP-counterparts of a thing need not be (whole) persons, but must have the same temporal extent as that thing. Which counterpart relation we use in evaluating a *de re* modal claim generally depends on many factors, including features of the containing sentential context and extra-sentential features of the context of utterance. In the present case, the counterpart relation used in evaluating *de re* modal claims about Descartes can depend on the term used to denote him. For occurrences of 'Descartes', we use the P-counterpart relation; for occurrences of 'D' we use the TP-counterpart relation. Thus, lines (iii) and (iv) in the argument become, respectively:

(iii′) In any world, *w*, D's TP-counterpart, *x*, and Descartes's P-counterpart, *y*, are such that: *it is not the case that in any world w, x's TP-counterpart is identical to y's P-counterpart*

(iv′) In any world, *w*, Descartes's P-counterpart, *x*, and Descartes's P-counterpart, *y*, are such that: *in any world w′, x's P-counterpart is identical to y's P-counterpart*

But now, we cannot use Leibniz's Law to move from these premises to the translation of (vi):

(vi′) In any world *w*, D's TP-counterpart, *x*, is distinct from Descartes's P-counterpart, *y*

for the italicized condition laid down on *x* and *y* in (iv′) is different from that denied of *x* and *y* in (iii′).

Recall the point from Chapter 4, Section 8 that counterpart theory is not strictly needed to make this sort of response to van Inwagen. Any view on which modal predicates like 'being necessarily identical to Descartes' are equivocal, changing their reference depending on what they are attached to, would block the argument. Alternatively, one could claim that *de re* modal predications are univocal, accept the conclusion that Descartes is indeed modally inductile, but then go on to claim that ordinary intuitions about *de re* modality vary depending on what terms one uses to denote Descartes.[12] I prefer the counterpart theoretic response, but the others are reasonable as well.

5.   MOTION IN HOMOGENEOUS SUBSTANCES

For the temporal parts theorist, the world is a four-dimensional manifold of stages. The career of any persisting object is a sequence of instantaneous objects in this manifold—a path through spacetime. But it is only a small minority of paths through spacetime that correspond to careers of persisting objects. This point will be put differently by worm and stage theorists. The worm theorist will say that only a small minority of all the mereological sums of instantaneous stages count as continuants (objects of our ordinary ontology)—namely, those sums whose temporal parts stand in some 'unity' or 'genidentity' relation. The stage theorist will

---

[12] This is in fact Mark Heller's (1990) response to van Inwagen. See also Jubien (1993).

say that of all the paths through spacetime intersecting a given continuant (stage), only some of these paths include all and only that continuant's counterparts, where the relevant counterpart relation is just the worm theorist's genidentity relation.

Thus an integral part of any four-dimensionalist view is the genidentity relation. The question of the nature of that relation is generally separable from the question of whether temporal parts exist, but one objection to four-dimensionalism threatens to rule out the possibility of *any* criterion of genidentity.

By 'genidentity' let us here understand just the genidentity relation for matter: that relation that holds between stages iff they are parts of some continuing portion of matter. (This is how the worm theorist would put it. The stage theorist would call this relation the matter-counterpart relation—the counterpart relation relevant when thinking of an object as a hunk of matter. From now on I will simplify the discussion by pretending that the worm theory is true. Nothing turns on this.) It is natural to seek a reductive analysis of genidentity, for example the popular spatiotemporal continuity analysis on which (in its simplest form) stages are genidentical iff connected by a spatiotemporally continuous sequence of stages.

But imagine two duplicate, homogeneous, continuous, perfectly circular disks of uniform depth: one stationary, the other rotating. The genidentity relation must hold in different patterns among the temporal parts of the bits of the two disks: it must hold in straight lines through spacetime in the case of the stationary disk, and in a helical pattern in the case of the rotating disk. But this is impossible if genidentity is identified with spatiotemporal continuity, for the disks occupy duplicate, perfectly smoothly filled regions of spacetime that contain *both* straight and helical continuous sequences of stages.

The problem threatens other analyses of genidentity as well, for example those that supplement spatiotemporal continuity with momentary qualitative features (e.g. Hirsch 1982, chs. 1–2). And never mind analysis: the disks threaten claims of mere supervenience of genidentity on various factors. Let the disks be located in different possible worlds otherwise alike: since the disks occupy duplicate regions of spacetime there appears to be a difference in the holding of genidentity without a difference in other factors. One view thus threatened is David Lewis's (1994, 1986*b*, pp. ix–xvii) Humean Supervenience, according to which *all* facts, including facts about genidentity, supervene on the distribution of 'local qualities' throughout spacetime. But there is a more general challenge. What explains the difference between the disks?

The *three*-dimensionalist has an easy answer. There are no temporal parts, and so no genidentity relation, and so no need for an analysis of genidentity. The enduring parts of the disk will be located at different places depending on whether the disk rotates. Thus, the disks are distinguished by different patterns of occupation of spacetime points by their enduring material parts. Denis Robinson (1989: 400) objects to distinguishing the disks via differences in 'some non-qualitative, unifying, uniquely identifying characteristic or quasi-property, common to the different stages of the genuinely persisting individual', and goes on to say that 'Such "haecceitistic" views, real or imaginary, strike me as undesirable, indeed as bordering on unintelligibility'. But note that this is *not* what the endurantist does. The endurantist merely appeals to differing facts of occupation between enduring objects and spacetime points; no non-qualitative, haecceitistic identifying properties are needed. The four-dimensionalist cannot accept this story, and so faces the challenge of grounding the differences in the holding of the genidentity relation.

Someone who defended four-dimensionalism's truth in the actual world might claim that three-dimensionalism must be true at the disk worlds. But this would involve granting the possibility of endurance, and thus giving up on the possibility of purely conceptual arguments in favor of perdurance. Moreover, concerning persistence over time as it *actually* occurs, one would have thought it possible for there to be differences between rotating and non-rotating homogeneous disks. A four-dimensional solution must be sought.

The example of the rotating disk is Saul Kripke's, given in often cited but so far unpublished lectures; he also discusses an infinite homogeneous continuous river.[13] Contemporary discussion of this problem was stimulated by this and a similar case given by D. M. Armstrong (1980); but similar problems were discussed by Bertrand Russell (1914: 114–16, 1917, sect. xi), C. D. Broad (1925: 36–7), and even in Leibniz (1698, sect. 13). Russell and Armstrong give essentially the same solution, which many

[13] The arguments of Kripke and Armstrong are discussed in Lewis (1999, 1986*b*, p. xiii n. 5); Noonan (1988); Robinson (1989); Shoemaker (1979); and Zimmerman (1998*a*, 1999).

have followed since: the difference between the spinning and rotating disks is nomic/causal. According to Russell, a sequence of temporal parts counts as a continuant only if that sequence falls under a causal law, specifically a law of dynamics; according to Armstrong (1980: 77), a sequence of temporal parts is a continuant only if earlier stages are 'nomically required' for later stages. (The need for a causal or nomic requirement on genidentity relations is familiar for other reasons. As a number of philosophers have argued, spatiotemporal and qualitative continuity conditions are not sufficient on their own for genidentity since they may be satisfied 'accidentally', as in Armstrong's (1980: 76) example in which one deity destroys a certain person and another deity, by chance, creates a duplicate person at the precise place and time at which the first person was destroyed.)[14]

Whether this is the end of the story depends on the details of the causal account. Suppose that earlier stages of a continuant produce its later stages by means of a *sui generis* relation of 'immanent causation', whose holding does not depend in any way on other states of affairs, not even on the laws of nature.[15] This relation could differ between the two disks, and the problem would be solved. Of course, one would be giving up on Humean Supervenience, since immanent causation thus conceived would not supervene on the spatiotemporal arrangement of local qualities. More importantly, this 'singularism' about causation is hard to accept. The singularist postulates a relation between object stages, and tells us only negative things about it, that it reduces neither to laws nor to qualitative states of affairs. What then does it have to do with *causation*? And what does it have to do with genidentity?[16]

But as Dean Zimmerman (1998a, sect. V) has pointed out, if we abandon singularism and analyze causation in terms of the laws of nature, there is trouble. Consider a version of the example in which the disks inhabit the same possible world. The disks then obey the same laws. Moreover the temporal parts of the disks are qualitatively alike. But having set aside singularism, surely causal relations are determined by

---

[14] See also Armstrong (1997, sect. 7.23); Shoemaker (1979); Swoyer (1984).

[15] See Zimmerman (1997) for an extended discussion of 'immanent causation'; see Anscombe (1971) on singularism.

[16] A similar complaint applies to the postulation of a brute, non-supervenient genidentity relation. Either it is unclear what the relation has to do with genidentity, or one picks out the relation by its role in the laws of nature, in which case the proposal becomes like those discussed below.

the laws plus the qualitative features of the relata, in which case the parts of the disks will stand in the same causal relations.

It has been a presupposition so far that states of rotation do not themselves count as qualitative differences between the stages of the rotating and stationary disks. This presupposition is correct given the Russellian account of motion (discussed in Ch. 2, Sect. 2), on which velocity is not an intrinsic property of an object at a time, but is rather a matter of that object's locations at neighboring times. But if one accepted instead Tooley's non-reductionist theory of velocity, on which velocity is an irreducible vector quantity that is lawfully correlated with the first derivative of the position function, the disks become qualitatively distinguishable. One could then utilize these vector quantities in an account of genidentity, presumably via causal laws or causal relations governing those quantities. Note that the non-reductionist account of velocity is not really needed to solve the problem of the disk; all we need is that the vector quantities exist in the possible worlds containing the disks. Those vector quantities may be used in an account of genidentity (as in Denis Robinson 1989), and the Russellian theory of motion may be retained.[17] A related proposal would be that of Katherine Hawley (1999), to postulate a non-spatiotemporal external relation between stages in the worlds in question, which could be picked out by its role in the laws of nature, and which could be used in an account of genidentity.[18]

Dean Zimmerman has objected that Tooley and Robinson's vector quantities cannot be invoked non-circularly in an account of genidentity since the laws they use to pick out their vector quantities appear to involve genidentity (1998a: 282–4). Laws of dynamics do not hold of arbitrary sums of stages (e.g. the sum of my stages to date plus all future stages of a distant star), and must therefore be restricted to physical continuants, that is, *genidentity*-interrelated sums of stages. The circularity may be avoided, however, by conceiving of a law of dynamics (for example T_1, from Ch. 2, Sect. 3) as saying that if there is a stage located at a certain spacetime point, and that stage has a certain velocity, then

---

[17] I am indebted to David Lewis for this point.

[18] This isn't quite Hawley's response. First, Hawley invokes her relations in the *actual* world. Secondly, although Hawley claims that the relations ground causal relations and counterfactuals, it is not clear whether this is intended as a theoretical *definition* of the relations as those which play a certain nomic role.

there will exist other stages, whether genidentical or not, at appropriate places in the infinitesimal vicinity of the first stage. The vector quantity may then be picked out as that quantity that plays the role of velocity in this law, and may then be used non-circularly in an account of genidentity.[19] And Hawley's relation may be picked out as that relation R over stages such that there exist laws of dynamics governing R-interrelated sums of stages.

Thus, Tooley, Robinson, and Hawley can allow differences in rotation between homogeneous disks in possible worlds containing the quantities they postulate. Apparently, however, their quantities conflict with Humean Supervenience. Hawley's relations clearly do not supervene on the distribution of local qualities throughout spacetime. And as noted by Robinson (1989: 407–8), even if his irreducible vector quantities are instantiated by point-sized things, they seem not to be *local* qualities since they have *directions*; they appear to involve relations to points or lines or objects outside the point-particles (or points of spacetime) that instantiate them. Lewis (1999: 209) claims that the threat to Humean Supervenience here is no worse than that already posed by the vector fields of classical electromagnetism. I think the threat is more pressing, though, because electromagnetic vector fields may supervene on the existence of the charged point-particles that generate them.

Lewis's response to the rotating disk is to construe Humean Supervenience as a claim only about possible worlds in the 'inner sphere'—the set of worlds in which no 'alien' natural properties or relations are instantiated, that is, natural properties or relations not instantiated in the actual world. Within the inner sphere no two worlds can differ without differing in their distribution of local qualities; outside the inner sphere there can be alien natural relations or non-local alien natural properties whose instantiation can make a difference to the world without resulting in a difference in the distribution of local qualities (Lewis 1986*b*, pp. x–xiii). If Hawley's relation and Robinson and Tooley's vector quantities are not actually instantiated then worlds in which they are instantiated would be outside the inner sphere.

The upshot is that Hawley, Robinson, and Tooley have two options. Option 1: their non-Humean quantities are instantiated in the *actual* world, and are tied up with actual motion. Option 2: their non-Humean

---

[19] Compare Lewis (1999).

quantities are not actually instantiated, and thus allow differences in rotation between homogeneous disks only in worlds outside the inner sphere. Option 1 requires giving up Humean Supervenience since disk worlds differing only in the distribution of the non-Humean quantities would be located in the inner sphere. This should be avoided if possible. The whole point of defending Humean Supervenience is to avoid being pushed by philosophical arguments into making posits beyond those forced by physics (Lewis 1986*b*, p. xi). A physically conservative onto-logy would avoid Hawley, Robinson, and Tooley's quantities.

I would live with Option 2 if I had to. But Option 2 does not give me everything I would have liked. I would have thought that differences in rotation between homogeneous disks could have occurred in a world like *ours*. Obviously the homogeneity of the disks would require the world to be *somewhat* different from actuality. But intuitively, alien properties or relations should not be required. What would be really nice is a theory allowing differences in rotation between homogeneous disks in worlds without non-Humean quantities.

This is in fact the sort of theory I will defend. Let us begin with three elements. (1) Lewis's version of Frank Ramsey's best-system theory of laws (1973, sect. 3.3, 1986*c*, postscript C, 1994). On this view, a law of nature is a consequence of the deductively closed set of propositions that achieves the best combination of *strength* and *simplicity* (for now, ignore refinements involving chance). Strength is a measure of how much is said about the contingent world; simplicity is determined by how simply the set may be axiomatized in a language whose predicates express natural properties and relations. (2) The laws of dynamics must be restricted to physical continuants—that is, genidentity-interrelated spacetime worms. (3) There should be a causal or nomic component in the definition of genidentity. These elements may be combined in a joint account of laws and genidentity. We need to specify *both* genidentity and the laws. Since genidentity requires playing a role in the laws and the laws concern genidentity, we cannot define one without presupposing the other. So we follow a familiar strategy and define the two at once. Consider various ways of grouping stages together into physical contin-uants. Relative to any such way, there are candidate laws of dynamics. The correct grouping into physical continuants is that grouping that results in the best candidate set of laws of dynamics; the correct laws are the members of this candidate set.

More carefully. Any law of dynamics is a statement restricted to physical continuants, which may be rewritten in terms of the predicate
'genidentity' as follows: 'for any maximal genidentity-interrelated sum,
$x, \ldots$'. Let S be any axiomatization of any candidate set of laws of nature.
Let S(genidentity) be the result of rewriting any dynamical laws in S in
terms of the genidentity predicate. Where G is a two-place predicate
variable, let S(G) be the result of replacing all occurrences of 'genidentity' in S(genidentity) with G. S(G) is thus a set of formulas, some of
which may have the variable G free. It may not, therefore, have a strength
simpliciter, for strength is defined as a measure of the truths implied, and
members of S(G) with free variables do not have truth values *simpliciter*.
But relative to any assignment of a two-place relation **G** to the variable
G, we can evaluate the strength of the resulting system S(**G**). We
now define the best system and genidentity at once: they are the pair
<S(**G**), **G**>, where **G** is a two-place relation over stages and S(**G**) is the
system that achieves the best combination of strength and simplicity.

To see how stages are grouped into physical continuants at a given
possible world, we must look *globally*, across the entire world, to find
what assignment yields the best candidate laws of dynamics. Thus,
although the states of a spinning disk may qualitatively match those of
a stationary disk, what is going on elsewhere in the world may result in
differences in rotation. Suppose, for example, that a stationary disk
with a small hole is impacted by an object that seamlessly lodges itself
in the hole, resulting in a perfectly homogeneous disk, as in Figure 6.1.
Suppose further that, in the possible world in question, collisions generally result in transfer of momentum. The best simultaneous assignment of genidentity and laws of dynamics will then be one according to
which this disk is spinning, for a pair of a genidentity assignment and
set of laws on which the disk does not spin will not contain exception-
less laws governing transfer of momentum. Now suppose further that,
elsewhere in the same world, a disk with an empty niche had initially
been spinning, and that a perfectly fitting object moving opposite to the
direction of rotation collided with the disk (Fig. 6.2). If the speeds and
masses are appropriate, the best assignment of genidentity plus laws
will have the result that this second disk is stationary after the colli-
sion. The present view, therefore, allows the possibility of differences
in rotation between homogeneous disks without appealing to non-
Humean quantities.

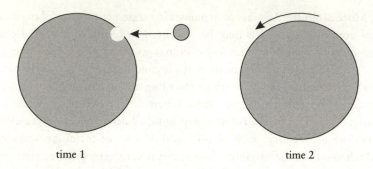

time 1   time 2

FIG. 6.1. Subsequently spinning disk

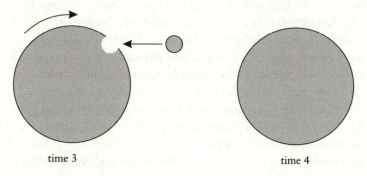

time 3   time 4

FIG. 6.2. Subsequently stationary disk

The candidate genidentity assignments had better be restricted in some way; otherwise, bogus laws of dynamics would result from gerry-mandered genidentity assignments. But the restriction cannot be to *perfectly* natural relations over stages. In the case just considered, the candidate genidentity assignment does not seem to follow any 'joint in reality'. The restriction must be only to more-or-less natural relations over stages.

Two other examples in which states of rotation can be distinguished without extra vector fields or relations: (1) The disk is in one case grasped by a person and spun, and is not spun in the other. (2) The disk in one case initially has deformities, and is spinning; as it spins, the deformities gradually fade away until the disk is homogeneous. In all these cases it is crucial that the world contain plenty of unproblematic cases *not* involving uniform homogeneous matter. Once a certain candidate pair of laws and genidentity gets its foothold in these unproblematic cases, it then can be projected into the problematic cases involving homogeneous objects, for this projection increases the strength of the candidate laws and does not decrease their simplicity.

Note that my account allows the possibility of discontinuous motion. Imagine a world in which objects regularly disappear, and in which objects materialize 'out of thin air' in spatiotemporal locations that are a uniform function of the locations of disappearance. The best assignment of genidentity-cum-laws will unite these stages into spatiotemporally gappy objects. Moreover, the account does not require deterministic laws of dynamics. Imagine that sequences of particle stages invariably occupy spatiotemporally continuous paths through spacetime, but the shapes of these paths exhibit no recurring patterns. Since the paths are always continuous, the best genidentity–laws pair will contain laws of dynamics requiring that position functions be continuous, but these laws will not constrain the directions traveled by particles. The laws will therefore be partly indeterministic. There might, on the other hand, be merely statistical patterns in the directions through spacetime of sequences of stages, in which case the best laws-plus-genidentity pair will contain probabilistic laws of dynamics.[20]

The examples considered so far have been based solely on patterns in the spatiotemporal locations of stages, but the candidacy of laws–genidentity pairs could be enhanced by subsuming other qualitative features as well. A set of laws might predict that the qualitative features of continuants are generally preserved, or change in regular ways. In certain cases laws *must* concern these qualitative features to account for facts about motion; otherwise a winning candidate pair of laws of dynamics and genidentity could never emerge in a world completely filled with continuous matter.

What the present view cannot do is distinguish states of rotation in cases where there is not enough else going on in the world to give candidate pairs of genidentity and laws a foothold. In a very simple world that contains only a homogeneous disk, the facts will not be sufficiently rich to allow one candidate pair to win out; there will therefore be no unique

---

[20]   At this point we will need the version of the best-system theory refined to account for probabilistic laws. See Lewis (1994), Hall (1994), Thau (1994).

facts about genidentity, no unique spacetime worm that counts as a given spatial part of the disk, and no fact of the matter whether the disk spins or rotates. Likewise, in Zimmerman's (1999) world consisting at all times of a uniform homogeneous fluid, there will be no basis to choose between genidentity–laws pairs on which there are currents and pairs on which the fluid is stationary. A second feature of the account some might find objectionable is that persistence becomes an extrinsic matter: whether a disk rotates depends on what goes on in parts of spacetime external to that occupied by the disk.

How bad are these two consequences? Not terribly bad, I think. The defender of the best-system account of laws is already accustomed to biting similar bullets. Consider simple worlds first. A completely empty world with exactly the laws of the actual world cannot be admitted, for lack of a rich enough set of facts to produce a winning candidate set of laws.

Consider next extrinsicality. On my account of motion, it may be that a disk is now spinning because it was shoved millions of years ago. Note that it is wrong to object, as Robinson (1989: 405–6) and Hawley (1999: 60) have, that this would amount to objectionable action at a temporal distance. Though the winning laws–genidentity assignment itself does hold in virtue of the totality of facts including the temporally distant shoving, those laws need not allow action at a distance. They may specify the positions of stages in the disks as a function of immediately temporally preceding genidentical stages. Still, the causal relations between stages of parts of the disk will not supervene, on my account, on the intrinsic properties of and local relations between those stages. But assuming causal relations are law-governed, *any* defender of the best-system theory of laws must admit this: duplicate pairs of events may be embedded in worlds with different arrays of qualitative facts, resulting in different sets of laws, and thus in different causal relations.

The best-system theory on its own stretches our intuitions about simple worlds and extrinsicality of causal connections. We should be slow to say: so much the worse for the best-system theory! Non-Humean accounts of lawhood and causation are shrouded in mystery and obscurity.[21] Instead, we should regard Humean laws and causation as that which best satisfies, however imperfectly, our concepts of law and causation.

---

[21] See e.g. Lewis (1986*b*, p. xii) and van Fraassen (1989, ch. 5).

Similarly for persistence. What we seek is a believable account of persistence that vindicates as many ordinary beliefs as possible. There is no denying that endurance theories do a better job of capturing our intuitions about motion in homogeneous substances. If objects endure, then even in very simple worlds the parts of homogeneous disks may differ in their successive positions; and this fact would be intrinsic to the regions of spacetime in question. If there were no other considerations we should favor endurance. But there are other considerations. The balance, I say, still favors perdurance. That is why it is worth showing *how close* a four-dimensionalist can get to capturing ordinary beliefs about motion. Metaphysics is like horseshoes: close counts.

In various places in this book I have complained that rival theories have implausible consequences with respect to certain distant possible worlds. Some of these worlds have been 'simple' worlds, as in discussion of the problem of cross-time relations for presentism (Ch. 2, Sect. 2), when I argued that presentists could not distinguish accelerated from unaccelerated motion in certain simple worlds. Others were 'exotic' (Ch. 4, Sect. 7). Now I myself must 'bite the bullet', and admit that four-dimensionalism has implausible consequences with respect to certain possible worlds. Some may suspect an unscrupulous accounting of theoretical costs and benefits, but I don't agree. It would be inconsistent to claim that four-dimensionalism's counterintuitive consequences in distant worlds represents *no cost at all* to accepting four-dimensionalism while at the same time upholding arguments based on distant worlds against my rivals. I do not claim this; I admit four-dimensionalism's weaknesses, hoping for victory in the final reckoning.

If Hawley, Robinson, and Tooley's relations are actual or possible, my solution to the problem of the rotating disk incorporates them. The distribution of the vector quantities and relations they postulate is, like other qualitative facts, up for being subsumed under the best system. Consider a world with a vector field that always points in a direction of emergence of stages, and suppose there to be plenty of cases of this in non-homogeneously filled regions of spacetime, to give a best system a foothold. Differential facts about motion could emerge where they could not have without the vector field.

But in other cases this injection of information into the Humean array will not help. Return to the simple world with just a disk, and let the vectors in the disk point in a direction of rotation. One candidate pair of laws plus genidentity would contain laws on which a vector is always succeeded by genidentical stages in the direction of the vector. But another candidate pair would 'interpret' the vectors differently. According to this pair, a vector is always succeeded by a genidentical stage with the same vector at the same place. These pairs will be equally good candidates; unless we give up on the Ramsey–Lewis theory of lawhood in favor of a more robust account, neither can be regarded as providing *the* correct laws. Since the first but not the second pair judges the disk to be rotating, there will be no fact of the matter about the disk's rotation. So even if we accept the possibility of the vectors, we will need to give up determinacy in the facts about motion in certain cases.

References

ADAMS, ROBERT MERRIHEW. 1986. 'Time and Thisness', in P. French, T. Uehling, and H. Wettstein, eds., *Midwest Studies in Philosophy*, xi (Minneapolis: University of Minnesota Press), 315–29.

ANSCOMBE, G. E. M. 1971. *Causality and Determination: An Inaugural Lecture* (London: Cambridge University Press).

ARMSTRONG, D. M. 1997. *A World of States of Affairs* (Cambridge: Cambridge University Press).

—— 1989. *A Combinatorial Theory of Possibility* (New York: Cambridge University Press).

—— 1983. *What is a Law of Nature?* (Cambridge: Cambridge University Press).

—— 1980. 'Identity through Time', in Peter van Inwagen, ed., *Time and Cause: Essays Presented to Richard Taylor* (Dordrecht: D. Reidel), 67–78.

—— 1978*a*. *Nominalism and Realism (Universals and Scientific Realism*, i) (Cambridge: Cambridge University Press).

—— 1978*b*. *A Theory of Universals (Universals and Scientific Realism*, ii) (Cambridge: Cambridge University Press).

BAKER, LYNNE RUDDER. 2000. *Persons and Bodies* (Cambridge: Cambridge University Press).

—— 1997. 'Why Constitution is not Identity', *Journal of Philosophy*, 94: 599–621.

BALASHOV, YURI. 2000. 'Enduring and Perduring Objects in Minkowski Space-Time', *Philosophical Studies*, 99: 129–66.

—— 1999. 'Relativistic Objects', *Noûs*, 33: 644–62.

BAXTER, DONALD. 1988*a*. 'Identity in the Loose and Popular Sense', *Mind*, 97: 575–82.

—— 1988*b*. 'Many-One Identity', *Philosophical Papers*, 17: 193–216.

BEALER, GEORGE. 1996. '*A Priori* Knowledge and the Scope of Philosophy', *Philosophical Studies*, 81: 121–42.

BIGELOW, JOHN. 1996. 'Presentism and Properties', in James E. Tomberlin, ed., *Philosophical Perspectives, 10, Metaphysics* (Cambridge, Mass.: Blackwell), 35–52.

—— 1988. *The Reality of Numbers* (Oxford: Oxford University Press).

BROAD, C. D. 1938. *Examination of McTaggart's Philosophy*, vol. ii, part i (Cambridge: Cambridge University Press).

BROAD, C. D. 1933. *Examination of McTaggart's Philosophy*, i (Cambridge: Cambridge University Press).

—— 1925. *Mind and its Place in Nature* (London: Routledge & Kegan Paul).

—— 1923. *Scientific Thought* (New York: Harcourt, Brace, and Company).

BURGESS, JOHN P. 1984. 'Basic Tense Logic', in D. Gabbay and F. Guenthner, eds., *Handbook of Philosophical Logic*, ii (Dordrecht: D. Reidel Publishing Company), 89–133.

BURKE, MICHAEL. 1994a. 'Preserving the Principle of One Object to a Place: A Novel Account of the Relations Among Objects, Sorts, Sortals, and Persistence Conditions', *Philosophy and Phenomenological Research*, 54: 591–624; reprinted in Rea 1997.

—— 1994b. 'Dion and Theon: An Essentialist Solution to an Ancient Puzzle', *Journal of Philosophy*, 91: 129–39.

—— 1992. 'Copper Statues and Pieces of Copper: A Challenge to the Standard Account', *Analysis*, 52: 12–17.

BUTTERFIELD, J. 1984. 'Spatial and Temporal Parts', *Philosophical Quarterly*, 35: 32–44.

CARNAP, RUDOLF. 1967. *The Logical Structure of the World*, trans. Rolf A. George (Berkeley: University of California Press).

—— 1950. 'Empiricism, Semantics and Ontology', *Revue Internationale de Philosophie*, 4: 20–40; reprinted in his *Meaning and Necessity*, 2nd edn. (Chicago: University of Chicago Press, 1956).

CARTER, WILLIAM, and HESTEVOLD, H. S. 1994. 'On Passage and Persistence', *American Philosophical Quarterly*, 31: 269–83.

CARTWRIGHT, RICHARD. 1975. 'Scattered Objects', in Keith Lehrer, ed., *Analysis and Metaphysics* (Dordrecht: D. Reidel Publishing Company), 153–71.

CHALMERS, DAVID. 1996. *The Conscious Mind* (Oxford: Oxford University Press).

CHISHOLM, RODERICK. 1979. 'The Indirect Reflexive', in Cora Diamond and Jenny Teichman, eds., *Intention and Intentionality* (Ithaca, NY: Cornell University Press).

—— 1976. *Person and Object: A Metaphysical Study* (La Salle, Ill.: Open Court Publishing Co.).

—— 1975. 'Mereological Essentialism: Further Considerations', *Review of Metaphysics*, 28: 477–84.

—— 1973. 'Parts as Essential to Their Wholes', *Review of Metaphysics*, 26: 581–603.

—— 1971. 'Problems of Identity', in *Identity and Individuation*, ed. M. Munitz (New York: NYU Press), 3–30.

—— 1968. 'Identity through Possible Worlds: Some Questions', *Noûs*, 1: 1–8.

CHURCHLAND, PAUL M. 1988. *Matter and Consciousness*, rev. edn. (Cambridge, Mass.: MIT Press).

COPELAND, B. J. ed. 1996. *Logic and Reality: Essays on the Legacy of Arthur Prior* (Oxford: Clarendon Press).

CORTENS, ANDREW, and O'LEARY-HAWTHORNE, JOHN. 1995. 'Towards Ontological Nihilism', *Philosophical Studies*, 79: 143–65.

COVER, J. A., and O'LEARY-HAWTHORNE, JOHN. 1998. 'A World of Universals', *Philosophical Studies*, 91: 205–19.

CUSHING, JAMES T. 1994. *Quantum Mechanics: Historical Contingency and the Copenhagen Hegemony* (Chicago: University of Chicago Press).

DAU, PAOLO. 1986. 'Part-Time Objects', in P. French, T. Uehling, and H. Wettstein, eds., *Midwest Studies in Philosophy*, xi (Minneapolis: University of Minnesota Press), 450–74.

DELLA ROCCA, MICHAEL. 1996. 'Essentialists and Essentialism', *Journal of Philosophy*, 93, 186–202.

DOEPKE, FREDERICK. 1982. 'Spatially Coinciding Objects', *Ratio*, 24: 45–60.

DRETSKE, FRED. 1977. 'Laws of Nature', *Philosophy of Science*, 44: 248–68.

DUMMETT, MICHAEL. 1981. *The Interpretation of Frege's Philosophy* (London: Duckworth).

—— 1978. *Truth and Other Enigmas* (London: Duckworth).

—— 1969. 'The Reality of the Past', *Proceedings of the Aristotelian Society*, 69: 239–58.

EARMAN, JOHN. 1995. 'Recent Work on Time Travel', in Steve Savitt, ed., *Time's Arrows Today: Recent Physical and Philosophical Work on the Direction of Time* (Cambridge: Cambridge University Press), 268–324.

EDWARDS, JONATHAN. 1758. *Doctrine of Original Sin Defended*. Parts reprinted in Clarence H. Faust and Thomas H. Johnson, eds., *Jonathan Edwards* (New York: American Book Company, 1935).

EVANS, GARETH. 1978. 'Can there be Vague Objects?' *Analysis*, 38: 208.

FINE, KIT. 1994. 'Compounds and Aggregates', *Noûs*, 28: 137–58.

—— 1975. 'Vagueness, Truth and Logic', *Synthese*, 30: 265–300.

FORBES, GRAHAM. 1987. 'Is There a Problem about Persistence?', *Aristotelian Society*, suppl. vol. 61: 137–55.

—— 1985. *The Metaphysics of Modality* (Oxford: Clarendon Press).

—— 1984. 'Two Solutions to Chisholm's Paradox', *Philosophical Studies*, 46: 171–87.

FRIEDMAN, MICHAEL. 1983. *Foundations of Space-Time Theories* (Princeton: Princeton University Press).

GALE, RICHARD. 1968. *The Language of Time* (London: Routledge & Kegan Paul).

GALLOIS, ANDRÉ. 1998. *Occasions of Identity* (Oxford: Clarendon Press).

GEACH, P. T. 1980. *Reference and Generality*, 3rd edn. (Ithaca, NY: Cornell University Press).

GEACH, P. T. 1972*a*. 'Some Problems about Time', in Geach 1972*b*.

—— 1972*b*. *Logic Matters* (Oxford: Basil Blackwell).

GIBBARD, ALLAN. 1975. 'Contingent Identity', *Journal of Philosophical Logic*, 4: 187–221.

GODFREY-SMITH, PETER. 1979. 'Special Relativity and the Present', *Philosophical Studies*, 36: 233–44.

GOODMAN, NELSON. 1951. *The Structure of Appearance* (Cambridge, Mass.: Harvard University Press).

GRAHAM, GEORGE. 1977. 'Persons and Time', *Southern Journal of Philosophy*, 15: 308–15.

GRIFFIN, NICHOLAS. 1977. *Relative Identity* (Oxford: Oxford University Press).

GUTHRIE, W. K. C. 1962. *A History of Greek Philosophy*, i (Cambridge: Cambridge University Press).

HALL, NED. 1994. 'Correcting The Guide to Objective Chance', *Mind*, 103: 505–18.

HASLANGER, SALLY. 1994. 'Humean Supervenience and Enduring Things', *Australasian Journal of Philosophy*, 72: 339–59.

—— 1989*a*. 'Endurance and Temporary Intrinsics', *Analysis*, 49: 119–25.

—— 1989*b*. 'Persistence, Change, and Explanation', *Philosophical Studies*, 56: 1–28.

—— 1985. 'Change, Persistence, and Possibility', University of California doctoral dissertation.

HAWLEY, KATHERINE. 1999. 'Persistence and Non-Supervenient Relations', *Mind*, 108: 53–67.

—— 1998. 'Why Temporary Properties are not Relations between Physical Objects and Times', *Proceedings of the Aristotelian Society*, 98: 211–16.

HAZEN, ALLEN. 1979. 'Counterpart-Theoretic Semantics for Modal Logic', *Journal of Philosophy*, 76: 319–38.

HELLER, MARK. 1993. 'Varieties of Four Dimensionalism', *Australasian Journal of Philosophy*, 71: 47–59.

—— 1992. 'Things Change', *Philosophy and Phenomenological Research*, 52: 695–704.

—— 1990. *The Ontology of Physical Objects: Four Dimensional Hunks of Matter* (Cambridge: Cambridge University Press).

—— 1984. 'Temporal Parts of Four Dimensional Objects', *Philosophical Studies*, 46: 323–34.

HINCHLIFF, MARK. 1996. 'The Puzzle of Change', in James Tomberlin, ed., *Philosophical Perspectives* 10, *Metaphysics* (Cambridge, Mass.: Blackwell).

HIRSCH, ELI. 1982. *The Concept of Identity* (Oxford: Oxford University Press).

HUDSON, HUD. Forthcoming. *A Materialist Metaphysics of the Human Person* (Ithaca, NY: Cornell University Press).

HUDSON, HUD. 1999. 'Temporal Parts and Moral Personhood', *Philosophical Studies*, 93: 299–316.

HUGHES, G. E., and CRESSWELL, M. J. 1996. *A New Introduction to Modal Logic* (London: Routledge).

HUME, DAVID. 1978. *A Treatise of Human Nature*, ed. by L. A. Selby-Bigge, this edn. 1st pub. 1888 (Oxford: Clarendon Press).

JOHNSTON, MARK. 1992. 'Constitution Is Not Identity', *Mind*, 101: 89–105.

—— 1987. 'Is there a Problem about Persistence?' *Aristotelian Society*, suppl. vol. 61: 107–35.

JUBIEN, MICHAEL. 1993. *Ontology, Modality, and the Fallacy of Reference* (Cambridge: Cambridge University Press).

KAPLAN, DAVID. 1989. 'Demonstratives', in Joseph Almog, John Perry, and Howard Wettstein, eds., *Themes from Kaplan* (New York: Oxford University Press), 481–563.

KAZMI, ALI AKHTAR. 1990. 'Parthood and Persistence', *Canadian Journal of Philosophy*, supp. vol. 16: 227–50.

KIRK, G. S. 1960. 'Popper on Science and the Presocratics', *Mind*, 69: 318–39.

KRIPKE, SAUL. 1982. *Wittgenstein on Rules and Private Language: An Elementary Exposition* (Cambridge, Mass.: Harvard University Press).

—— 1972. *Naming and Necessity* (Cambridge, Mass.: Harvard University Press).

LE POIDEVIN, ROBIN. 1991. *Change, Cause and Contradiction* (New York: St Martin's Press).

—— and MACBEATH, MURRAY. 1993. *The Philosophy of Time* (Oxford: Oxford University Press).

LEIBNIZ, GOTTFRIED WILHELM. 1698. 'On Nature Itself, Or On the Inherent Force and Actions of Created Things', in Leroy E. Loemker, ed., *Gottfried Wilhelm Leibniz: Philosophical Papers and Letters* (Dordrecht: Kluwer Academic Publishers, 1989), 498–508.

LEONARD, HENRY, and GOODMAN, NELSON. 1940. 'The Calculus of Individuals and its Uses', *Journal of Symbolic Logic*, 5: 45–55.

LEWIN, KURT. 1923. 'Die zeitliche Geneseordnung', *Zeitschrift für Physik*, 13: 62–81.

LEWIS, DAVID. Forthcoming. 'Tensed Quantifiers', in Dean Zimmerman, ed., *Oxford Studies in Metaphysics*, i (Oxford: Oxford University Press).

—— 2000. 'Things qua Truthmakers', forthcoming in Hallvard Lillehammer and Gonzalo Rodriguez-Pereya, eds., *Real Metaphysics: Essays in Honour of D. H. Mellor* (London: Routledge, 2002).

—— 1999. 'Zimmerman and the Spinning Sphere', *Australasian Journal of Philosophy*, 77: 209–12.

Lewis, David. 1994. 'Humean Supervenience Debugged', *Mind*, 103: 473–90.

Lewis, David. 1993. 'Many, But Almost One', in Keith Campbell, John Bacon, and Lloyd Reinhardt, eds., *Ontology, Causality and Mind: Essays in Honour of D. M. Armstrong* (Cambridge: Cambridge University Press).

—— 1992. Review of D. M. Armstrong, *A Combinatorial Theory of Possibility*, *Australasian Journal of Philosophy*, 70: 211–24.

—— 1991. *Parts of Classes* (Oxford: Basil Blackwell).

—— 1988*a*. 'Rearrangement of Particles: Reply to Lowe', *Analysis*, 48: 65–72.

—— 1988*b*. 'Vague Identity: Evans Misunderstood', *Analysis*, 48: 128–30.

—— 1986*a*. *On the Plurality of Worlds* (Oxford: Basil Blackwell).

—— 1986*b*. *Philosophical Papers*, ii (Oxford: Oxford University Press.)

—— 1986*c*. 'A Subjectivist's Guide to Objective Chance', with postscripts, in Lewis 1986*b*: 83–132.

—— 1984. 'Putnam's Paradox'. *Australasian Journal of Philosophy*, 62: 221–36.

—— 1983*a*. 'Survival and Identity', plus postscripts, in his *Philosophical Papers*, i (Oxford: Oxford University Press), 55–77.

—— 1983*b*. 'Extrinsic Properties', *Philosophical Studies*, 44: 197–200.

—— 1983*c*. 'New Work for a Theory of Universals', *Australasian Journal of Philosophy*, 61: 343–77.

—— 1979. 'Attitudes *De Dicto* and *De Se*', *Philosophical Review*, 88: 513–43.

—— 1976. 'The Paradoxes of Time Travel', *American Philosophical Quarterly*, 13: 145–52.

—— 1973. *Counterfactuals* (Cambridge, Mass.: Harvard University Press).

—— 1971. 'Counterparts of Persons and Their Bodies', *Journal of Philosophy*, 68: 203–11.

—— 1970. 'How to Define Theoretical Terms', *Journal of Philosophy*, 67: 427–46.

—— 1968. 'Counterpart Theory and Quantified Modal Logic', *Journal of Philosophy*, 65: 113–26.

Locke, John. 1975. 'On Identity and Diversity' (ch. 27 of his *Essay Concerning Human Understanding*), in Perry 1975: 33–52.

Lombard, Lawrence. 1999. 'On the Alleged Incompatibility of Presentism and Temporal Parts', *Philosophia*, 27: 253–60.

—— 1994. 'The Doctrine of Temporal Parts and the "No-Change" Objection', *Philosophy and Phenomenological Research*, 54: 365–72.

—— 1986. *Events: A Metaphysical Study* (London: Routledge & Kegan Paul).

Lotze, Hermann. 1887. *Metaphysic, Book 1 (Ontology)*, ed. Bernard Bosanquet (Oxford: Clarendon Press).

Lowe, E. J. 1995. 'Coinciding Objects: In Defence of the "Standard Account" ', *Analysis*, 55: 171–8.

—— 1989. *Kinds of Being* (Oxford: Blackwell).

—— 1988a. 'The Problems of Intrinsic Change: Rejoinder to Lewis', *Analysis*, 48: 72–7.

—— 1988b. 'Substance, Identity, and Time', *Aristotelian Society*, suppl. vol 62: 61–78.

—— 1987. 'Lewis on Perdurance versus Endurance', *Analysis*, 47: 152–4.

—— 1983a. 'On the Identity of Artifacts', *Journal of Philosophy*, 80: 220–32.

—— 1983b. 'Instantiation, Identity, and Constitution', *Philosophical Studies*, 44: 45–59.

Lukasiewicz, Jan. 1967. 'On Determinism', in Storrs McCall, ed., *Polish Logic* (Oxford: Oxford University Press), 19–39.

Markosian, Ned. Forthcoming. 'A Defense of Presentism', in Dean Zimmerman, ed., *Oxford Studies in Metaphysics*, i (Oxford: Oxford University Press).

—— 1998. 'Brutal Composition'. *Philosophical Studies*, 92: 211–49.

—— 1995. 'The Open Past', *Philosophical Studies*, 79: 95–105.

—— 1993. 'How Fast Does Time Pass?' *Philosophy and Phenomenological Research*, 53: 829–44.

—— 1992. 'On Language and the Passage of Time', *Philosophical Studies*, 66: 1–26.

Martin, C. B. 1996. 'How It Is: Entities, Absences and Voids', *Australasian Journal of Philosophy*, 74: 57–65.

McCall, Storrs. 1994. *A Model of the Universe* (Oxford: Clarendon Press).

McTaggart, J. M. E. 1927. *The Nature of Existence*, ii (Cambridge: Cambridge University Press).

—— 1921. *The Nature of Existence*, i (Cambridge: Cambridge University Press).

—— 1908. 'The Unreality of Time', *Mind*, 18: 457–84.

Mellor, D. H. 1998. *Real Time*, II (London: Routledge).

—— 1981. *Real Time* (Cambridge: Cambridge University Press).

Merricks, Trenton. 1999. 'Persistence, Parts and Presentism', *Noûs*, 33: 421–38.

—— 1995. 'On the Incompatibility of Enduring and Perduring Entities', *Mind*, 104: 523–31.

—— 1994a. 'Endurance and Indiscernibility', *Journal of Philosophy*, 91: 165–84.

—— 1994b. 'Enduring Objects'. Notre Dame Ph.D. diss.

Mulligan, Kevin, Simons, Peter, and Smith, Barry. 1984. 'Truth-Makers', *Philosophy and Phenomenological Research*, 44: 287–321.

MUNDY, BRENT. 1983. 'Relational Theories of Euclidean Space and Minkowski Space-Time', *Philosophy of Science*, 50: 205–26.

MYRO, GEORGE. 1986. 'Identity and Time', in Richard E. Grandy and Richard Warner, eds., *The Philosophical Grounds of Rationality* (New York: Clarendon Press).

NOONAN, HAROLD. 1993. 'Constitution is Identity', *Mind* 102: 133–146.

—— 1991. 'Indeterminate Identity, Contingent Identity, and Abelardian Predicates', *The Philosophical Quarterly*, 41: 183–93.

—— 1989. *Personal Identity* (London: Routledge).

—— 1988. 'Substance, Identity and Time', *Aristotelian Society*, suppl. vol. 62: 79–100.

—— 1980. *Objects and Identity* (The Hague: Martinus Nijhoff).

OAKLANDER, L., SMITH, NATHAN, and QUENTIN. 1994. *The New Theory of Time* (New Haven: Yale University Press.)

ODERBERG, DAVID. 1996. 'Coincidence under a Sortal', *Philosophical Review*, 105: 145–71.

—— 1993. *The Metaphysics of Identity over Time* (New York: St Martin's Press.)

PARFIT, DEREK. 1984. *Reasons and Persons* (Oxford: Oxford University Press).

—— 1976. 'Lewis, Perry, and What Matters', in Amelie O. Rorty, ed., *The Identities of Persons* (Berkeley: University of California Press), 91–107.

—— 1975. 'Personal Identity', in Perry 1975: 199–223.

PARSONS, JOSH. 2000. 'Must a Four-Dimensionalist Believe in Temporal Parts?' *The Monist*, 83: 399–418.

PARSONS, TERENCE. 1987. 'Entities without Identity', in James Tomberlin, ed., *Philosophical Perspectives*, 1, *Metaphysics* (Atascadero, Calif.: Ridgeview Publishing Company).

PEACOCKE, CHRISTOPHER. 1999. *Being Known* (Oxford: Clarendon Press).

—— 1997. 'Metaphysical Necessity: Understanding, Truth and Epistemology', *Mind*, 106: 521–74.

—— 1988. 'The Limits of Intelligibility: A Post-Verificationist Proposal', *Philosophical Review*, 97: 463–96.

PELLETIER, FRANCIS JEFFRY. 1989. 'Another Argument against Vague Objects', *Journal of Philosophy*, 86: 481–92.

PERRY, JOHN. 1979. 'The Problem of the Essential Indexical', *Noûs*, 13: 3–21.

—— ed. 1975. *Personal Identity* (Berkeley: University of California Press).

—— 1972. 'Can the Self Divide?', *Journal of Philosophy*, 69: 463–88.

PLANTINGA, ALVIN. 1974. *The Nature of Necessity* (Oxford: Oxford University Press).

POLLOCK, JOHN. 1986. *Contemporary Theories of Knowledge* (Totowa, NJ: Rowman & Littlefield).

PRIOR, A. N. 1996. 'Some Free Thinking about Time', in Copeland 1996: 47–51

—— 1970. 'The Notion of the Present', *Studium Generale*, 23: 245–8.

—— 1968*a*. 'Changes in Events and Changes in Things', in Prior 1968*c*.

—— 1968*b*. 'Quasi-propositions and Quasi-individuals', in Prior 1968*c*.

—— 1968*c*. *Papers on Time and Tense* (London: Oxford University Press).

—— 1967. *Past, Present and Future* (Oxford: Clarendon Press).

—— 1959. 'Thank Goodness That's Over', *Philosophy*, 34: 12–17.

—— 1957*a*. *Time and Modality* (Oxford: Clarendon Press).

—— 1957*b*. 'Opposite Number', *Review of Metaphysics*, 11: 196–201.

PUTNAM, HILARY. 1987*a*. 'Truth and Convention: On Davidson's Refutation of Conceptual Relativism', *Dialectica*, 41: 69–77.

—— 1987*b*. *The Many Faces of Realism* (La Salle, Ill.: Open Court).

—— 1981. *Reason, Truth and History* (Cambridge: Cambridge University Press).

—— 1980. 'Models and Reality', *Journal of Symbolic Logic*, 45: 464–82.

—— 1978. *Meaning and the Moral Sciences* (Boston: Routledge & Kegan Paul).

—— 1975. 'The Meaning of "Meaning" ', in K. Gunderson, ed., *Language, Mind and Knowledge, Minnesota Studies in the Philosophy of Science*, vii (Minneapolis: University of Minnesota Press), repr. in Hilary Putnam, *Mind, Language and Reality: Philosophical Papers*, ii (Cambridge: Cambridge University Press, 1975).

—— 1967. 'Time and Physical Geometry', *Journal of Philosophy*, 64: 240–7.

QUINE, W. V. O. 1981. *Theories and Things* (Cambridge, Mass.: Harvard University Press).

—— 1976*a*. 'Worlds Away', *Journal of Philosophy*, 73: 859–63.

—— 1976*b*. 'Whither Physical Objects', in R. S. Cohen, P. K. Feyerabend, and M. W. Wartofsky, eds., *Essays in Memory of Imre Lakatos* (Dordrecht: D. Reidel Publishing Company), 497–504.

—— 1963. 'Identity, Ostension, and Hypostasis', in his *From a Logical Point of View*, 2nd edn., rev. (Evanston, Ill.: Harper & Row), 65–79.

—— 1960. *Word and Object* (Cambridge, Mass.: MIT Press).

—— 1953. 'Mr Strawson on Logical Theory', *Mind*, 62: 433–51.

—— 1950. *Methods of Logic* (New York: Henry Holt and Company).

REA, MICHAEL. 2000. 'Constitution and Kind Membership', *Philosophical Studies*, 97: 169–93.

—— 1998. 'Temporal Parts Unmotivated', *Philosophical Review*, 107: 225–60.

—— ed. 1997. *Material Constitution* (Lanham, Md.: Rowman and Littlefield Publishers).

—— 1995. 'The Problem of Material Constitution', *Philosophical Review*, 104: 525–52.

RIETDIJK, C. W. 1976. 'Special Relativity and Determinism', *Philosophy of Science*, 43: 598–609.

RIETDIJK, C. W. 1966. 'A Rigorous Proof of Determinism Derived from the Special Theory of Relativity', *Philosophy of Science*, 33: 341–4.

ROBINSON, DENIS. 1989. 'Matter, Motion, and Humean Supervenience', *Australasian Journal of Philosophy*, 67: 394–409.

—— 1985. 'Can Amoebae Divide without Multiplying?' *Australasian Journal of Philosophy*, 63: 299–319.

—— 1982. 'Re-identifying Matter', *Philosophical Review*, 91: 317–42.

RUSSELL, BERTRAND. 1927. *The Analysis of Matter* (New York: Harcourt, Brace & Company).

—— 1923. 'Vagueness', *Australasian Journal of Philosophy and Psychology*, 1: 84–92. Repr. in Rosanna Keefe and Peter Smith, eds., *Vagueness: A Reader* (Cambridge, Mass.: MIT Press, 1996), 61–8.

—— 1918. *The Philosophy of Logical Atomism*. 1st pub. in *The Monist*, repr. in David Pears, ed., *The Philosophy of Logical Atomism* (La Salle, Ill.: Open Court, 1985).

—— 1917. 'The Relation of Sense-Data to Physics', in his *Mysticism and Logic, and Other Essays* (New York: Longman's, Green and Co.)

—— 1915. 'On the Experience of Time', *The Monist*, 25: 212–33.

—— 1914. *Our Knowledge of the External World* (London: Allen & Unwin Ltd.)

—— 1903. *The Principles of Mathematics* (Cambridge: Cambridge University Press).

SALMON, NATHAN U. 1986. 'Modal Paradox: Parts and Counterparts, Points and Counterpoints', in P. French, T. Uehling, and H. Wettstein, eds., *Midwest Studies in Philosophy*, xi (Minnesota: University of Minnesota), 75–120.

—— 1981. *Reference and Essence* (Princeton: Princeton University Press).

SAVITT, STEVEN. 2000. 'There's No Time Like the Present (in Minkowski Spacetime)', *Philosophy of Science*, 67, suppl. vol., *Proceedings of the 1998 Biennial Meetings of the Philosophy of Science Association*, 5563–74.

—— 1994. 'The Replacement of Time', *Australasian Journal of Philosophy*, 72: 463–74.

SCHLESINGER, GEORGE. 1980. *Aspects of Time* (Indianapolis: Hackett Publishing Co.)

SELLARS, WILFRID. 1962. 'Time and the World Order', in Herbert Feigl and Grover Maxwell, eds., *Minnesota Studies in the Philosophy of Science*, iii: *Scientific Explanation, Space, and Time* (Minneapolis: University of Minnesota Press), 527–616.

SHOEMAKER, SYDNEY. 1999. 'Self, Body, and Coincidence', *Aristotelian Society*, suppl. vol. 73: 287–306.

—— 1988. 'On What There Are', *Philosophical Topics*, 16: 201–23.

—— 1979. 'Identity, Properties, and Causality', in P. French, T. Uehling, and H. Wettstein, eds, *Midwest Studies in Philosophy*, iv (Minnesota: University of Minnesota Press), 321–42.

SIDER, THEODORE. 2001. 'Criteria of Personal Identity and the Limits of Conceptual Analysis', in James Tomberlin, ed., *Philosophical Perspectives*, xv, *Metaphysics* (Cambridge, Mass.: Blackwell).

—— 2000a. 'Reducing Modality'.

—— 2000b. 'The Ersatz Pluriverse'.

—— 2000c. 'The Stage View and Temporary Intrinsics', *Analysis*, 60: 84–8.

—— 1999a. Critical Study of Michael Jubien's *Ontology, Modality, and the Fallacy of Reference*, *Noûs*, 33: 284–94.

—— 1999b. 'Presentism and Ontological Commitment', *Journal of Philosophy*, 96, 325–47.

—— 1999c. 'Global Supervenience and Identity across Times and Worlds', *Philosophy and Phenomenological Research*, 59: 913–37.

—— 1997. 'Four-Dimensionalism', *Philosophical Review*, 106: 197–231.

—— 1996a. 'All the World's a Stage', *Australasian Journal of Philosophy*, 74: 433–53.

—— 1996b. 'Naturalness and Arbitrariness', *Philosophical Studies*, 81: 283–301.

—— 1993. 'Van Inwagen and the Possibility of Gunk', *Analysis*, 53: 285–9.

SIDES, C. BROCK. 1997. 'Mereological Nihilism and the Limits of Paraphrase', http://philarete.home.mindspring.com/philosophy/nihilism.html

SIMONS, PETER. 1987. *Parts: A Study in Ontology* (Oxford: Oxford University Press).

SKLAR, LAWRENCE. 1981. 'Time, Reality, and Relativity', in Richard Healy, ed., *Reduction, Time, and Reality* (New York: Cambridge University Press), 129–42.

—— 1974. *Space, Time, and Spacetime* (Berkeley: University of California Press).

SMART, J. J. C. 1972. 'Space-Time and Individuals', in Richard Rudner and Israel Scheffler, eds., *Logic and Art: Essays in Honor of Nelson Goodman* (New York: Macmillan Publishing Company), 3–20.

—— 1963. *Philosophy and Scientific Realism* (London: Routledge & Kegan Paul).

—— 1962. 'Tensed Statements', *The Philosophical Quarterly*, 12: 264–5.

SMITH, QUENTIN. 1993. *Language and Time* (New York: Oxford University Press).

SORENSEN, ROY A. 1988. *Blindspots* (Oxford: Clarendon Press).

SOSA, ERNEST. 1993. 'Putnam's Pragmatic Realism', *Journal of Philosophy*, 90: 605–26.

SOSA, ERNEST. 1987. 'Subjects among Other Things', in James Tomberlin, ed., *Philosophical Perspectives, 1, Metaphysics* (Atascadero, Calif.: Ridgeview Publishing Company).

STALNAKER, ROBERT. 1988. 'Vague Identity', in D. F. Austin, ed., *Philosophical Analysis: A Defense by Example* (Dordrecht: Kluwer): 349–60.

—— 1986. 'Counterparts and Identity', in P. French, T. Uehling, and H. Wettstein, eds., *Midwest Studies in Philosophy*, xi (Minneapolis: University of Minnesota), 121–40.

STCHERBATSKY, T. 1992. *Buddhist Logic*, i, 1st Indian edn. (Delhi: Motilal Banarsidass Publishers).

—— 1970. *The Central Conception of Buddhism*, 4th edn. (Delhi: Indological Book House).

STEIN, HOWARD. 1970. 'A Note on Time and Relativity Theory', *Journal of Philosophy*, 67: 289–94.

—— 1968. 'On Einstein-Minkowski Space-Time', *Journal of Philosophy*, 65: 5–23.

STRAWSON, P. F. 1959. *Individuals* (London: Methuen and Company).

SWOYER, CHRIS. 1984. 'Causation and Identity', in P. French, T. Uehling, and H. Wettstein, eds., *Midwest Studies in Philosophy*, ix (Minneapolis: University of Minnesota), 593–622.

TAYLOR, RICHARD. 1955. 'Spatial and Temporal Analogies and the Concept of Identity', *Journal of Philosophy*, 52: 599–612.

THAU, MICHAEL. 1994. 'Undermining and Admissibility', *Mind*, 103: 491–503.

THOMASON, RICHARD. 1982. 'Identity and Vagueness', *Philosophical Studies*, 42: 329–32.

THOMSON, JUDITH JARVIS. 1998. 'The Statue and the Clay', *Noûs*, 32: 149–73.

—— 1983. 'Parthood and Identity Across Time', *Journal of Philosophy*, 80: 201–20.

TOOLEY, MICHAEL. 1997. *Time, Tense and Causation* (Oxford: Clarendon Press).

—— 1988. 'In Defense of the Existence of States of Motion', *Philosophical Topics*, 16: 225–54.

—— 1987. *Causation: A Realist Approach* (Oxford: Oxford University Press).

UNGER, PETER. 1990. *Identity, Consciousness, and Value* (New York: Oxford University Press).

—— 1980. 'The Problem of the Many', in P. French, T. Uehling, and H. Wettstein, eds., *Midwest Studies in Philosophy*, v (Minneapolis: University of Minnesota), 411–67.

—— 1979a. 'I Do Not Exist', in G. F. Macdonald, ed., *Perception and Identity: Essays Presented to A. J. Ayer with His Replies to Them* (New York: Macmillan), 235–51.

—— 1979*b*. 'Why There are No People', in P. French, T. Uehling, and H. Wettstein, eds., *Midwest Studies in Philosophy*, iv (Minneapolis: University of Minnesota Press).

—— 1979*c*. 'There are No Ordinary Things', *Synthese*, 41: 117–54.

VAN CLEVE, JAMES. 1986. 'Mereological Essentialism, Mereological Conjunctivism and Identity Through Time', in P. French, T. Uehling, and H. Wettstein, eds., *Midwest Studies in Philosophy*, xi (Minneapolis : University of Minnesota Press).

VAN FRAASSEN, BAS. 1989. *Laws and Symmetry* (Oxford: Clarendon Press).

VAN INWAGEN, PETER. Forthcoming. 'The Number of Things', in Ernest Sosa, ed., *Philosophical Issues*, xii: *Realism and Relativism* (Oxford: Blackwell).

—— 1998. 'Modal Epistemology', *Philosophical Studies*, 92: 67–84.

—— 1994. 'Composition as Identity', in J. E. Tomberlin, ed., *Philosophical Perspectives*, viii, *Logic and Language* (Atascadero, Calif.: Ridgeview), 207–20.

—— 1990*a*. *Material Beings* (Ithaca, NY: Cornell University Press).

—— 1990*b*. 'Four-Dimensional Objects', *Noûs*, 24 (1990), 245–55.

—— 1987. 'When are Objects Parts?', in J. Tomberlin, ed., *Philosophical Perspectives*, 1, *Metaphysics* (Atascadero, Calif.: Ridgeview Publishing Co.).

—— 1981. 'The Doctrine of Arbitrary Undetached Parts', *Pacific Philosophical Quarterly*, 62: 123–37.

WEINGARD, ROBERT. 1972. 'Relativity and the Reality of Past and Future Events', *British Journal for the Philosophy of Science*, 23: 119–21.

WELLS, H. G. 1895. *The Time Machine: An Invention* (London: William Heinemann).

WHITEHEAD, A. N. 1920. *The Concept of Nature* (Cambridge: Cambridge University Press).

WIGGINS, DAVID. 1980. *Sameness and Substance* (Cambridge, Mass.: Harvard University Press).

—— 1968. 'On Being in the Same Place at the Same Time', *Philosophical Review*, 77: 90–5.

WILLIAMS, BERNARD. 1975. 'The Self and the Future', in Perry: 179–98.

—— 1973*a*. *Problems of the Self* (Cambridge: Cambridge University Press).

—— 1973*b*. 'Bodily Continuity and Personal Identity', in B. Williams 1973*a*: 19–25.

WILLIAMS, DONALD C. 1951. 'The Myth of Passage', *Journal of Philosophy*, 48: 457–72.

WILLIAMSON, TIMOTHY. 1994. *Vagueness* (London: Routledge).

WILSON, N. L. 1955. 'Space, Time and Individuals', *Journal of Philosophy*, 52: 589–98.

WITTGENSTEIN, LUDWIG. 1961. *Tractatus Logico-Philosophicus*, trans. D. F. Pears and B. F. McGuinness (London: Routledge & Kegan Paul).

WOODGER, J. H. 1952. *Biology and Language* (Cambridge: Cambridge University Press).

—— 1937. *The Axiomatic Method in Biology* (London: Cambridge University Press).

WRIGHT, CRISPIN. 1987. *Realism, Meaning and Truth* (Oxford: Basil Blackwell).

YABLO, STEPHEN. 1987. 'Identity, Essence, and Indiscernibility', *Journal of Philosophy*, 84: 293–314.

YI, BYEONG-UK. 1999. 'Is Mereology Ontologically Innocent?' *Philosophical Studies*, 93: 141–60.

ZIMMERMAN, DEAN W. 1999. 'One Really Big Liquid Sphere: Reply to Lewis', *Australasian Journal of Philosophy*, 77: 213–15.

—— 1998a. 'Temporal Parts and Supervenient Causation: The Incompatibility of Two Humean Doctrines', *Australasian Journal of Philosophy*, 76: 265–88.

—— 1998b. 'Temporary Intrinsics and Presentism', in Zimmerman and Peter van Inwagen, eds., *Metaphysics: The Big Questions* (Cambridge, Mass.: Blackwell).

—— 1997. 'Immanent Causation', in James Tomberlin, ed., *Philosophical Perspectives*, xi (Cambridge, Mass.: Blackwell).

—— 1996. 'Persistence and Presentism', *Philosophical Papers*, 25: 115–26.

—— 1995. 'Theories of Masses and Problems of Constitution', *Philosophical Review*, 104: 53–110.

Index